PENGUIN CLASSIC

# CICERO: ON THE GOOD LIFE

MARCUS TULLIUS CICERO (106–43 BC), Roman orator and statesman, was born at Arpinum of a wealthy local family. He was taken to Rome for his education with the idea of a public career and by 70 BC he had established himself as the leading barrister in Rome. In the meantime his political career was well under way and he was elected praetor for the year 66. His ambitious nature enabled him to obtain those honours which would normally only have been conferred upon members of the Roman aristocracy, and he was duly elected consul for 63. One of the most permanent features of his political life was his attachment to Pompey. As a politician his greatest failing was his consistent refusal to compromise; as a statesman his ideals were more honourable and unselfish than those of his contemporaries. Cicero was the greatest of the Roman orators, possessing a wide range of technique and an exceptional command of the Latin tongue. He followed the common practice of publishing his speeches. The information that they give us about contemporary social and political life is greatly increased by his letters, of which we have 900, published posthumously. They reflect the changing personal feelings of an emotional and sensitive man. His deeper thoughts are revealed by a considerable number of writings on moral and political philosophy, on religion and on the theory and practice of rhetoric. In addition to the great influence these have exercised on subsequent European thought, they are of profound intrinsic interest, as the selected works in the present volume reveal.

MICHAEL GRANT has been successively Chancellor's medallist and Fellow of Trinity College, Cambridge, Professor of Humanity at Edinburgh University, first Vice-Chancellor of Khartoum University, and President and Vice-Chancellor of the Queen's University of Belfast. Until 1966 he was President of the Virgil Society. He has also translated Cicero's *Selected Works* and *Selected Political Speeches* and Tacitus's *Annals of Imperial Rome* for the Penguin Classics; his other books include *The World of Rome* (1960), *Myths of the Greeks and Romans* (1962), *The Civilizations of Europe* (1965), *Gladiators* (1967), *Roman Readings* and *Roman Literature* (the last three available in Pelicans), *The Climax of Rome* (1968), *The Ancient Mediterranean*, *Julius Caesar* (both 1969), *The Ancient Historians*, *The Roman Forum* and *Nero* (all 1970).

# CICERO

## ON THE GOOD LIFE

*Translated with an introduction*
*by Michael Grant*

*Penguin Books*

Penguin Books Ltd, Harmondsworth, Middlesex, England
Penguin Books Inc., 7110 Ambassador Road, Baltimore, Maryland 21207, U.S.A
Penguin Books Australia Ltd, Ringwood, Victoria, Australia

—

First published 1971

—



—

Made and printed in Great Britain by
Hazell Watson & Viney Ltd
Aylesbury, Bucks
Set in Monotype Bembo

# CONTENTS



## APPENDICES

# INTRODUCTION

CICERO believed in individual human beings. He believed in their rights and their responsibilities and their freedom to make decisions without detailed interference from heaven or destiny. (In his fragmentary essay *On Fate* he says, in effect, 'You will see a doctor, and get better: both are decreed by Fate.')[1] Leaving aside, for the moment, the towering influence of this attitude upon subsequent generations, an influence which has bequeathed us much of the vast range of ideas suggested by words like humanity and humanism, it must be observed that his concern for human beings was a splendid contribution to an age dominated by autocrats like Sulla and Caesar.

Cicero was able to offer a theoretical justification for faith in human entitlements and powers – though it sometimes rather looks as if the belief came first and the justification followed afterwards. His explanation lay in the belief that each and every human being possesses a spark of divinity: that is to say, a spark of the divine mind, or of God, the force that pervades and animates the whole of nature. Cicero's thoughts about God and the gods are shifting and elusive. His view that it is important for the Roman people to worship the divinities of the Roman state was a matter of patriotic morale, not belief. He was aware that the widespread belief in a god or gods is insufficient reason for accepting that they exist;[2] and whether any deity does much for mortals he sometimes felt inclined to doubt, especially in bad times.[3]

For Cicero is a doubter, an undogmatic man. He often

1. *On Fate*, 13, 30.
2. *On the Nature of the Gods*, I, 23, 62.
3. *Letters to Friends*, XIV, 4, 1, *Letters to Atticus*, IV, 10. On this correspondence, see *Cicero: Selected Works* (ed. M. Grant, Penguin Books, reprinted 1969), pp. 58ff.

writes scathingly about people who accept the first view they hear or who swallow whole the declaration of some authority.[1] 'I am no Pythagoras pronouncing his oracles to a believing band of disciples.' Opinion is free, and disagreement legitimate. He is prepared to refute and be refuted without anger. Suspicious of certainties, he intends to be directed by probabilities (p. 28).

Nevertheless, while not prepared to offer dogmatic assertions about the nature of the gods, Cicero strongly believed that the universe is governed by a divine plan, and this belief is reflected in the *Dream of Scipio*, which is translated in the present volume. When he looked round him at the marvels of the cosmos he could only conclude, adopting the 'argument from design', that they must be of divine origin.[2] He was happy to adopt this form of religion, purified and illuminated by the knowledge of nature,[3] because it justified his confidence in human beings, which was based, as has been seen, on the conviction that the mind or soul of each individual person is a reflection, indeed a part, of the divine mind. 'We must now conceive of this whole universe as one commonwealth – of which both gods and men are members.'[4]

> All are but parts of one stupendous whole
> Whose body Nature is and God the Soul.[5]

Since the universe is wholly filled with the Eternal Intelligence and the Divine Mind, it must be that human souls are influenced by their contact with divine souls. . . .[6]

That animal which we call man, endowed with foresight and quick intelligence, complex, keen, possessing memory, full of reason

1. *On the Nature of the Gods*, I, 5, 10; cf. *Tusculans*, IV, 4, 7, *On the Chief Good and Evil*, I, 5, 15, I, 8, 27 (*De Finibus Bonorum et Malorum* can perhaps be translated 'Different Views regarding the Chief Good and Evil').

2. *Tusculans*, I, 29, 70.

3. *On Divination*, II, 72, 148, etc.

4. *On Laws*, I, 7, 23.

5. Alexander Pope, *Essay on Man*.

6. *On Divination*, I, 49, 110.

and prudence, has been given a certain distinguished status by the supreme God who created him; for he is the only one among so many different kinds and varieties of living beings who has a share in reason and thought, while all the rest are deprived of it. But what is more divine, I will not say in man only, but in all heaven and earth, than reason? And reason, when it is full grown and perfected, is rightly called wisdom. Therefore, since there is nothing better than reason, and since it exists both in man and God, the first common possession of man and God is reason.[1]

Reflecting on the wonderful achievements of this human reason, Cicero deduced from its divine origin the conclusion that every individual must do everything in his power to develop the higher faculties that distinguish him from animals. This meant, on the one hand, making sure that one holds fast to the quality of mind and the education which befits a truly civilized man – not only the frills of good taste which some of Cicero's critics have unfairly fastened upon, but the really basic requirements as well. But it was also clear to him that this human responsibility implies a tremendous social and communal obligation. For the fact that every human being possesses a spark of the divinity means that he is also bound by an essential, indissoluble bond with all his fellows, and this in turn demands that he must treat them decently.

There is no single thing so like another, so closely corresponding to it, as are all of us to one another.[2]

Consequently, to take something away from someone else – to profit by another's loss – is more unnatural than death, or destitution, or pain, or any other physical or external blow. To begin with, this strikes at the roots of human society and fellowship. For if we each of us propose to rob or injure one another for our personal gain, then we are clearly going to demolish what is more emphatically nature's creation than anything else in the whole world: namely, the link that unites every human being with every other. ... Nature's law

1. *On Laws*, I, 7, 22 (translated by C.W. Keyes).

2. *On Laws*, I, 10, 29.

promotes and coincides with the common interest. . . . If people claim (as they sometimes do) that they have no intention of robbing their parents or brothers for their own gain, but that robbing their compatriots is a different matter, they are not talking sense. For that is the same as denying their common interest with their fellow-countrymen, and all the legal or social obligations that follow therefrom: a denial which shatters the whole fabric of national life. Another objection urges that one ought to take account of compatriots but not of foreigners. But people who put forward these arguments subvert the whole foundation of the human community – and its removal means the annihilation of all kindness, generosity, goodness and justice.[1]

This was the spirit in which Immanuel Kant, too, declared that 'It is necessary to treat humanity, whether in your own person or in that of any other, in every case as an end, never as a means only.'

The idea that all men are brothers has become pretty faded and threadbare in modern times, when the ideal has seemed so singularly unrealizable. But its reassertion is timely in an age like the present, in which the popular urge towards peace, even if it still totally fails to dominate events, is exceptionally strong. One of the last influential statements of the theme was by H. G. Wells in his *Outline of History* (1920); but even he lost heart and cut the passage out of his later editions.

In the background of the consciousness of the world, waiting as silence and moonlight wait above the flares and shouts, the hurdy-gurdys and quarrels of a village fair, is the knowledge that all mankind is one brotherhood, that God is universal and impartial, Father of mankind, and that only in that universal service can mankind find peace, or peace be found for the troubles of the individual soul.

When this conception was first formulated by the ancient philosophers, it was heady stuff; and far the most eloquent of its expounders was Cicero. He moved on to the conclusion

1. *On Duties*, III, 5, 21, III, 6, 31, III, 6, 28 (see *Cicero: Selected Works*, op. cit.).

that, since all men have to treat each other properly, there is one law for everyone.

> Our natural inclination to love our fellow-men is the foundation of justice. . . . Those who have reason in common must also have right reason in common. And since right reason is law, we must believe that men have law also in common with the gods. . . . Justice is one: it binds all human society, and is based on one law, which is right reason applied to command and prohibition.[1]

And elsewhere Cicero asserts this universal and absolute standard of right and wrong in a statement which is as significant to our own life and happiness as almost anything else that has ever been said in western Europe.

> True law is reason, right and natural, commanding people to fulfil their obligations and prohibiting and deterring them from doing wrong. Its validity is universal; it is unchangeable and eternal. Its commands and prohibitions apply effectively to good men and have no effect on bad men. Any attempt to supersede this law, to repeal any part of it, is sinful; to cancel it entirely is impossible. Neither the Senate nor the Assembly can exempt us from its demands; we need no one to interpret or expound it but ourselves. There will not be one law at Rome, one at Athens, or one now and one later, but all nations will be subject all the time to this one changeless and everlasting law.[2]

*

Cicero, then, who put forward this point of view more forcibly, persuasively and durably than anyone else, is a writer peculiarly relevant to the problems that the world faces today. He wrote those words during the catastrophic years of the late fifties BC when the vast Roman empire, covering the whole of southern Europe and northern Africa and western Asia, was sliding hopelessly into the civil war which led to the dictatorship of Caesar and the elimination of

1. *On Laws*, I, 5, 16, I, 7, 23, I, 15, 42.
2. *On the State*, III, 22, 33.

many of the human rights that Cicero valued above everything else. For he knew that autocracy is the same thing as general slavery.[1] Moreover, when civil strife threatened, there was less and less scope for the political activities which seemed to him the most important of all occupations. And then, after Caesar had finally won the war and confirmed his own position as dictator, there was no longer any scope for such activities at all. So Cicero retired to the country, and particularly to his house at Tusculum, not far from Rome; and there he wrote.

He had other reasons, too, for taking refuge in writing. He had divorced his first wife Terentia, had quarrelled with his brother Quintus, had suffered the worst grief of his life because of the death of his daughter Tullia, and had divorced his juvenile second wife Publilia because she showed little sympathy with his bereavement. But his political misery was equally bad, or worse, and it was this more than anything else which drove him to authorship. The result was an astonishing proliferation of treatises on themes which may roughly be grouped together as philosophical. 'The history of civilization,' said the Polish scholar Tadeusz Zielinski, 'knows few moments equal in importance to the sojourn of Cicero at his houses in the country during the brief period of Caesar's sole rule.' And the work went on after Caesar's death, until near the end of 44 BC – a year before Cicero himself met his end at the hands of Caesar's autocratic successors, Antonius, Octavian (the future Augustus) and Lepidus, the members of the Second Triumvirate. During this period of about twenty months he dictated not only a variety of minor works, but eight major ones.[2] Three of these writings, *Discussions at Tusculum*, *On Duties* and *On Friendship*, are represented here, the first two by their fifth and second volumes ('books') respectively, and the third in its entirety.

1. *On the State*, I, 27, 43.
2. See Appendices I, II, III, pp. 356ff.

The essays contain Greek philosophy. In one of many remarkable letters written by Cicero to his friend Atticus, he is engagingly modest about his own personal contribution (it is only in his politics that he is immodest, since he could never find enough people to blow his political trumpet on his behalf).[1] 'Make your mind easy about my Latin,' he reassures Atticus. 'You will say, "What, when you write on such subjects?" But they are copies, and don't give me much trouble. I only supply words, and of them I have plenty.'[2] These words in a private letter cannot, however, be elevated into a rule explaining away and disparaging every treatise that Cicero ever wrote. Granted that his remark refers to this philosophical branch of his writings at all (which cannot be proved but is likely enough), it may only allude to some single and particular work in which he was engaged at the time (May 45). But in any case the remark is casual, and not to be taken too seriously.

In one respect the observation does himself rather more than justice, because if he had 'copied' Greek philosophers he would presumably also have reproduced their rigour of thought and logic and definition, all of which qualities his renderings lack. The concept of the brotherhood of man, for example, rests on an arbitrary and incomplete classification of natural impulses. There is no clear statement of what moral goodness is – perfection of virtue is not demonstrated theoretically. Nor is it explained how the holding of private property is compatible with the interests of society. It is also confusing to find Cicero often stating as a conclusion something he is in the middle of trying to prove. Indeed, what he writes is scarcely cohesive enough to be what we should call philosophy.

1. On this subject see *Cicero: Selected Political Speeches* (ed. M. Grant, Penguin Books, 1969), pp. 11ff.

2. *Letters to Atticus*, XII, 52, 3. Atticus had apparently commented on the problems of rendering Greek terms into Latin (p. 21). On the letters see *Cicero: Selected Works*, op. cit., pp. 58ff.

For one thing, he does not mind if he is inconsistent (p. 22); though it is true that my present selection has not quite done him justice as a philosopher, because I have omitted the more technical *Academics* and *Nature of the Gods*, in which the reasoning is closer and more exact.[1]

At the same time, however, Cicero's comment that he writes mere 'copies' is far too modest. For it does not begin to do justice to his distinction, not indeed as an 'original' thinker, but as a man who took in hand the rebarbative, contradictory and usually ill-written Greek philosophy that had come down to him (pp. 22), and, without slavishly translating,[2] paraphrased, selected, blended, and summed it up, with his own distribution of emphasis. 'As is my custom, I shall at my own option and discretion draw from these sources in such measure and in such manner as shall suit my purpose.'[3] The gifts which he himself brought to these transpositions have made them works of genius. Contemporaries had a further, special reason for admiring them, since they considered the transposition of a *whole literary genre* from Greek to Latin – which is what Cicero achieved – as sufficient proof of originality in itself. Indeed, even 'mere' translators were greatly respected; and Cicero, although he undertook such work at times (p. 24), regarded himself as much more than that.

It was his practice to adapt what he read and learnt to his Roman environment and his own views and tastes: those of a sensitive, experienced man, who possessed unique powers of expression, and infused what he was adapting with his own earnest purpose and keen sense of personal involvement. To work out solutions for isolated philosophical problems was

1. *On Duties*, III (the contents of which are largely original) and *Cato the Elder*: *On Old Age* are both translated in *Cicero: Selected Works*, op. cit., pp. 159ff., 213ff.

2. *On Duties*, II, 17, 60, III, 2, 7.

3. *On Duties*, I, 2, 6.

not his aim. But it seemed to him a desirable thing to set out, edit, and assess in his own Latin language the various systems of Greek philosophy, presenting their best and most applicable parts for the benefit of his fellow-citizens and the world.[1] And we, who can savour the fruits of his endeavours, can see that he was right: it would be a mistake to dismiss for lack of originality writings that contain so much truth and commonsense.

*

When Cicero had returned gloomily to Italy to endure the tyranny of Caesar, a friend of the dictator named Gaius Marius urged him to write philosophy;[2] and this was the startlingly abundant result. Amid the evils of the times, Cicero became more engrossed in the task every day.[3] But his interest in philosophy was not new; it was a renewal, for he had always been keen on such studies.[4]

It was an interest amounting to passion, and in the first work chosen for translation here Cicero enlarges on the glories of philosophy (p. 49). Indeed, at the very outset of this fertile period he had written a work especially devoted to praising the subject and exhorting people to turn to its study. This treatise, the *Hortensius*, is now lost – though not before it had revolutionized St Augustine's life (p. 33) – but one of the surviving fragments describes such researches as divine, remarking that it is only through their knowledge of the universe that even the gods are enabled to lead good lives.[5] And as for men, 'philosophy is a physician of souls, takes away the load of empty troubles, sets us free from desires, banishes

1. *On Divination*, II, 1, 1 and 5, II, 2, 5, *Tusculans*, II, 3, 6, *On the Chief Good and Evil*, I, 3, 7.

2. *Letters to Friends*, XI, 27, 5.

3. *Letters to Friends*, IV, 4 (September 45 BC).

4. *On Divination*, II, 2, 7, *For Murena*, 30, 63.

5. Fragment 42 (Orelli).

fears'.[1] 'Philosophy! Without you, what would I ever have amounted to and what, indeed, would have become of all human life?'[2] This is the spirit of the Psalmist: 'One day in thy courts is better than a thousand in the tents of ungodliness'.[3]

Philosophy was Greek, and Cicero, however much he might look down on some of the more feeble manifestations of Hellenism in his own day, repeatedly shows his enormous admiration for classical Greek culture,[4] which it was his proud purpose to transmit, in popularized form, to Rome. He was known as a phil-Hellene, and not always to his credit.[5] A lot of Romans thought badly of statesmen who went in for a literary career and studied Greek literature. Cicero knew this,[6] and was therefore at pains, first, to emphasize his patriotic motives, secondly, to deplore Romans who hellenized themselves too completely,[7] and thirdly, to explain reassuringly that their own ancestors would have done just as well as the Greeks if they had not been engaged in other occupations.

And as regards philosophy, in particular, Cicero had to contend with severe Roman disapproval. This he frequently seeks to dispel (p. 18),[8] partly by insisting that the study was a venerable feature of the Roman tradition itself. But in fact, as late as 155 BC, when the Greek philosopher Carneades visited Rome and gave the arguments for and against injustice (pointing out that empires are unavoidably amoral), he and his fellow-delegates were expelled from the city; though shortly afterwards the Stoic Panaetius had close contacts with

1. *Tusculans*, II, 4, 11.
2. *Tusculans*, V, 2, 5.
3. *Psalms*, 84, 10.
4. For example in the speech *For Archias*. See *Cicero: Selected Political Speeches*, op. cit., pp. 147ff.
5. Plutarch, *Cicero*, 5.
6. *Academics*, II, 2, 5.
7. *On the Chief Good and Evil*, I, 3, 9.
8. *On Duties*, II, 1, 2, etc.

a number of eminent Romans, including Scipio Africanus the younger.[1] In Cicero's own day hostile prejudice still existed in leading men, especially if there seemed to be any question of philosophy taking precedence over political life; for example Hortensius, the leading orator until Cicero, was dead against the subject.[2]

On the other hand there was, by now, a fairly wide interest in philosophy among the Roman upper class. Indeed this interest was very much wider than anything that can be found in most other cities and epochs, including our own. For the leading personages of the Roman Republic, collapsing though it was, were formidably able and versatile people. Cicero was not the only man to find time for philosophy and general culture in an active political life. Nevertheless he claimed that no Roman before himself had seriously presented Greek thought to Roman readers. The claim does not bear too close scrutiny, but is true enough if one discounts a few isolated works of single schools, short monographs or pieces written for special occasions, or pieces that were too badly written to be worth considering. In other words Cicero was the first person to do the job comprehensively; and of course no one (except Lucretius who spoke for the Epicureans only)[3] had approached his incomparable eloquence, or, for that matter, ever approached it afterwards.

Unfortunate though the causes for Cicero's retirement were, this was the occupation in which he preferred to spend the spare time thus thrust upon him, because he saw philosophical writing as a continuation of his public and political career by other means. It offered the same scope for the ideas that had hitherto governed his life, since in those days, in sad contrast to our own, philosophy was regarded as a strictly practical study – something which, if approached in the right

1. For these philosophers, see below, pp. 27, 28.
2. *On the Chief Good and Evil*, I, 1, 2.
3. On Lucretius, see below, p. 26.

way, was perfectly capable of guiding and improving people's lives. Indeed Cicero, declaring that no man can be at the same time wise and not involved in politics, condemns worrying over abstruse philosophical side-issues that will yield little practical result.[1] Writing to his son, it is true, Cicero might maintain that, although one ought to know what philosophy teaches, it is necessary to live by one's own national traditions,[2] but elsewhere his passion overrides these more prosaic Roman moods. That is why, 'after serious and long continued reflection as to how I might do good to as many people as possible and thereby prevent any interruption of my service to the State, no better plan occurred to me than to conduct my fellow-citizens in the ways of the noblest learning.'[3] And he was most of all keen to present these splendours to the young. The whole task of transmission was particularly inviting, because, as A. E. Douglas remarks, this sort of 'philosophy' geared to practical guidance 'comes near to a reader, to *any* reader, in a way that metaphysical or Utopian speculations do only to a few'.[4] It is exciting because, unlike the precepts of the revealed religions, it is fully applicable and realizable in our daily lives (and less likely than they are, if one may judge from history, to lead to wars).

*

But in order to bring such a message right home it was absolutely essential, as any writer ought to know, that the material be presented in palatable and attractive form. Otherwise, how could it win acceptance? Here lay Cicero's strong point. He was the first and greatest exponent of the process of popularization that is so widely discussed and in demand today, and the artistry he devoted to this task is what has made his

1. *On Duties*, I, 6, 19.
2. Cicero in Lactantius, *Divine Institutions*, III, 14, 17.
3. *On Divination*, II, 1, 1.
4. *Cicero*, ed. T. A. Dorey, Routledge & Kegan Paul, 1964, p. 166.

works so enduring. Although they were undertaken and completed within such an astonishingly short period, they have been, throughout the ages, among the world's best sellers. More than any other Latin prose writer, more than any other Latin writer at all with the possible exception of Virgil, Cicero gathered up and passed on the best of the ancient world (p. 31). He supremely embodies the virtues of Latin literature in the range, form and spirit of his work. This included not only the philosophical treatises but his incomparable speeches and letters as well.[1] All three sets of writings possess distinct and remarkable merits of their own. The treatises stand out for their unique blend of practicality and human sympathy.

The *Tusculans* and *Laelius: On Friendship* (like the earlier work *On the Orator*, which also appears in this book) are ostensibly in the form of dialogues, a form of 'sugar on the pill' now much in favour again (for example, among advertisers on the television and radio of Cicero's own country). We must not look, in these discussions, for the dramatic interplay of Plato's *Protagoras* or *Symposium*, for we shall not find it. Indeed, even Plato himself had abandoned the method long before the end of his life, rejecting it as a fruitful means of attacking serious philosophical problems, and turning to monologue and exposition instead. These are also the methods of Cicero, but his special models are rather Plato's earliest successors. As he himself tells us, the presentation of a work set in a contemporary scene, like the *Tusculans*, is based on Aristotle, whereas those staged in the past, like *On Friendship* and *On the Orator*, are modelled on his contemporary Heraclides of Pontus.[2]

1. See *Cicero: Selected Works*, op. cit., and *Cicero: Selected Political Speeches*, op. cit. He also wrote poetry (p. 79).

2. *Letters to Atticus*, XIII, 19, 4; cf. *Letters to Friends*, I, 9, 23. Heraclides Ponticus (c.390–310 BC), from Heraclea on the Black Sea, came to Athens and became the pupil of Speusippus and later of Plato. The

In discussions of the latter kind, those placed within a historical framework, the participants are Romans of what Cicero regarded as the great days of the Republic, either in the time of his boyhood or before he was born. 'Those were the days' is a not uncommon sentiment at any epoch. But a conviction that there had been a decline from the grand Roman past was particularly deep-rooted in the troubled first century BC; and this view was held with especial fervour by Cicero himself, who believed intensely, though over-optimistically, that the Republic would recover if men would only behave as the heroes of old had behaved, the two Scipios and all the rest. Besides, setting the dialogue in the past had a further advantage, for it avoided possible offence to powerful contemporaries. Cicero's historic settings were based on careful research, and given well calculated dramatic dates. The spokesmen, surrounded by country-house luxury, are polite, decorous, serious though occasionally indulging in mild badinage, and rather self-conscious. Here are the masters of the world, out to absorb the best of Greek civilization. They are a literary device: there is no reason to suppose that they ever really said any of the things attributed to them, and Cicero, for all his care to make his speakers resemble their characters, was sometimes quite prepared, as he got a work into shape, to scrap one set of speakers in favour of another. He was also willing to admit, privately, that he made them talk above their own heads.[1]

*

This was the Roman element, intended to show that the message of philosophy did not find Rome 'alien soil'. But Cicero's models were Greek. His achievement in converting

---

Hellenistic popular dialogues of exposition, which may have served as more immediate models, are lost.

1. *Letters to Atticus*, XIII, 12, 3.

them into Latin, which, powerful though it was, had no familiarity with such matters, was a colossal one. Some believed he had set himself an impossible task;[1] but they were wrong, because Cicero carried it out. His success meant that Latin was established as a language of general ideas, capable of giving lucid and splendid voice to a massive array of human thought.

In order to achieve his purpose he had to create new words. We owe him the terms quality, individual, vacuum, moral, property, induction, element, definition, difference, notion, comprehension, infinity, appetite, instance, science, image, species. He was fully conscious that the problems of translating technical Greek were severe,[2] but often an invented word would do the trick.[3] A few problems could not, it is true, be surmounted, since *Officia* (Duties), for instance, is not quite the same thing as *kathekonta*, and there are difficulties about *De Finibus* and *peri telon* (p. 8n.). Nevertheless Cicero concluded, with an assurance which Lucretius had by no means shared,[4] that, regarded as a vehicle for philosophy, Latin was actually superior to Greek.[5]

Nevertheless the philosophy itself was Greek; and indeed Cicero is our earliest and fullest source for the views of the later Greek philosophers whom he followed. He would be even more informative on this subject if we could always disentangle what he owed to whom; but we cannot. The attempt is often made. Indeed, in recent years, scholarly attention has very largely been concentrated on this endeavour to identify the Greek authorities whose writings Cicero had in front of him when he was compiling and dictating his

1. *On the Nature of the Gods*, I, 3, 8.
2. *Academics*, II, 6, 17; but see above, p. 13.
3. *Academics*, I, 6, 24.
4. Lucretius, *On the Nature of the Universe*, I, 139, I, 318ff., III, 261.
5. *On the Chief Good and Evil*, I, 3, 10, III, 2, 5, *Tusculans*, II, 15, 35, III, 5, 10.

treatises. This concentration has meant that other aspects have tended to be ignored (p. 43), and the results the search has yielded are not always conclusive – though it is obviously worth undertaking. Here, however, all that can be done is to indicate very briefly the philosophical situation that Cicero inherited and the positions that he himself adopted.

In keeping with his refusal to be dogmatic (p. 8), he refuses with equal determination to commit himself to any single school. He possesses in very marked degree the ability of the intellectual, and the lawyer, to see things from more than one point of view. 'As is my custom, I shall, at my own option and discretion, draw from the various sources in such measure and in such manner as shall suit my purpose.'[1]

'He is an eclectic,' remarked Einar Löfstedt, 'like most wise people.' But if Cicero will not be bound by the dogmas of any one sect, he also, rather more disconcertingly, declines to be bound by what he himself has said on earlier occasions. He values his freedom to change his mind, and openly admits to the resulting contradictions (p. 14).[2] Consequently he feels at liberty to draw upon whatever philosophical points of view are relevant to his topic, even when they conflict with one another.

A little must now be said about the various Greek schools, sects and systems that were available for him to study.

*

PYTHAGORAS of Samos (6th century BC), the historic but half-legendary leader of a strictly disciplined religious community at Croton in south Italy, had believed that the soul is condemned to a cycle of reincarnations from which it can be rescued by the cultivation of a noble way of life. This doctrine is Romanized in Cicero's *Dream of Scipio*.

HERACLITUS of Ephesus (c. 500) anticipated and helped to

1. *On Duties*, I, 2, 6.
2. *Tusculans*, V, 11, 33.

direct the belief of the Stoics (p. 26) and Cicero that 'all the laws of men are nourished by one law, the divine law'.[1]

SOCRATES the Athenian (469–399 BC) wrote nothing down, and it is disputed how much of his actual teaching is reflected in the extensive but contradictory reports of Plato and Xenophon. Cicero, with some exaggeration, hails him as the first to call philosophy down from the heavens and set her in the cities and homes of men and compel her to ask ethical questions (p. 9),[2] and the Academy, which he followed (p. 29), claimed that their method of arguing both sides, with a tentative summing up in favour of one of them, went back to Socrates.[3]

PLATO (c. 429–347 BC), founder of this Academy, lays down in his *Republic* and *Gorgias* the doctrine, assumed by Cicero and a number of later thinkers (notably Mill) to be correct, that all our deliberate acts aim at our happiness,[4] and that we are therefore always searching for the *beata vita* which is identifiable with the Good. Plato inherited from Socrates, and handed on to his successors, the problem of establishing a rational basis for morality. He also grappled with two obstacles to knowledge: the transitory nature of the physical world, and the apparent uncertainty of our apprehension of it. Modern philosophy is often thought of as starting with Descartes' discussion of the reliability of the senses, but this had already been the theme which Cicero's study of the Academy's doctrines, his *Academics* (p. 29), derived from Plato and his successors. Although Cicero had not read all Plato's dialogues (and especially not all the later ones), his

1. Fragment 114 (G. S. Kirk and J. E. Raven, *The Presocratic Philosophers*, Cambridge University Press, 1966, p. 213, no. 253).

2. *Tusculans*, V, 4, 10; cf. *Academics*, I, 1, 3, I, 4, 15.

3. *Letters to Atticus*, II, 3, 3.

4. 'Wellbeing' or 'welfare' is sometimes preferred as a translation: cf. H. Sidgwick, *History of Ethics*, Macmillan, 6th edn, reprinted 1967, pp. 48 n. 1, 56 n. 2.

interest in them was deep and real, and his knowledge considerable. He translated Plato's *Protagoras* and *Timaeus*, and thought of himself as going back beyond the mechanical methods of later days to the classical, Platonic ideal.[1] However, in affairs relating to the State, though diffident of offering criticisms of the master, he regarded Plato's Utopian *Republic* as wholly unpractical.[2] (Nevertheless, the Myth of Er in the same work, reflecting the influence of Pythagorean doctrines of transmigration (p. 22), served Cicero as a general model for the revelation of immortality in the *Dream of Scipio*.)

ARISTOTLE of Stagirus (384–322 BC), founder of the Peripatetic School (peripatos = 'covered arcade', where their discussions were held), and his chief pupil THEOPHRASTUS of Eresus (369–285 BC), contributed a new scientific approach. Although Cicero found Aristotle's ethical writings rather too hard for him, much of the argument in the fifth *Tusculans* revolves round the Peripatetic belief that virtue, although the highest good, is not the only good – in contrast to the Stoic view that it is the only good (p. 26). But Cicero, although attracted by the Aristotelian doctrine of 'the Mean', scarcely recognizes the Peripatetics as a separate school, treating them as barely distinguishable in some passages from the Stoics, and in others from the Academy. His own philosophy, though based on the two latter schools (pp. 26, 29), 'is not very different', he remarked, 'from that of the Peripatetics: for both they and I claim to be followers of Socrates and Plato'. This observation appears in the treatise *On Duties*,[3] dedicated to the son whom Cicero had entrusted to the Peripatetic Cratippus at Athens, an arrangement which may have encouraged him, out of politeness, to join contemporary Academics in playing down the differences between the schools (p. 30).

1. Plutarch, *Cicero*, 2: by character he was a Platonic lover of learning and wisdom.

2. *On the State*, II, 11, 21; cf. I, 22, 36.

3. *On Duties*, I, 1, 2.

The Epicureans and Stoics bring us into a more modern and more easily understandable world in which the values of individualism and universalism (both reflected in the social life of the great Hellenistic states) had now begun to prevail over those of the independent, closely knit, city states so dominant in previous periods. But although these developments brought ethics into the first place, the contrast frequently drawn between these 'ethical' schools and the earlier 'metaphysicians' Plato and Aristotle is too simple. For on the one hand, Plato and Aristotle had possessed many other interests besides metaphysics, and it is equally true that the post-Aristotelians and Cicero were deeply concerned not only with ethics but with physics, theology and the theory of knowledge; and the Stoics were interested in logic as well.

The Epicureans and Stoics agreed with one another to the extent that, in answer to Plato's question, they both believed that sensory perceptions *are* reliable: and that meant that philosophy tended to become more dogmatic.

Accepting this guidance by the senses, EPICURUS of Samos (341–270 BC), founder of 'the Garden', believed that they indicate the supreme good to be happiness,[1] which he identified with the absence of pain and trouble. The Epicureans believed that the world is composed of material atoms obeying their own laws, and maintained that there is no evidence for divine intervention or interest in human affairs, a doctrine which has won them sympathy from materialist and Marxist thinkers today.

At the age of sixteen Cicero went to the lectures of the Epicurean Phaedrus, who remained his friend. His companion at the lectures was his friend Atticus, who remained an Epicurean and obeyed the Garden's injunction to shun public life (though he contravened their further instruction to 'flee

1. This doctrine went back to Aristippus, founder of the Cyrenaic school, grandson of a companion of Socrates of the same name. For difficulties of terminology, see above, p. 23n.

from all forms of culture'). Cicero also had the good fortune to be presented with an important library by another Epicurean friend, Lucius Papirius Paetus. Cicero had read and privately praised the great poem on the universe by his Epicurean contemporary Lucretius;[1] but his treatises strangely ignore this supreme Latin exposition of the school, perhaps because it did not cover a wider range (p. 17). He refers disparagingly to another popularizer of Epicurean doctrine, Gaius Amafinius. Though anxious to disclaim partisan hostility to the holders of these views,[2] Cicero disagreed with them almost totally, being repelled equally by their reliance on the senses, their idealization of pleasure (however austerely interpreted), their negation of any sort of providence, their subversive questioning of the state religion, and their abstinence from public affairs. And he disliked their authoritarian attitude.

ZENO of Citium in Cyprus (335–263 BC) established the Stoic school (*stoa* = 'porch') in c. 300 BC. He and his successors Cleanthes and Chrysippus taught the doctrine of divine providence, and above all propagated the concept of the human brotherhood inspired by a shared divine spark, a belief which was particularly dear to Cicero (p. 7).[3] After the Epicurean Phaedrus, Cicero's next master was the Stoic Diodotus; and the impersonal nature religion of the school left its impression on him.[4] As to its belief that moral goodness or virtue is the *supreme and only* good, the simple moral grandeur of the theory tempts him. However, in his *Tusculans* and elsewhere, he leaves the final decision open between this view and the Academic–Peripatetic opinion that, although virtue is the highest good, there are other goods also (pp. 24, 30). Virtue is based on knowledge.

It was a feature of the times to stress the need for self-

1. *Letters to his brother Quintus*, II, 9, 3.
2. *Tusculans*, III, 21, 50.
3. It was foreshadowed by Plato, *Philebus*, 30, etc.
4. e.g. Cleanthes's *Hymn to Zeus*.

sufficiency, and Cicero admired the autonomous, proud, impregnable, passionless sage of the Stoics, echoing their conviction that the good life, in order to be secure, must be independent of chance and circumstances.[1] By such means it is possible to attain human perfection: human nature is not unavoidably flawed, as the Jewish and Christian doctrines insisted. Nevertheless, Cicero found many of the Stoic tenets too rigid and inflexible – absolute virtue, for example, is an unrealistic and unrealizable ideal.

However, PANAETIUS of Rhodes (c. 185–109), of the 'Middle Stoa', modified this doctrine for the requirements of Roman society by leaving room for imperfect virtue, 'progression towards virtue'. He also devoted much attention to the practical obligations and possible conflicts of obligation that this idea involves. He is followed fairly closely by Cicero in the first two volumes of *On Duties*, of which the second is translated here.[2] Cicero welcomed this practical approach, and approved of Panaetius's demonstration that the rights of the individual (including private property) are reconcilable with the needs of society.[3] Like innumerable educated Romans after him, he found it easy to accept a good deal of this modified Stoicism, stripped of its more extreme and paradoxical tenets and adapted to make sense of his own and his country's experience.

POSIDONIUS of Syrian Apamea (c. 135–50 BC), Cicero's teacher at Rhodes in 79, was a remarkable polymath who absorbed and summed up past Stoicism, and much other philosophy as well, and handed down the composite product to posterity. He did not exclude the passions altogether, as the original Stoics had preferred to do, but reverted to Plato by

1. This had been stressed by Diogenes of Sinope (c.400–325 BC), founder of the Cynic school, who urged the renunciation of all material possessions.

2. For the third volume see *Cicero: Selected Works*, op. cit., pp. 159ff.

3. Though the point was not philosophically worked out (p. 13).

asserting that these feelings must be controlled by reason. While Cicero was writing the third volume of his treatise *On Duties*, a summary of Posidonius's book on the same subject was in his hands.[1] Posidonius identified the human brotherhood or Stoic cosmopolis with the Roman empire, regarding this as a reflection of the commonwealth of God, to which, as later in Cicero's *Dream of Scipio*, deserving statesmen and philosophers were eligible for admission after the completion of their tasks upon earth. Cicero also followed Posidonius's belief that philosophy had been the inventor of the arts of civilization (p. 54).[2]

ARCESILAUS of Pitane (315–241 BC) led the Middle Academy, which claimed descent from Plato.[3] His main attack was directed against the dogmatic theory of knowledge on which the Stoics based their ethics. Arcesilaus introduced a strong sceptical spirit, denying the possibility that one could know anything at all.[4] In practical life, he maintained, it is enough to find the most sensible, 'reasonable' reasons for an action. Claiming to uphold the Socratic spirit of clear thinking, his logical scepticism transformed the whole direction of Academic thought.

But this negative attitude was not enough for the practical spirit of the age, and the founder of the Third or 'New' Academy, CARNEADES of Cyrene (213–129 BC), added an emphasis on *probability*. It is true that, in opposition to the Stoics and Epicureans, suspended judgement was still the order of the day – 'you can never be sure', 'there are two sides to

1. *Letters to Atticus*, XVI, 11, 4.
2. Seneca, *Letters*, 90, 7.
3. The first Academics after Plato had concentrated on mathematics.
4. This had been the belief of Pyrrho of Elis (c. 360–270 BC), founder of the Sceptical school. Isocrates too (436–338 BC), claiming to adopt a Socratic attitude, had believed that absolute knowledge is impossible (*Busiris*, 24).

every question' – and indeed this element of philosophical doubt was developed and systematized by Carneades. But at the same time he mitigated the negative factor by making a distinction between different stages of clearness in human perception: 'man may infer the nature of the objects of sensation from the evidence of his experience', and some of these perceptions will deserve to be called 'convincing or likely'. In spite of hostility from Roman traditionalists who found him subversive (p. 16), when Carneades visited Rome in 155 his independent realistic attitude, eloquent delivery, and dialectical skill made a considerable impression. Subsequently, after his teaching had been recorded by his pupil Clitomachus, this combination of undogmatic scepticism and practicality exercised great influence over Cicero, who, in spite of his admiration for many features of Stoicism, declared himself a supporter of this version of the Academy and expounded its merits in his *Academics*, making himself the spokesman for the school in the second edition of the work.[1]

The validity of sensory perception remained a vigorous debating point in the Fourth Academy of PHILO of Larissa (c. 160–80 BC). He too avoided Stoic dogma; but, fearing that Carneades's polemics had weakened the Academy's footing, he claimed that his own compromising, pragmatic interpretation of probability (defined as 'knowable' but not in the rigid Stoic sense) was a return to the true Platonic position. Cicero had attended Philo's lectures at Rome, and defended his case in the first edition of the *Academics*.

Later at Athens (79–78) Cicero studied under ANTIOCHUS

1. i.e. *Academics*, I, as it has come down to us; *Academics*, II (the 'Lucullus'), forms part of the first edition (which was written in two volumes, subsequently expanded to four). Cicero is prepared to allow the speakers in his dialogues to accuse the Academy of introducing confusion, *On the Laws*, I, 13, 39. H. J. Blackham, (*Objections to Humanism*, Penguin Books, 1965, p. 11) restates Cicero's preference for the probable.

of Ascalon (c. 130–68 BC), head of the Fifth Academy, which he (and Cicero) misleadingly described as the 'Old' Academy because Antiochus, too, claimed to be going back to Plato. But Antiochus, who influenced Brutus and the polymath Varro[1] as well as Cicero, carried Philo's tentative move towards Stoicism a stage further – far enough, indeed, for Cicero to comment that although the Ascalonian was called an Academic he was virtually a Stoic.[2] That is to say, Antiochus more or less accepted the validity of perception in the Stoic sense, since he argued that even if the senses are fallible they can be corrected by reason. Cicero regretted this move away from scepticism and probability in the direction of Stoic dogma.

In the field of ethics, however, Antiochus's reliance on the senses led him to a different opinion from the Stoics, since he concluded that moral worth could not be regarded as the *only* good thing, because there are no grounds for placing it in a realm apart from the senses. That is to say, even if moral worth is the best of goods, there are other goods (bodily, and external or accidental) as well. This conclusion had also been reached by the Peripatetics at Aristotle's Lyceum (p. 24), and Antiochus asserted that the Academy and Lyceum had originally been one and the same thing, and that their basic teaching was therefore similar.

Cicero had personal reasons for welcoming this reconciliation (p. 24), which he celebrated by calling the two gymnasiums in his Tusculan garden the Academy and the Lyceum; and he largely devoted the fifth volume of the *Tusculans*, translated here, to the resultant dispute between the Academic–Peripatetics and the Stoics as to whether virtue is the *only* good or not. He was attracted by the more simple, coherent and consistent Stoic view, but was not prepared to say that

1. *Academics*, I, 4, 13.
2. *Academics*, II, 43, 132.

the other attitudes were wrong (p. 22) – comforting himself by Antiochus's own remark that the dispute was largely a matter of terminology (p. 21).[1] And he must also have welcomed the advice of Antiochus (who was a friend of statesmen such as Lucius Licinius Lucullus) that there was nothing better than the life of action exemplified by great Romans of the past.[2] Furthermore, Cicero approved of the Academy's sympathetic attitude towards literature and oratory (p. 233). But above all, and despite reservations about this or that individual phase of Academic doctrines, he liked the school because it encouraged his belief in a system of truth which man's reason is too imperfect to grasp altogether, but may nevertheless approach.

*

It would have been possible to begin this introduction by pointing out the extraordinary influence exerted by these works throughout the ages. Instead I have preferred to start by indicating how important they still are for us today.

But something must also be said about their unparalleled history during these two thousand years, and the dominance they have exerted upon the thought of successive generations.[3] For Cicero, through these treatises, has been the greatest of all conservers and transmitters of cultural values, the greatest unifying force of Europe, the shaper of its civilized speech.[4] It is writings such as *On Duties* which, through their effects on our ancestors and forerunners, have made us, for better or worse, what we are.

From Caesar, whose politics he so deplored, Cicero earned

1. *Tusculans*, V, 41, 120.

2. Plutarch, *Cicero*, 4.

3. For the influence of his speeches see *Cicero: Selected Works*, op. cit., pp. 24ff. Here I have expanded the information about his philosophical treatises.

4. For his style, ibid., pp. 20ff.

a magnificent tribute: 'It is better to extend the frontiers of the mind than to push back the boundaries of the empire.'[1] A quarter of a century after the two men's deaths, Virgil provided the poetic dynamic which helped many of Cicero's attitudes to endure, following the *Dream of Scipio* with his own profound vision of the after-life.[2] But Cicero's ambition to commend 'philosophy' to the younger generation was not fulfilled. He himself had been conscious that his undogmatic 'Platonism' bore an old-fashioned air and, in spite of lip-service from some quarters, his treatises made little immediate impact. This was partly because those who were interested could read about the various systems in the original Greek. But in any case the ravages of civil war had made people tired of argument – and all too ready for the dogmas of imperial orthodoxy.[3]

The younger Seneca (d. AD 65) did not find Cicero sharp enough for his tastes.[4] But he was greatly admired by Pliny the elder (d. AD 79), who placed him alongside Homer, and then by the greatest of Roman educationalists, Quintilian, who coupled his philosophy with Plato's.[5] In the second century AD Cicero's philosophical views and political theory were not understood very well, but Gellius was attracted by his broad culture, and Fronto allowed him every merit except exactitude: he did not find that Cicero had taken sufficient care to track down the *mot juste*. The emperor Severus Alexander (AD 222–35) was said, though the source is not reliable, to read *On Duties* and *On the State* in preference to anything else.[6]

Lactantius (c. 250–317) praised Cicero's treatises very highly,

1. Pliny the elder, *Natural History*, VII, 31.
2. Virgil, *Aeneid*, VI, 703ff.
3. cf. Seneca the elder, *Suasoria*, VI, 1, 22, 24, 26.
4. Seneca the younger, *Moral Letters*, 40, 11; 114, 16.
5. *Institutio Oratoria*, X, 1, 123.
6. *Scriptores Historiae Augustae*, *Severus Alexander*, 30, 2.

declaring that they contained important original features.[1] He himself wrote a sort of supplement to *On the State*, from which he quoted many passages, earning himself the designation of 'the Christian Cicero'. He also found *On Duties* adaptable to the needs of the Church. Ambrose's *On the Duties of Ministers*, a manual for the clergy, owes a great deal to the same work, and it was at this time, the end of the fourth century AD, that Cicero experienced his first major revival; his works were kept alive and transmitted, becoming an important ingredient in Christian doctrine. The early Fathers were caught in a tension between Christianity and paganism which was not unlike earlier tensions between Roman tradition and Greek culture, except that now the field of conflict was religious rather than patriotic. For Jerome and Augustine, Cicero symbolized the culture whose vanities Christianity had rejected. And yet Jerome, withdrawing from the world, had not been able to give up these precious books, and used to fast in order to justify reading them at the end of his day; and one night he dreamt that before the Seat of Judgement he was accused of being more Ciceronian than Christian.[2] Augustine, though his *City of God* was written to oppose Cicero's conception of Providence, writes that it was the exhortation to philosophy in the *Hortensius* (now lost) which first turned his attention from worldly frivolity to the study of religion and wisdom.[3]

The *Dream of Scipio*, too, was very well known in the later empire. Christians were impressed by its Platonic and Pythagorean doctrines, and shortly after 400 the vision was expounded by Macrobius in a strange mixture of erudition, pseudo-science and mysticism. His principal aim was to support Cicero's assertion of a life beyond the grave, and to demonstrate, in a manner dear to the medieval mind but scarcely accurate, that Cicero had already known religious

1. *Divine Institutions*, I, 17, 3, I, 15, 6, III, 14, 10.
2. *Letters*, XXII, 30.
3. *Confessions*, III, 4, 7, VIII, 7, 17.

contemplation to be on a higher plane than political life. The *Dream* was also well known to Boethius (c. 480–524), who lived at the watershed between antiquity and the Middle Ages and conveyed so much of the ancient world's thought to posterity. And he made considerable use of the *Tusculans* as well.

But Pope Gregory I the Great (590–604) wanted to suppress Cicero's writings, since the charm of their style diverted young men from the scriptures. This heralded a period, continuing throughout the latter half of the first millennium AD, when Cicero, though his influence can be traced here and there, was not one of the greatest favourites. At most, during this epoch, his work still served to transmit rather tenuously certain leading ethical ideas, until Europe again became capable of more critical thinking. Quotations are usually at second hand; he was little more than a great name of shadowy prestige.[1] From the eleventh century onwards, however, interest in Cicero began to increase steadily. Hitherto the civic world of Rome had been forgotten, but now Cicero's idealized Republic, his good sense, public spirit, and portrayal of a civilized community appealed to the rising urban peoples of the later Middle Ages – merchants, professional men, administrators, all struggling, in their different ways, for an independent, stable and rational existence. The non-technical essays *On Friendship* and *On Old Age* remained far the most popular works. But in contrast to Peter Abelard (1079–1142), who still cited Cicero as an open opponent of the toil of active

1. The Carolingian Paschasius Radbertus converted the 'active leisure' of *On Duties* to the monastic ideal. Sedulius Scottus knew many of the treatises. Einhard quotes the *Tusculans* in the preface of his *Life of Charlemagne*, and manuscripts of it (and *On the Orator*) were acquired in the ninth century by Servatus Lupus of Ferrières. The Presbyter Hadoardus of the Western Franks quotes extensively from the same work, and in the eleventh century Meinhard of Bamberg reported it as valuable training for Christian philosophy.

life, Guido of Pisa (1118) was already quoting a passage from *On Duties* (known to him from Ambrose) which suggested that men's efforts ought to be devoted to human society. For this work, almost as much as Augustine's *City of God*, now began to figure as an interpretation of the Christian faith which dominated western thought. It is true that the tension was still there. For example, the Prior of Hildesheim felt obliged to reassure Wibald, Abbot of Corvey on the Weser (c. 1150): 'Though you desire to have the books of Cicero, I know that you are a Christian and not a Ciceronian. You go over to the camp of the enemy not as a deserter but as a spy!'

Medieval philosophy owed Cicero a great deal of its terminology, and medieval education a great part of its teaching programmes. Although, on the rhetorical side, these curricula were largely based upon the juvenile *On Invention* rather than upon the mature treatise *On the Orator*,[1] John of Salisbury (c. 1115–80) owned a manuscript of the latter work and bequeathed it to Chartres. John, who plainly reveals the medieval sense of continuity with the Roman past, knew the philosophical treatises equally well, and his favourite Latin author was Cicero – who would, in his opinion, have been one of the greatest of the great, if only his conduct had not fallen short of his wisdom. John found in these works support for his own ideals of statesmanship, his natural love of literature, and his antipathy to dogmatism and specialization.[2]

Meanwhile more and more readers felt profoundly attracted to Cicero as the plain man's interpreter of ancient thought, and as a writer of popular stories and anecdotes. Guillaume de Loris, who wrote the first part of that uniquely important

1. *On Invention* (on which see also p. 233) and another textbook *To Herennius*, which was wrongly attributed to Cicero, far exceeded the more mature rhetorical works in popularity.

2. Herbord of Michelsberg (d. 1168) quoted whole chapters of *On Duties*, and then Alexander of Neckham recommended a curriculum including this and five other treatises of Cicero.

love romance, the *Roman de la Rose* (c. 1225), began his poem with a reference to the *Dream of Scipio* (of which he believed Macrobius to have been the author) and when the second part of the poem was written by Jean de Meun (c. 1270), his models included *On Friendship* and *On Old Age*. During this period, as scholastic erudition and logic reached their zenith, the revival of Cicero as a Roman figure was in full swing. In 1238 Albertano da Brescia found *On Duties* a pre-eminent guide for the active public career, supporting his own conviction that man may freely choose between this and the spiritual life;[1] and the theme was again present in the most widely circulated encyclopaedia of the later thirteenth century, the *Speculum* of Vincent de Beauvais. St Thomas Aquinas (1226–74) used *On Duties* to point out how exceptional Cicero was for his championship of an active existence and 'justice', but in considering the *Dream of Scipio* (a hero to the later Middle Ages) Aquinas replaced Scipio's commendation of civic activity by praise of the 'rule of souls'. He quoted Cicero more frequently than any other Latin writer, and at times even preferred him to Aristotle himself.

An anonymous biography of Cicero written after 1300, though unaware of the facts of his political career, sees him as Roman statesman as well as author. Dante (d. 1321) compares him to Orpheus, and declares that the chief philosophical influence operating upon his own thought had been the essay *On Friendship*, supplemented by Boethius (p. 34).[2] Dante also knew several of Cicero's other treatises, admiring him as 'Rome's best Aristotelian'. The classification of sins in the *Inferno* is taken from *On Duties*, and Dante's whole poetic vision of the voyage of the soul is the largest and most complex of all the many adaptations from the *Dream of*

1. *On Duties* was used by the Paris Arts Faculty in the mid thirteenth century as its guide to social ethics, Aristotle's *Ethics* being employed for the study of the inner life.

2. *Convivio*, II, 13.

*Scipio*. The same work, with Macrobius's commentary, was read by Chaucer, who summarized it at the beginning of his *Parliament of Fowls*, thus setting the birds' debate on love against a background of philosophical inquiry.

*

One of the very strongest forces contributing to the ideals of the Italian Renaissance, and thus to the whole intellectual, scientific and social development of western Europe, was Cicero's thought as interpreted by Petrarch (d. 1374). Though Petrarch was inspired by Cicero's thought because of its affinities with his own, the novel element in his humanism was his devoted determination to use the Roman as his guide in interpreting the present through the past.

For Cicero seemed to him the inimitable paragon of eloquence, the delineator of a perfect human relationship based on speech, the portrayer of an ideal enlightened Roman social system and way of life. Petrarch also welcomed him as the spokesman for civilized, active leisure, and, in his essay *On the Solitary Life* and elsewhere, quoted him in order to show that the highest aim of leisure is to be busy. No one since Roman times had praised activity so highly, or stressed so greatly the desirability of renown won by inborn merit – though Petrarch himself, an exile from Florence, 'the hermit of Vaucluse', was disposed to reject the life of community and family in favour of the activity of the mind. In keeping with his own situation, Petrarch for a time accepted the medieval picture of Cicero as a sort of philosophical anchorite – a picture based on parts of the *Tusculans* and on the *Dream*. But when he first read the *Letters to Atticus* he was shocked to learn how Cicero had returned to politics after Caesar's death. For Petrarch had previously liked to suppose that all the literary works of Cicero's last years were written in glorious scholarly solitude. And it was, above all, as the stimulating thinker on moral questions that he admired the

Roman.[1] But then Petrarch managed to adjust himself to the new point of view.

Like later humanists in Renaissance times, he was a devout Christian. But he reconciled Cicero with his religion by declaring, 'You would fancy sometimes that it is not a pagan philosopher but a Christian apostle speaking.' However, he himself preferred ethics to theology, and felt that salvation must come through right conduct. Petrarch did not know the Platonic writings well, but, prompted by Cicero's praise of the Academy, he saw the orator, and Plato before him, as opponents of the 'arid theorizing' of Aristotelian scholasticism.[2] Aristotle, at this time, was reaching the climax of his dominance in Italy, but Petrarch, who wanted a guide to life – someone who could demonstrate the ideal way of living – preferred Cicero on the grounds that Aristotle, though more skilled in defining virtue, was less effective in urging its cultivation.

The next generation of Italians brought Cicero right out of the study, since they readily found his patriotic responsibility the fulfilment, not the negation, of his moral teaching. Florence was one of the last Italian city-states to remain free of dictatorial rule, and Petrarch's pupil, the Chancellor Coluccio Salutati (1331–1406), saw his city as heir to the Roman Republic and champion of individual liberties: a fact to which he attributed Florentine cultural pre-eminence. So Cicero, whose *Letters to his Friends* were discovered by Salutati's agent at Vercelli in 1392, earned the Chancellor's admiration because he had taken part in political life and civil war, and had thirsted for political renown. A pupil of Salutati, Pier Paolo Vergerio, again cited Cicero to illustrate a civic culture which

1. His prose style was mainly inspired by Cicero's philosophical treatises and Seneca's *Moral Letters*.

2. Acceptance of Cicero's arguments in favour of the Latin language in *On the Chief Good and Evil* (I, 3, 10 and III, 2, 5) caused him to believe that Latin literature was far superior to Greek.

needs no scholarly retreat but thrives in the very midst of the activities of daily life (1402–3). And so the ideal of the liberally educated secular administrator gained strength, and Leonardo Bruni Aretino, who likewise studied with Salutati and was also a friend of the English humanist Duke Humphrey of Gloucester, hailed this 'new version of Cicero' (1415), admiring his union of political action and literary creation as an ideal blend, and later commenting that 'among the stay-at-homes, withdrawn from human society, I have never seen one who could count up to three'.[1] In this atmosphere the first complete text of *On the Orator*, found at Lodi in 1421, attracted wide popularity. Then Matteo Palmieri, in his *Della Vita Civile* (c. 1430), combines *On Duties* and the *Dream of Scipio* in a crowning chapter portraying Dante, on the field of battle, receiving a message from the other world.

The dazzling outbursts of creative vitality in the fifteenth-century Italian city-states was believed by their inhabitants themselves to be a rebirth, a Renaissance, of classical activity.[2] And this Renaissance meant, above all, a fresh look at Cicero, his revival as a guide to the times, his elevation to be the chief liberator of the human mind from the shackles of blindly accepted authority, and his acceptance as champion of free thought, free will, individualism, rationality and style. Cicero's concept of the whole man, combining mastery of language with a sense of public responsibility and a cultivated employment of leisure, was what infused the philosophical studies of the day with their powerful humanistic element.[3]

1. The argument went on. In the dialogue of Cristoforo Landino (1434–1504), staged at Camaldoli in imitation of the *Tusculans*, Lorenzo the Magnificent praises the life of action and L. B. Alberti the life of contemplation.

2. Venice particularly saw itself as the modern counterpart of Cicero's State.

3. A medallion portrait of Pier Candido Decembrio by Pisanello, before 1450, shows one of the first applications of the term *humanitas* to Renaissance Latin studies.

This same ideal also became the kernel of the education of the Renaissance upper class, through the school of Vittorino da Feltre (c. 1373–1446) at Mantua (on which numerous academies of Europe were later based), as well as the university-style college of Guarino Veronese (1374–1460) at Ferrara. The only prose works included in the Ferrara curriculum were two of Cicero's treatises, *On Duties* and the *Tusculans*, and his *Letters*. Guarino had English admirers and pupils, including John Tiptoft who translated *On Friendship* (c. 1481), and he and men like him ensured that Cicero had pride of place in the educational system of England.

*

Translations into several languages were now under way,[1] and soon there were printed editions of the originals. Within the very first year in which classical books were printed (1465), *On Duties* was published twice, at Subiaco and Mainz, and in the same year Subiaco published *On the Orator*. Before the end of the century, printers in Italy had produced more than 200 editions of Cicero; for in royal courts, chanceries, embassies, churches and universities his Latinity was dominant. The Italian humanist Politian (Angelo Poliziano) felt it necessary to rebel against people who tried to ape Cicero too exactly (1490). 'Someone will say "You do not express Cicero." I answer: "I am not Cicero, what I really express is myself."'[2] And away to the north another who protested against mere mechanical imitation was Erasmus of Rotterdam, in his *Ciceronianus* (1528). This protest earned a shocked denuncia-

1. *On Friendship* into French (c.1418) and English (before 1460, printed 1481), *On Duties* into Spanish (c.1456) and German (1488). Theodorus of Gaza (c.1400–1475) translated *On Friendship* and *On Old Age* into Greek.

2. The dispute was renewed by the eclectic Pico della Mirandola and the ultra-Ciceronian papal secretary Cardinal Bembo (1512). At Ferrara in 1542, Olimpia Morata was trying to imitate the dialogues of Cicero and Plato at the age of fourteen.

tion from the French classical scholar Scaliger, who described Cicero as wholly flawless and Erasmus as a parricide, parasite and mere corrector of proofs. Nevertheless, Erasmus was extremely devoted to Cicero – more so than to any other writer, and as he grew older his devotion increased. For one thing, *On Duties* seemed to him to embody every single principle that a youth embarking on a public career could need; and the *Tusculans* caused him to declare, 'I do not know what others feel, but when I read this work I cannot doubt that a divinity inspired the man who wrote such beautiful things.' Erasmus praised Cicero for being such a good popularizer – for bringing philosophy within reach of the common man; and he insisted that this pagan's moral doctrines were more truly Christian than many a discussion by theologians and monks.

The Dutchman bears witness to the Ciceronian influences that spread so widely in the sixteenth century outside Italy, bringing humanity and style to northern lands. Martin Luther considered Cicero's treatises superior even to those of Aristotle, and Melanchthon described *On Duties* as a masterpiece that could not possibly be excelled. Between 1553 and 1610 this essay ran into ten editions, a figure equalled by no other work. In Richard Fox's statutes for Corpus Christi College, Oxford (1517), *On Duties* had been established as set reading. Then from the middle of the century it is often found in English school curricula. Yet this and the other writings were prominent not only in Protestant places of education but also among Jesuit instructors, who taught *On Friendship* in their top grammar forms (1551) and the *Tusculans* in the Humanities class to which pupils went next. Montaigne (1533–92), though he complained that Cicero's essays were verbose and 'languidly beat about the bush', quoted him 312 times, grew fonder and fonder of him as he grew older (like Erasmus), and derived from *On Duties* (I) his concern with discovering, and remaining true to, one's own self.

Edward Herbert (1583–1648) based much of his natural history of religion on Cicero, and John Locke (1632–1704) was another who owed a great deal to his influence. 'A beautiful soul always,' pronounced Montesquieu (1689–1755), 'when it was not weak.' Humanists, deists of all kinds, free-thinkers, and the cool rationalists of the day, all had something to draw from this rich store. 'I desire,' wrote David Hume, 'to take my Catalogue of Virtues from Cicero's *Offices* (*On Duties*).' The 'amiability of virtue' admired by eighteenth-century philosophers comes from Cicero, and any Whig statesman of the time had much in common with a Roman of Cicero's day – and was conscious of the fact. Diderot was an admirer, and so was Voltaire. 'We honour Cicero,' he said, 'who taught us how to think,' and he remarked (with fervent agreement from Frederick the Great) that no book on moral questions ever written has equalled *On Duties* in value.

Kant was influenced by the same work (p. 10), and so was the youthful Schiller (1759–1805). Thomas Jefferson infused the American Declaration of Independence (1776) with Ciceronian natural law and an acknowledgement of 'certain unalienable rights' of man, and filled his own notebook with references to the *Tusculans*; and John Adams, quoting Cicero extensively in his *Preface on Government* (1786), observed that 'all ages of the world have not produced a greater statesman and philosopher combined'. Meanwhile Cicero, often the model of spiritual rebels as well as of establishments, old or new, was no stranger to young Frenchmen fired by the Revolution, such as Camille Desmoulins who described *On Duties* as a masterpiece of common sense.[1]

Macaulay (1800–1859) was another who greatly admired the same work, and during his lifetime commentaries on this and the other treatises attained new heights of efficiency. A good deal of Cicero's influence could still be detected, though

1. Johan Madvig's edition of *On the Chief Good and Evil* (1839) was particularly important.

it had passed through several hands, in the patriotic nationalism of the Germans, the moral public-school training of the imperial English, and the French enthusiasm for rhetoric[1].

*

Yet the nineteenth century witnessed an eclipse of Cicero's reputation, especially as regards his philosophical writings. His lack of 'originality' was now for the first time seriously held against him, with the result that his true merits were neglected (p. 15). Furthermore, the originals had been Greek, and this was such a phil-Hellenic age that a Latin interpreter and adapter of the Greeks stood no chance. The greatest of all ancient historians, Theodor Mommsen (1817–93), had another reason for objecting to Cicero – because the orator's Republican politics were distasteful to a man who disliked the Prussian Junkers of his own day. However understandable, that condemnation of Cicero helped German liberalism on its disastrous downward path. But an attitude even more common in the later nineteenth century was the willingness to leave him to one side, on the grounds that he 'has in great measure been absorbed into the fabric of civilized society'.[2]

Society has subsequently shown that it has not learnt Cicero's principal messages. In England, particularly, the neglect of his treatises has continued. Perhaps they are *too* relevant : they strike near the bone, since few people have the time or inclination to reflect about the practical principles that ought to be governing their lives. Cicero's ideals do not dwell in Utopias, but in the real world. His treatises are for people who possess mature and independent minds, who have no desire to follow other minds slavishly, and who are compelled, in the course of their daily existences, to grapple with problems which are complex – rarely admitting of a purely intellectual solution – and which call on all the resources of their humanity.

1. The word 'humanism' first appeared in German, c.1808.

2. J. W. Mackail, *Latin Literature*, 1895, p. 73.

For it is usually only with increasing experience, maturity, and above all with the ever-increasing network of ties and responsibilities that life as a member of a family, a profession and a community brings to a man, that the real difficulties of moral decision are felt and understood, and that there comes, if it ever comes, the realization that most people most of the time do not live in a world of chivalric selfless endeavour – but they have their problems of 'what to do' which merit consideration. ... *On Duties* is a work on adult topics for readers with adult tastes.

I owe that quotation to Mr A. E. Douglas.[1] And I am grateful to him for letting me see a proof of his recent survey of Ciceronian studies.[2] I also appreciate the kindness of Professor F. H. Newark in advising me about legal terminology. And finally I want to thank my wife for a great deal of invaluable help.

*Gattaiola, 1971* MICHAEL GRANT

1. *Cicero*, op. cit., p. 149.
2. 'Cicero', *Greece and Rome* (New Surveys in the Classics, No. 2), Oxford University Press, 1968.

# LIST OF LATIN AND GREEK TERMS

ACADEMY: see p. 28.
AEDILES: Officials ranking over quaestors and below praetors (q.v.). concerned with the care of the city of Rome, its corn-supply and its Games. The original plebeian aediles, representing the plebs (like the tribunes), were augmented in 367 BC by two 'curule aediles', representing the whole people.
AS: The basic denomination of currency, of which the regular coining (in bronze) ceased early in the first century BC. Four *asses* comprised one *sestertius* (q.v.), and sixteen *asses* made one silver *denarius*.
ASSEMBLY: An Assembly of the Roman people, ie. citizens summoned in various sorts of group (eg. tribes, q.v.) by a senior official. The Assembly enacted laws, elected to offices of state, and declared war and peace; but under the dictators and triumvirs (q.v.) it was powerless.
AUGURS: The official Roman diviners; one of the four Orders of Priesthood. They consulted the divine will by taking the auspices at the request of a state official.
BOARD OF ONE HUNDRED: see Centumviri.
BOARD OF TEN (*decemviri*): see Twelve Tables.
CENSORS: Officials appointed every five (earlier every four) years to draw up and maintain the list of citizens (*census*) and revise the list of senators.
CENTUMVIRI: This 'Board of One Hundred' – actually numbering 105 members, and later 180 – was an annually appointed special court of justice for certain types of important legal case. The Board may have been founded in the mid second century BC.
CHIEF PRIEST: The Pontifex Maximus, head of the Board of Priests (see Priests), and head of the whole state clergy.
CLIENTS: These were dependents whose moral and legal relation to the leading Romans who were their patrons, with its powerful and hereditary mutual obligations, formed a vital element in Roman social and political life. Freed slaves became the clients of their former masters, and towns throughout Italy and the empire had their

patrons at Rome; whole communities in the provinces and on the frontiers were 'clients' of the Roman state itself.

CONSULS: The supreme civil and military officials ('magistrates') of the Roman Republic, two in number, holding office for one year and giving their names to that year.

CYNICS: see p. 27n.

CYRENAICS: see p. 25n.

DICTATOR: Originally a temporary, extraordinary, supreme office for an emergency, restricted to six months. Sulla retained the power for two years, and Caesar, after three renewals, assumed it permanently shortly before his death.

EPHOR: At Sparta the ephors were a body of five magistrates exercising control over the kings.

EPICUREANS: see p. 25.

FORUM: The Forum Romanum, the chief public place of Rome, surrounded by important temples and halls. The term 'Forum' is often used to signify the centre of public, legal and other business.

FREEDMEN: Liberated ('manumitted') slaves.

IUS CIVILE: This originally meant 'the law of the Roman citizen', i.e. of Rome as opposed to the law of any other state. It does not mean 'civil law' in any of the four senses in which this term is found in English and American usage. It can sometimes be translated 'common law', referring to good old rules that are still operative or contrasting such rules with more recent statutes, but it is usually best translated 'law', conveying the idea that the matter in question is not a matter of morals or social convention but is subject to rules imposed by the State.

KINGS: Traditionally the earlier rulers of Rome, from its foundation by Romulus until the expulsion of Tarquinius Superbus (510 BC: though monarchic rule may not have ended until the 5th century BC). The kings are partly mythical and partly historical.

KNIGHTS (*equites*): A powerful Order with financial interests as well as career ambitions (minimum property qualification 400,000 *sestertii*, q.v.). They were outside the Senate and from the 2nd century BC (and especially from the time of the Gracchi) often conflicted with its interests; though the pattern of alliances and conflicts was a complex one.

MINA (MNA): A large unit of Greek currency. At Athens, from the time of Solon, it consisted of 100 silver drachms.

OSTRACISM: At Athens, banishment without loss of citizen rights or property for ten years. Each citizen inscribed on a piece of broken earthenware (*ostrakon*) the name of the person whose banishment he favoured.

PATRICIANS: A privileged class of distinguished houses at Rome – the inner aristocracy. The same clan (*gens*) could comprise or develop both patrician and non-patrician (plebeian) families or branches.

PATRONS: see Clients.

PERIPATETICS: see p. 24.

PLEBEIANS: see Patricians.

PRAETORS: The annually selected state officials, in Cicero's time eight in number, who were next in importance to the consuls; largely concerned with the administration of justice. The senior member was the city (urban) praetor.

PRIESTS (*pontifices*): One of the four Orders of Roman Priesthood (see also Augurs), presided over by the Pontifex Maximus or Chief Priest (q.v.). The younger Quintus Mucius Scaevola was known as 'the Priest' (Pontifex) to distinguish him from his older relative of the same name called 'the Augur'.

PYTHAGOREANS: see p. 22.

QUAESTORS: The lowest annually elected state office in the senator's career; in Cicero's time comprising twenty officials.

SCEPTICS: see p. 28n.

SENATE: The chief Council of the State, its numbers raised to 600 by Sulla and 900 by Caesar. Sulla made admission depend mainly on tenure of the quaestorship (q.v.). The Senate was technically an advisory body, but by tradition it wielded great influence over the executive Assembly (q.v.) – an influence which the Gracchi, deplored by Cicero, tried to weaken and which the two triumvirates, and the intervening dictatorship of Caesar, wholly undermined.

SESTERTIUS (*sesterce*): A unit of currency, containing four *asses* (q.v.).

STOICS: see p. 26.

TRIBES: All Roman citizens were registered in one of the thirty-five territorial 'tribes' (four urban and the others rural), which were the units for voting on certain matters in the Assembly. The allocation of freedmen (q.v.) to tribes was a major issue in Cicero's youth.

TRIBUNES, MILITARY (*tribuni militum*): The senior officers of the legions in the army of the Roman Republic. Six knights (q.v.), elected by the Assembly, were assigned to hold these posts in each legion.

TRIBUNES OF THE PEOPLE (*tribuni plebis*, generally translated as 'tribunes'): They possessed ancient 'democratic' powers entitling them to 'protect the people' by intercessions and vetos directed against officers of state. The Gracchi revived these long obsolete powers, and the dictator Sulla abolished them; but the tribunes made themselves felt again in the years 70–49 BC.

TRIUMPH: The processional return of a victorious Roman general, when he sacrificed to Jupiter on the Capitol. Triumphs were awarded by the Senate.

TRIUMVIRS: The informal First Triumvirate was established by Cnaeus Pompeius Magnus, Marcus Licinius Crassus and Gaius Julius Caesar in 60–59 BC, and the Second Triumvirate by Marcus Antonius (Mark Antony), Octavian (the future Augustus) and Marcus Aemilius Lepidus in 43 BC.

TWELVE TABLES: The earliest Roman code of law, drawn up, at least in part, by a Board of Ten (*decemviri*) in 451–450 BC.

TYRANT: The name (of non-Greek origin) given to the individuals who assumed autocratic powers in many Greek city-states in the seventh and sixth centuries BC and then again from the time of Dionysius I of Syracuse (405–367 BC).

# DISCUSSIONS AT TUSCULUM

THE *Tusculans* are intended to raise people to a higher level; to strengthen them and inspire them to a better way of life. Cicero himself describes the contents of these five books or volumes:

They examine the essentials for a happy life. The first volume shows that death is not to be feared, and the second that pain is endurable. The third indicates how sorrow can be alleviated, the fourth deals with other disturbances of the mind, and the fifth handles a proposition which brilliantly illuminates the entire field of philosophy – the proposition that moral goodness, by itself, is sufficient to make anyone happy.[1]

That is to say, the first four parts of the treatise have stated the view that human beings are capable of acting rationally despite the influence of fears, pains and emotional disturbances in general. The fifth book, which is translated here, is the culmination of this attempt to show how these distractions, which militate against happiness, must be confronted. The entire work is gathered up in the single thought that moral goodness is *in itself* sufficient for a happy life. But one of the principal points that remains at issue is whether it is the *only* good or whether there are others as well (pp. 24, 26).[2]

A book which Erasmus regarded as superlative must indeed be worth reading. But 'Tusculan Disputations' is a forbidding title which during recent years (in remarkable contrast to earlier times) has helped to get this treatise left on the shelf

1. Cicero, *On Divination*, II, 2. For 'happiness' see above, pp. 23, 25.

2. It seems impossible to discover what sources Cicero was drawing upon. He quotes the Peripatetic Dicaearchus, Aristotle's pupil (*Tusculans*, I, 10, 21), and on 29 May 45 BC he was asking Atticus for some of Dicaearchus's works. But he is likely to have used a number of other authorities as well.

(p. 43).[1] Yet it is the least demanding of Cicero's studies, and if we can overcome a modern distaste for being edified, it is also one of the most entertaining, in addition to being highly characteristic of its author.[2]

The *Tusculans* date from a time which Cicero found terrible – the last year of Caesar's dictatorship and life, when the orator had no part to play in politics (p. 15). The work is dedicated to the austere Brutus who was shortly to become Caesar's murderer, and had already, in the previous year, been invited by Cicero to emulate his two great ancestors, Lucius Brutus who drove out the tyrant Tarquinius and Lucius Ahala who killed the would-be tyrant, Maelius.[3] But meanwhile, in February 45, Cicero had suffered a shattering bereavement when his daughter Tullia died. In a moment of complete despair he declared that, with Tullia dead and the way to public life barred,[4] death itself would come as a blessing. Nevertheless, he makes it the purpose of the *Tusculans* to explain how life's great unhappinesses ought to be confronted. He is consoling himself, and consoling others as well, and indeed the world has often eagerly taken comfort from what he wrote.

But apart from these contemporary circumstances Cicero had a special reason for turning to this sort of subject. In his immediately preceding book, giving different views *On the Chief Good and Evil* (*De Finibus*; p. 8n), he had considered the theoretical side of ethics and enunciated the broad principles on which human conduct should rest. Now was the time to seek the practical applications of these doctrines.

The scene is Cicero's country villa at Tusculum near

1. This title should really be translated 'Discussions at my country house at Tusculum'.

2. Cicero consciously gave the work a decorative, rhetorical character (*Tusculans*, I, 4, 7).

3. *Brutus*, 96, 331. See also p. 192n.

4. *Tusculans*, I, 34, 84.

Frascati, thirteen miles from Rome. He had a good many residences (mostly not very large, though even so he could ill afford them), but this was his favourite. He had acquired it in 68 BC on valuable land with the money of his wife Terentia. Once he thought of selling the house when it was damaged by political rowdies during his exile; but he repeatedly wrote in his letters how dear it was to him. He spent the greater part of the years 46 and 45 at this place where, as Merivale pointed out, 'he could see the seven hills fade in haze on the horizon'. The villa itself, and buildings in the grounds, were full of Greek works of art, including a statue of Hermathena on a square pillar of which he was particularly proud. A roof-tile inscribed with Cicero's name was found at Tusculum in the 1740s, and consequently one set of remains has been identified as his house; but the identification is over-optimistic, since many other Romans had mansions there as well. They included the wealthy Lucius Licinius Lucullus, whose magnificent library was available for Cicero to consult. In 46 Cicero had his son-in-law Publius Cornelius Dolabella and Caesar's lieutenant Aulus Hirtius to stay, and tells us that he gave them lessons in rhetoric in return for instruction in dining. The present work, we are given to understand by Cicero, is the product of five days of similar debate, this time on philosophical subjects;[1] though probably the whole dialogue is just a fictitious framework for the author's thoughts (p. 20).

We do not know who, if anyone, the two participants in the discussion are meant to be, though the principal speaker (who tends to monologue) speaks with Cicero's own voice. In manuscripts from the sixth century AD onwards the two men are sometimes described as 'M(agister)' and D(iscipulus)', the Latin for 'master' and 'pupil' (the initials written in Greek). Renaissance manuscripts altered the initial *delta* of 'Discipulus' into 'A', thus puzzling future commentators. Here I call the two personages 'Cicero' and 'Friend'.

1. *Tusculans*, I, 7.

# DISCUSSIONS AT TUSCULUM (V)

HERE we are, Brutus, on the fifth and last day of our discussions at Tusculum. And this was the day when we discussed the subject that is nearest of all to your heart. For the book you wrote with such care and dedicated to myself, as well as our numerous conversations with one another, have shown me the strength of your conviction that in order to live a happy life the only thing we need is moral goodness.[1]

Certainly, after all the varied blows of fortune that have descended on our heads, it is a hard thing to prove! All the same, we have simply got to do everything we can to make people accept this conclusion, because the entire range of philosophy contains nothing more essential or more sublime. That is why the very first philosophers who ever existed dismissed all other considerations into the background and devoted themselves entirely to the search for the best way to live. The reason why they decided to dedicate all their care and concentration to this quest was because they believed it would reveal to them how happiness could be attained. And if, as I argue, happiness can only come from what is morally right – an idea which they invented and elaborated – nobody can fail to admit that philosophy, which they founded and we have carried on, is a very glorious activity indeed.

But just suppose, on the other hand, that the good way of life lay at the mercy of a whole lot of unpredictable accidents, so that if the appropriate accidents were not forthcoming this goodness would lack sufficient strength to maintain itself independently on its own account. If that were really so, all we could do then to achieve a happy life, it seems to me, would be merely to hope for the best and pray heaven that

1. Brutus's essay *On Virtue*, now lost. The doctrine is that of the Stoics (p. 26).

happiness might somehow come our way. For in such a situation to behave decently would not benefit us in the least.

And indeed as I think of my personal experiences, and all the formidable hazards to which fortune has subjected me, there are moments when I begin to doubt this moral theory myself – the feebleness and frailty of mankind seem too terrifying. What disturbs me most is the fact that nature, not content with giving us bodies that are weak and liable to incurable illnesses and unendurable agonies, has also endowed us with hearts and souls which not only share these physical sufferings but are involved, besides, in additional, separate, pains and troubles of their own.

However, when such considerations seem too depressing I check myself, and try to reflect that I have perhaps been judging the power of moral goodness not by its own real strength at all, but on the basis of this or that defect shown by individual human beings, not excluding myself. For if such a thing as moral goodness really exists – and it was your uncle, Brutus, who dispelled my doubts on this point[1] – then it surely possesses the ability to rise above the accidents that can befall human beings. It can look down upon them all, with complete contempt for the hazards of mortal life: it is incapable of any shortcomings whatever, and dependent on nothing but itself.

We mortals, however, do not come up to this standard. When misfortunes appear on the horizon, we exaggerate them from sheer fright, and when they are right upon us we exaggerate them once more, because of the pain they are causing us. These feelings impel us to put the blame on circumstances when what we ought to be blaming is a deficiency in our own character.

*

1. Marcus Porcius Cato the younger, who committed suicide at Utica in 46 BC.

The cure for this fault and for all our other failings and offences is philosophy. From my earliest youth I threw myself into its arms: it was my own deliberate enthusiastic choice. And now again, in my present miseries, when I am tossed by all the fury of the tempest, I have sought refuge in the very same harbour from which I first set out to sea.

Philosophy! The guide of our lives, the explorer of all that is good in us, exterminator of all evil! Had it not been for your guidance, what would I ever have amounted to – and, what, indeed, would have become of all human life? It was you who brought cities into existence. Before that, people had been scattered far and wide, but you made them come together into communities. First you united them by making them live in the same houses, and next by getting them to marry, and then by enabling them to communicate with one another by language and writing. Inventor of laws, teacher of morals, creator of order! You were all these things. And now, you are *my* refuge and rescuer. I have already relied on you so much in past years; and now my dependence is total and complete. One day well spent in obeying your rules is better than an eternity of error. Your aid is the most precious in all the world. It is you who have brought peace into our lives; you who have relieved us of the fear of death.

And yet it would be over-optimistic to suppose that philosophy gets the praise its service to mankind deserves. On the contrary, most people pay it no attention at all; and some actually subject it to abuse. And yet it seems inconceivable that anyone should abuse the begetter of his own life! To revile what, as even the dimmest mind must comprehend, unquestionably demands reverence, is sheer base ingratitude, no better than killing one's own parent. The reason, I suppose, why uneducated people have fallen into this darkest of all errors is because they are incapable of looking far enough back into the past; this is what makes them fail to realize that the people who first created civilization were the philosophers.

*

Nevertheless, although we see that philosophy itself is of extreme antiquity, it has to be admitted that its name is of recent origin. If, on the other hand, you prefer to call it 'wisdom' instead, you are using a name which is as old as the thing itself. For it was in very ancient times that this wonderful designation was given to the study of all heavenly and earthly phenomena, and their beginnings and causes. And so the famous Seven were called *sophoi*, meaning wise, by the Greeks, and were estimated and named Wise Men by our own countrymen as well.

Indeed, already many centuries before that, according to the tradition, Lycurgus had been a wise man and was accepted as one – even before the foundation of our city, in the days when Homer is thought to have lived; and earlier still the same could be said of Ulysses and Nestor. Nor, surely, would we have all the stories of Atlas holding up the sky and Prometheus nailed down on the Caucasian range and Cepheus elevated among the stars in the company of his wife and daughter and her husband, if these had not been men who, in their mortal days, achieved some genuine, marvellous discoveries of supra-terrestrial truths, capable of giving rise to these fictitious fairy-tales. They, therefore, are the heroes who must be considered pioneers among that whole succession of researchers into natural phenomena who were hailed and described as 'wise'.[1]

The term was still being used in the time of Pythagoras. He, according to a tale reported by Plato's learned pupil

1. For the Seven Wise Men, see p. 178. Lycurgus was the legendary or semi-legendary founder of the Spartan discipline, attributed to dates varying between 1100 and 600 BC (the seventh century is now favoured). According to Greek mythology Atlas was a Titan condemned by Zeus to support heaven on his head and hands in the far west, where he was identified with the mountain-range that still bears his name. Prometheus was his brother. Cepheus, king of Ethiopia, was husband of Cassiopea, and father of Andromeda who was married to Perseus.

Heraclides of Pontus,[1] came to the Peloponnesian city of Phlius, and engaged in lengthy and erudite discussions with its ruler Leon. Deeply impressed by his intellect and eloquence, Leon asked Pythagoras which subject he regarded as particularly important. He replied that he had no knowledge of any special subject, but was a *philosopher*. Leon was astonished at the word, which was unfamiliar to him, and inquired who philosophers were and how they differed from other people.

Then Pythagoras, the story continues, answered that human life seemed to him comparable with the festival to which people flocked from all over Greece in order to see those magnificent Games.[2] This is an occasion for which some people have gone into physical training in the hope of winning the splendid distinction of a crown, while others are attracted by the prospect of buying or selling for profit, whereas a further category again – and these represent an especially good class of person – are interested in winning neither applause nor profit, but come merely for the sake of the spectacle, to get a thorough look at what is going on and how it is done. And we too, said Pythagoras, as we enter this life from some other kind of existence,[3] behave like people who have moved out of town to join the crowds at this sort of show. Some of us are enslaved to glory, others to money. But there are also a few people who devote themselves wholly to the study of the universe, believing everything else to be trivial in comparison. These call themselves students of wisdom, in other words philosophers; and just as a festival attracts individuals of the finest type who just watch the proceedings without a thought of getting anything for themselves, so too, in life generally,

1. For Pythagoras of Samos see p. 22. Heraclides of Heraclea in Pontus (p. 19), though a philosopher of the Academy, based his molecular theory on Pythagorean doctrine.

2. The Olympic Games. The crown was of wild olive.

3. The Pythagorean doctrine of metempsychosis; see p. 22.

the contemplation and study of nature are far superior to the whole range of other human activities.

Nor did Pythagoras only invent the name of philosophy, for he extended its subject matter as well. After engaging in these discussions at Phlius, he went on to Italy,[1] where he enriched both the private and public life of the Greek part of the country, Greater Greece as we call it, with superb institutions and arts; I hope to say something about his doctrines on another occasion.

From its earliest beginnings right down to the time of Socrates, who attended the lectures of Anaxagoras's pupil Archelaus,[2] philosophy was accustomed to dealing with numerical questions and the laws of movement, and the problems of creation and decline; its practitioners also meticulously investigated the dimensions of the stars, and the distances which separate one from another, and the nature of their orbits and generally every sort of astronomical phenomenon.

Socrates, however, took the initiative in summoning philosophy down from the heavens. He transferred it to the actual cities inhabited by mankind, and moved it right into people's own homes; and he compelled it to ask questions about how one ought to live and behave, and what is good and what is bad. The variety of his methods of discussion, and the complexity of his material, and the greatness of his genius – all of which have been immortalized in Plato's writings – caused the emergence of a number of different philosophical schools, putting forward contradictory views. The school I myself have particularly followed is the one which in my view comes closest to Socrates in its methods: it allows me to refrain from expressing a personal opinion of my own, while I

1. Pythagoras settled at Croton in southwestern Italy.

2. Archelaus was either an Athenian or a Milesian who moved to Athens. His teacher Anaxagoras (d. 428 BC) came from Clazomenae in Ionia.

am at liberty to correct other people's mistakes and make my own search for the most probable solution, whatever subject may happen to be involved. This was the approach employed by Carneades,[1] with great penetration and eloquence, and I have repeatedly made use of it myself. Indeed, I have been employing this very method now, in these conversations of ours here at Tusculum.

*

The talks which occupied us for the first four days I have put into writing; and I sent them on to you. When the fifth day came, we sat down once again at the same spot, and discussed what subject we should tackle next. This is how our conversation went.

FRIEND: I don't believe that just being good is enough, in itself, to make anyone happy.

CICERO: You don't? Well, let me tell you that my friend Brutus believes it, and if you don't mind my saying so I consider his opinion far more valuable than yours.

FRIEND: That is what I should expect. But we aren't concerned at the moment with your affection for Brutus. The point before us now is the denial I have just expressed; and that is what I should like you to consider.

CICERO: So you really mean that moral goodness is not capable, by itself, of creating a happy life?

FRIEND: Yes, I insist that it can't do any such thing.

CICERO: Tell me this, then. Would you agree that being good is the same thing as living virtuously, honourably, laudably, and, in a word, *well*?

FRIEND: Of course; because a person is quite capable of living virtuously, honourably, laudably and well even when he is being tortured – provided you appreciate the sense in which I am now using the word 'well'. What I mean it to convey is staunchness, dignity, wisdom, courage. For these

1. Carneades of Cyrene was founder of the Third Academy (p. 28).

are qualities that need not desert a man even when he is being tormented on the rack: whereas, on the other hand, that is certainly not an experience the happy life aspires to!

CICERO: I see. Are you saying, then, that when staunchness, dignity, courage, wisdom and all the other virtues are hurried along to the torturer, and do not flinch from even the most dreadful torments and pains, happiness stays behind on the threshold outside the prison walls?

FRIEND: If you want to establish your point, you will really have to look for some new arguments! The ones you have just put forward totally fail to impress me. They are hackneyed, for one thing. And besides, these Stoic maxims remind one of a light wine which is no good in water – they are better sipped than drained in deep draughts.

Take your band of virtues, for example, and their willingness to be tormented on the rack. This makes a very edifying spectacle, and one is tempted to conclude that Happiness will surely rush off to join them because it will feel they ought not to be abandoned. But when you turn your gaze away from this allegorical picture and instead look at the hard facts, there remains this plain question: how can anyone who is being tortured possibly be happy? And that is the question we now have to ask.

As for the virtues, there is no need to worry about the possibility of their complaining and lamenting because Happiness has failed to stay with them. Because an essential element in every virtue is Prudence; and Prudence is perfectly capable, unaided, of detecting that it is *not* true to say that all good men are happy. It will easily be able, for example, to recall everything that happened to Marcus Atilius and Quintus Caepio and Manius Aquilius – whose fates prove that precisely the contrary is the case.[1] Consequently (if you still

1. Marcus Atilius Regulus was defeated by the Carthaginians in the First Punic War (255 BC). Quintus Servilius Caepio was defeated by the Cimbri (105 BC). (Cicero probably meant to cite another commander,

want to go on talking in terms of allegories rather than concrete facts) the endeavours by Happiness to place itself on the rack are thwarted by Prudence, which declares that it has nothing whatever to do with pain and torture.

CICERO: Very well, you are at liberty to take that line if you want to – although it is not quite playing fair when you lay down in advance the way in which you want me to conduct my inquiry! However, there's one thing that I do feel impelled to ask. Would you consider that our discussions on the previous days achieved any results or not?

FRIEND: Certainly they did, and substantial ones too.

CICERO: Well, if that is so, we surely ought to regard this particular question as having been already thrashed out and settled for good!

FRIEND: Whatever do you mean?

CICERO: I mean this. We concluded that violent commotions and upheavals of the soul, when it is agitated and troubled by some irrational impulse or other, are altogether incompatible with happiness. For example, anyone who fears pain or death must inevitably be unhappy, because pain is a frequent occurrence, and death always hovers not far off. Or if, as happens all too often, a man is afraid of poverty, disgrace and scandal, if he is terrified of bodily collapse and blindness and slavery – a disaster which often overtakes not merely individuals but whole powerful communities – no one, surely, who suffers from terrors such as these can possibly be happy.

And then there are the people who are not just frightened that these things will descend upon them in the future, but who actually have to support and endure such onslaughts here

---

Marcus Aemilius Scaurus, instead, since like the other two men he mentions, but unlike Caepio, he was captured and killed.) Manius Aquilius was captured by King Mithridates VI of Pontus (88 BC). The allegory quoted somewhat disparagingly by Cicero (but returned to later without protest) illustrates the Stoic dogma of the inseparability of the virtues.

and now. Add exile, if you wish, to the list of troubles – and bereavement, and childlessness. How can somebody suffering from such afflictions be anything but exceptionally unhappy? Or when you see a man driven to a mad frenzy by lust, so that he plunges himself insatiably into every sort of sensuality, and still, the deeper the draughts he takes from every source, the more furious and rabid his thirst becomes: there, obviously, is another thoroughly unhappy man. And consider the person who lets frivolities dominate him completely, until he becomes quite beside himself with all his pointless amusements and stupid crazes: such an individual may believe himself to be living happily, but the more he is convinced that this is so, the more desperately miserable his existence really is.

Now, the exact opposites to these unhappy people are the happy ones who are alarmed by no fears, anguished by no distresses, disturbed by no cravings, dissolved into no voluptuous languors by fatuous transports of delight. When there is not the smallest breeze to ruffle the waves of the sea one speaks of it as calm: and in the same way you are entitled to describe the condition of the soul as peaceful when no agitation disturbs its tranquillity. If, therefore, there exists any man who is capable of regarding all the hazards and accidents of fortune and human life as endurable, a man moreover who is troubled neither by fear nor by distress nor by passion, a man whom all empty pleasures of whatever kind leave utterly cold – then, if such a person exists, there is every reason why he should be happy. And the fact that this can be achieved by what is morally right leads up to the further point that this sort of goodness is enough, *by itself* and without any additional factor, to bring happiness to anyone in the world.[1]

FRIEND: Yes, one point at least is indisputable. That is to say, there is no denying that people who have no fears or distresses

1. Previous volumes of these *Discussions* have demonstrated that virtue produces happiness: it remains to show that it can do so on its own account, without any supplementation.

or desires or immoderate pleasures are happy. This I grant you. And the point you mentioned earlier, that an absence of disturbances in the soul is the source of true wisdom, does not need arguing out again from the beginning, because it was already established in our earlier discussions.

CICERO: So that is that, then. We seem to have reached the conclusion of our inquiry!

FRIEND: Very nearly so, at any rate.

CICERO: But not quite, all the same! Because that is how mathematicians would react: not philosophers. For when geometricians want to demonstrate some proposition, they take every relevant point they have dealt with in earlier demonstrations as granted and proved, and only go on to handle the matters which have not been considered before. Philosophers, on the other hand, when they have a problem to deal with, collect together and analyse all the points that are relevant to its solution, even if they have been the subjects of previous discussions.

If this had not been their practice, you would never find a Stoic going on at such length about the question whether moral goodness is enough to ensure the happy life. It would be enough for him to refer back to his previous demonstration that nothing is good except what is morally good, adding that once this point has been proved it follows that moral goodness is enough by itself to create the happy life; and then (he would go on) in just the same way as the second of those propositions has followed from the first, the fact that moral goodness is sufficient to produce happiness leads to the third conclusion that moral goodness is the only sort of good that there is. However, that is not, in fact, the way the Stoics proceed. Instead, their books allocate one separate set of studies to moral goodness and another set to the Supreme Good, and although it emerges from these studies that moral goodness *is* powerful enough to create happiness, nevertheless they reserve independent treatment for that question as well. Every single proposition, that is to say, has to be handled with its own different arguments and special appropriate considerations.

All the more so when the matter is as important as this one! For you must appreciate that what we are speaking of is the most glorious maxim, the most magnificent and fruitful promise, that has ever been pronounced in the entire history of philosophy. For what does the promise amount to? This: that, heaven willing, philosophy will ensure that the man who has obeyed its laws shall never fail to be armed against all the hazards of fortune: that he shall possess and control, within his own self, every possible guarantee for a satisfactory and happy life. In other words, that he shall always be a happy man.

The question how far philosophy actually *keeps* this promise I must reserve for some later occasion. Meanwhile, I would place on record that the mere fact that the promise has been *given* is already a matter of the very first importance.

The certainty that there is no gift in the world which can offer the same assurances as moral goodness is admirably illustrated by the story of Xerxes. Here was a man loaded with every privilege and favour that fortune could offer. But all his cavalry and infantry and fleets of ships and boundless stores of gold were not enough to satisfy him. And so he offered a reward to anyone who could discover some pleasure that was altogether new. Yet, even if such a thing had been found, he still would not have been content. For such cravings cannot ever be sated.

But I, on the other hand, would like us to offer a reward for the discovery of something totally different – a way of making it really abundantly clear to everyone that moral goodness is enough to ensure a happy life.

FRIEND: Yes, I too am very keen that we should demonstrate that. But meanwhile I've got a small request to make of you. I entirely agree that the two propositions you put forward follow from one another: that is to say, first, if moral good is the only good, then moral good is what creates happiness; and conversely, if moral good is what creates happiness, moral good is the only good. However, your friend Brutus, basing himself on Aristus and Antiochus, is not fully in agreement here. He believes, certainly, that moral good *does* create happiness. Yet he is also prepared to concede that there are other sorts of goodness *in addition to* moral good.[1]

CICERO: What do you want me to do then? Do you expect me to contradict Brutus?

FRIEND: No, you do whatever you think fit. I am certainly not going to prescribe how you ought to set about it!

CICERO: Well, then, the question who is the more consistent, Brutus or myself, we will talk about some other time. But as to the point you mention. I have often had occasion to disagree with Antiochus; and also recently with Aristus during my stay with him at Athens while I held my command.[2] What I pointed out to them was that no one who is suffering experiences that can be correctly defined as bad could possibly be happy. And if afflictions that overtake one's body, or things that go wrong owing to the operations of chance, have to be classified as bad, then it must be admitted that even the wisest of men are not exempt from bad experiences.

But they tried to explain to me – and Antiochus has often repeated the same argument in his writings – that moral goodness, while admittedly sufficient to produce a happy life, is not capable, by itself, of producing a *supremely* happy life. Most things, I was reminded, take their names from the elements that predominate in them, even when these are not

1. Aristus was the brother of Antiochus of Ascalon, the head of the Fifth Academy whose lectures Cicero attended in 79–78 BC. It was the Peripatetics, the followers of Aristotle, who believed that there were goods of body and accident (external goods) as well as moral goods of the soul (p. 24). They therefore described diseases, pain and poverty as evils, whereas the Stoics called them 'inconveniences'.

2. Cicero's governorship of Cilicia (southeastern Asia Minor, 51–50 BC).

present to the fullest possible extent. Take, for example, strength, health, wealth, honour or glory. These are all spoken of by people in general, indefinite, terms without reckoning up the exact quantity of each that may be present in any specific case. Now, the same applies to the happy life. Even if it may fall short of *perfect* happiness, nevertheless it is entitled to be called happy when happiness is the constituent which greatly exceeds all the others.

This is not the moment to investigate that theory carefully. But I must just point out that it doesn't seem to me entirely consistent. For one thing I don't understand what the happy man needs to make him happier: because if there is something missing, then the description of him as happy is wrong.[1] And then consider the assertion that all things are viewed in terms of their major component, and take their names from that. Sometimes this is true, certainly. But if, as we are told, there are three categories of good, there must be three categories of evil as well. Suppose then that a man is attacked by *two* of these sorts of evil – first, he is suffering gravely from external circumstances, or from accident; and secondly, his body is overwhelmed and consumed by fearful pains. Is it really possible to say that a person involved in troubles such as these *falls only a little short* of a happy life – not to mention a supremely happy life?

That is the position which Theophrastus found it impossible to defend. He was forced to conclude that floggings, tortures, the rack, banishment, childlessness, contribute a great deal to making life miserable and unhappy. His feelings on the subject were pessimistic and depressed, and he had not the heart to clothe them in fine or grand language.

Whether he was right to take that attitude is not the question we have to consider at the present moment. The point, for us, is that he was at least being logical: if you grant

1. This is the Stoic argument. The supreme good does not admit of degrees.

someone's premise, you have no right to reject what follows next. The premise of Theophrastus, who was, after all, a highly sophisticated and learned philosopher, was that goodness can be divided into three categories. Now that is an assertion which has aroused little criticism; and yet everybody criticizes the deductions he derived from it.

First of all, they take exception to his work *On Happiness*, in which he offers a long discussion of the reasons why a man who is being tortured and racked is not in a position to achieve happiness at all. In the course of this study Theophrastus is regarded as implying that the happy life has to keep right away from the Greek torturer's wheel of torment. He does not, it is true, at any point state this explicitly, yet what he does say amounts to the same thing. But once I have granted his point that bodily pains and ruinous accidental misfortunes must be regarded as evils, I do not see how I can then be angry with him for going on to deny that all good men are happy, seeing that these happenings – which he classifies as evils – can befall even the best of them.

And then again one philosopher after another writes books or delivers lectures attacking Theophrastus[1] because in his *Callisthenes* he expresses approval of the saying: 'Chance, and not wisdom, rules the life of men.' His critics declare that this is the most demoralizing utterance that any philosopher has ever made. Quite true! And yet, all the same, the declaration is thoroughly logical. For if so much good depends on the body, and so much else depends on sheer external accident, it is entirely consistent to conclude that chance, which is thus seen to dominate physical and non-physical occurrences alike, must be more powerful than any rational factor.

*

1. The Peripatetic philosopher, Aristotle's chief pupil (p. 24). His essay *On Happiness* and his memorial to the historian Callisthenes of Olynthus are lost.

Or do we prefer to follow Epicurus? He often makes imposing pronouncements – for the very good reason that he does not bother to be too consistent or logical! For example, he praises plain living. That is good philosopher's language: but only if it is on the lips of Socrates or Antisthenes[1] – not of the man who believes the supreme good is identical with pleasure. It is true that Epicurus then goes on to explain that no one can get pleasure out of life unless his conduct is honourable, wise and just. This is thoroughly noble, the sort of thing that is very appropriate to philosophy. Or rather, it would be, if only he did not see these virtues of honour, wisdom and justice *in terms of pleasure*. He made another splendid observation too: 'Over a man who is wise, chance has little power.' But the man who said that is also on record as asserting that pain is not merely the greatest of evils but the only evil that there is! And yet it would be perfectly possible to imagine a situation in which a man was suffering the acutest pain at the very moment when he was uttering his loudest defiance of all that chance might bring.

The same sentiment was expressed even more felicitously by his supporter Metrodorus. 'I've got the better of you, Fortune!', he declared. 'I've captured and sealed off every possible route by which you could approach me. You can't get anywhere near!' This would be an admirable sentiment in the mouths of Stoics like Aristo of Chios, or Zeno himself who wholly identified evil with moral wickedness.[2] But you, Metrodorus, were convinced that the only thing that can be described as good is what is piled up in the guts and entrails of the human body. According to you, the supreme good is sound physical health plus the confident hope that nothing will interfere with it in the future. How on earth, then, can

1. Antisthenes of Athens was a pupil of Socrates.

2. Metrodorus of Lampsacus (c.331–278 BC) was the principal follower of Epicurus. Aristo of Chios (different from Aristo of Ceos) was a pupil of Zeno, who founded Stoicism.

you suppose that you have cut off Fortune's access? Your ideal might easily vanish into thin air at any moment.

All the same, inexperienced people do get deceived by statements of this sort; the mere fact that they are uttered at all is enough to ensure that a considerable number of people are taken in. But anyone capable of accurate reasoning will not be satisfied just to listen to what this or that philosopher actually says. He will want to go on to consider the implications behind their remarks.

Take, for example, the argument I have been putting forward in our present discussions: that good men are always happy. What I mean by 'good men' is clear enough – if someone is equipped and endowed with all the virtues, then he is not only wise, he is good as well. Now let us see what we mean by happy. The happy man, I suggest, is someone who is equipped with all things that are good, without the slightest admixture of what is bad. When we say 'happy', the essential significance we attach to this word is that everything that is bad shall be excluded and everything good shall be included.

But goodness, in the moral sense, would not possess the capacity to create this condition if it were true that other kinds of goodness exist besides itself. For if they did exist, we should be attended by a host of evils – for that, evidently, is how we should have to regard them. I refer to poverty, failure, low birth, loneliness, bereavement, physical agony, ruined health, paralysis, blindness, national collapse, exile, slavery. All these states of affairs, and others besides, may easily befall even the wisest of men, since they are the products of chance, from which no man, however wise, enjoys immunity. If, therefore, they really deserve the name of evils, it is quite impossible to maintain that a person who is wise will always be happy – because, however wise he is, any of these happenings may very well overtake him at any moment: or indeed every single one of them, all at the same time.

Now, Brutus and the men who were his and my teachers, and earlier thinkers like Aristotle, Speusippus, Xenocrates and Polemo, did reckon these things as evils.[1] That being so, I cannot admit that they have any right to go on and make the further statement that the wise man is always happy. For since they are so keen on this fine and imposing epithet 'wise', with its echoes of Pythagoras and Socrates and Plato, it is imperative that they should also make every effort to stop being dazzled by physical strength, health, beauty, riches, honours and possessions. They must learn to view these things with contempt instead. If they succeed in doing this, they will be able to disregard the so-called 'evils' that are the opposites of those alleged advantages: and then they really will be in a position to proclaim, as loudly as they like, that chance and public opinion and pain and poverty hold no terrors for them, and that they regard themselves as entirely self-sufficient and refuse to attach the designation 'good' to anything they do not completely control themselves.

As it is, however, the people who hold such views cannot be allowed, first, to make the sort of pronouncements that are appropriate to noble and lofty personages, and then, in the same breath, to offer precisely the same definitions of good and evil as we are accustomed to hear from the ordinary unenlightened man in the street.

Another writer who is fond of enunciating noble maxims is Epicurus, and even he, heaven forgive me for daring to mention the fact, likewise believes that the wise man is always happy. The beauty of the formula captivates him. But he could never have contrived to utter any such sentiment if only he listened to the words coming out of his own mouth. For it is the height of inconsistency for one and the same

1. 'The men who were his and my teachers' are Antiochus, Aristus, etc. Speusippus was the nephew of Plato, whom he succeeded as head of the Academy. Xenocrates of Chalcedon was head from 339 to 314 BC, and Polemo was his successor.

person to declare, first, that pain is the supreme or even the only evil, and, secondly, that the wise man, when he is in torments of agony, will cry 'What a pleasant time I am having!'

Philosophers, in other words, must not be judged by this or that individual utterance they may choose to offer. They must be judged, instead, by all their different statements put together, and by the degree of consistency and coherence which this whole body of doctrine displays.

*

FRIEND: You very nearly convince me. All the same, watch out, or you will get accused of inconsistency yourself.

CICERO: Why, how do you mean?

FRIEND: I mean this. I have just been reading the fourth volume of your book *On the Chief Good and Evil*. There you seemed to me to be arguing, in opposition to Cato, that there was no real difference between Zeno and the Peripatetic followers of Aristotle except that Zeno had introduced some new terminology. And I agreed with you. But if this is really so, and if Zeno, without damaging the rest of his argument, can declare that moral goodness is in a position to make life happy, why should the Peripatetics not be allowed to say the same? For surely we ought not merely to look at verbal points but should examine the substance of the matter which lies behind them.

CICERO: Ah, you're trying to refute me by quoting things I've said or written myself. That's confronting me with documents that have already been sealed![1] You can reserve that method for people who only argue according to fixed rules. But I live from one day to the next! If something strikes

1. It was a Roman practice to seal documents so as to prevent their subsequent alteration, for example when they were going to be produced in court.

me as probable, I say it; and that is how, unlike everyone else, I remain a free agent.

*

All the same, since we were speaking of consistency a little while back: I don't think this is quite the moment to ask whether Zeno and his disciple Aristo of Chios were right in thinking there is no good but the morally good. But I do feel it is appropriate to ask, on the assumption that they *were* right, whether logic does not require a further conclusion; that the happy life must depend on moral goodness and nothing else. However, let us at this point be content to concede Brutus the right to declare that the wise man is always happy – keeping an eye on his logic is his own business. The precept is a glorious one, and who deserves its glory better than he? But we, for our part, must hold fast to the additional doctrine that this happiness, which the wise man has in his grasp, is happiness to a complete, supreme degree.

If, however, you may happen to feel that Zeno of Citium was just a mere foreigner, an obscure coiner of words who somehow intruded his way into ancient philosophy, then instead you can go right back, if you like, to the authority of Plato himself, and there you will find exactly the same weighty principle – because Plato returns again and again to the assertion that moral good is the only good. In his *Gorgias*,[1] for example, when Socrates was asked whether he regarded Perdiccas's son King Archelaus (then considered the most fortunate person alive) as a happy man, he replied, 'I can't say; I have never spoken to him.' 'What do you mean? Haven't you any other way of deciding?' 'No.' 'Do you mean that you can't even say if the Great King of Persia is happy?' 'How can I, when I don't know how well educated he is, or how good?' 'What, do you really think *those* are the things

1. Plato, *Gorgias*, 470 D, E. Archelaus was king of Macedonia (c.413–399 BC).

happiness depends on?' 'Yes, I am absolutely convinced that good men are happy and bad men are miserable.' 'Is Archelaus miserable then?' 'Certainly, if he is bad.' So Socrates, as you see, makes happiness entirely dependent on moral goodness.

And then consider what he said in his Funeral Oration.[1] 'The man who is entirely self-sufficient as regards all the necessary ingredients for leading a happy life, so that these do not in any way depend on other people's good or bad luck or dangle at the uncertain mercy of someone else's fortune – he is the person who has found the right way to live. He has done so by making himself an exemplar of moderation, courage and wisdom. Such a man, as his possessions wax and wane and his children are born and die, will obediently submit to the ancient maxim which directs him to avoid extremes either of joy or grief: for he will always limit his hopes to the things his own unaided efforts can achieve.'

That is the doctrine formulated by Plato. It is like a venerated, holy fountain; and everything I shall have to say will flow from it.

*

Our surest starting-point is nature, the common parent of us all. All things that nature has brought into being, not only those which are animate but everyone of the other things, too, which emerge out of the earth but remain attached to it by their roots – all of these have been ordained by their begetter to be perfect, each after its own kind. And so, by nature's ordinance, some of the trees and vines, and some also of those humbler plants which cannot lift themselves much above the ground, are evergreen, whereas others get stripped bare in winter until the springtime comes to bring them warmth and clothe them in leaves again. Thanks to an internal urge which impels the seeds folded away inside each of these trees and shrubs, each one of them eventually puts forth its flowers or

1. Generally known as the *Menexenus* (247 E).

its fruits or its berries, and each one of them too, if allowed to develop unimpeded, attains its own sort of perfection.

But the unalloyed power of nature appears most clearly of all in animals, because nature has endowed them with sensation. It has decreed that some shall swim and inhabit the water, others shall fly and enjoy the freedom of the heavens, others again shall creep or walk. And among those which walk, nature has willed that some shall range alone, and some herd together; some shall be wild, and some tame; and others again shall live hidden lives, and burrow beneath the earth.

And all these categories of living being, each holding fast to its own established course and keeping itself distinct from other types of existence, abide equally by the law of nature, which has given to each kind its special distinguishing feature to retain permanently as its own peculiar possession. Man, however, has been endowed with something more outstanding. Yet it would be better, perhaps, to reserve the term 'outstanding' for things which admit of some comparison: whereas the human soul admits of none, since, being derived from the Divine Mind,[1] it can only be compared – if such a suggestion is permissible – with God himself.

Once, therefore, this human soul has received the appropriate training, once its vision has been seen to – so as to make sure it is blinded by no errors – the result will be perfect mind, flawless reason: which is the same thing as perfect moral goodness. And if the essence of happiness is that everything has to be complete, nothing missing, all filled up to its utmost capacity, and if those are also precisely the characteristics of moral goodness, then evidently all good men *are* happy.

Up to this point, then, I am in agreement with Brutus, that is to say with Aristotle, Xenocrates, Speusippus and Polemo.

*

But hereafter I part from them, because I next have to assert

1. The Stoic view (p. 26).

that good men are not only happy, but *supremely* happy. A man who has confidence in the good things inherent in his own self possesses all the necessities for the happy life. But once anyone starts trying to divide good into three categories (of which moral goodness then becomes only one) he must inevitably be lacking in such confidence. For how can he possibly feel certain about the other alleged kinds of good, the future of his health, or the durability of his luck? And yet, unless a good thing is durable and stable and lasting it is quite impossible for its possessor to be happy. Whereas there is no durability whatever in those bodily and external or accidental things, which occupy two of the three categories these philosophers insist upon.

Such people remind me of a certain Spartan who once heard a trader boasting of the large number of ships he had dispatched to many a distant coast. When the Spartan had listened to all this, he made a single comment: 'Your fortunes depend on hawsers; and that's an unenviable situation.' For nothing that there is the slightest possibility of eventually losing can be regarded as an ingredient of the happy life. It is inconceivable that any of the elements that make for happiness could ever be shrivelled up, snuffed out, annihilated. For once a man starts fearing that one of these supposedly 'good' possessions is going to vanish, it is out of the question for him to be happy any longer. For the happy man, as I see him, has to be safe, secure, inconquerable, impregnable: a man whose fears are not just insignificant but non-existent.

When we describe an individual as innocent, we are not envisaging somebody who is guilty of minor offences but a person who has not committed any at all. And by the same token, a fearless character is not someone who is only frightened of a few things; he is the man who is frightened of nothing whatever. That is what courage really means. It is the quality which enables one to face dangers and endure trouble and pain – without feeling the slightest fear.

Now, these are characteristics which simply could not exist if there were any valid standards of what is good and bad other than the moral standard. Because, if such other standards existed, it would be impossible for anyone who was assailed or menaced by disasters to enjoy that supreme object of our desires and aspirations, tranquillity; by which I mean the absence of distress: that is to say, the state which constitutes happiness. A man who lacks the absolute certainty that everything depends on himself and himself alone is in no condition to hold his head high and disdain whatever hazards the chances of human life may inflict.

When Philip of Macedonia sent a letter to the Spartans threatening to prevent them from acting in the way they wished to, they wrote back and asked if he proposed also to prevent them from dying! And they, who took this brave line, were a whole community; so it ought to be a good deal easier to find one single individual prepared to adopt the same intrepid attitude.

So much, then, for courage.

Supplement it with self-control – the power to keep every emotion in check – and then every ingredient you could need for the happy life is yours. For you will have courage as your defence against distress and fear, and self-control to liberate you from sensuality and keep you free of immoderate cravings. At this point I could go on to demonstrate that both these virtues are aspects of moral goodness. But I submit that this is not necessary, since our discussions on the previous days made the point perfectly plain.

In contrast to tranquillity, which brings happiness, mental and emotional disturbances make people wretched. Such disturbances can be of two kinds: distress and fear for supposed, imaginary, evils; and extravagant pleasures and crazes for things that are mistakenly interpreted as good. But all conditions of this kind are completely at variance with rational sense. They are merely disagreeable – and incidentally, one such feeling diametrically contradicts another. So it is perfectly legitimate to identify the freedom from such disturbances with happiness. Consequently a wise man, a man, that is to say, who enjoys this exemption permanently, cannot fail to be happy.

*

All good things are enjoyable. What is enjoyable deserves credit and pride; that is to say, it is glorious: and, if so, it must be praiseworthy. What is praiseworthy has to be morally good: therefore goodness means moral goodness.[1] The people I have been speaking about are prepared to talk of certain 'good' things which fall outside the category of the morally good. But in fact, moral good is the *only* good:[2] from which it follows that happiness depends on moral goodness and nothing else whatever.

As for the other so-called 'good' things, it is erroneous to describe or regard them as good, since it is perfectly possible to possess them in abundance and still to be miserable all the same! Imagine a man who is favoured with excellent health, great physical strength and extremely good looks, and whose senses are all vigorous and active. Then throw in wealth, distinctions, great offices of state, power and glory. But suppose also that the person thus endowed is at the same time unjust, intemperate, cowardly, and slow-witted or downright stupid. You will surely have to admit that he is an unhappy man. Well, then, if someone can be loaded with all those worldly honours and still be exceedingly unhappy, it would surely be quite wrong to classify him as good.

Take a heap of grain, any sort you like, and look at its ingredients: the particular kind of grain it contains gives its

1. This artificial form of reasoning, much used by the Stoic Chrysippus of Soli, was known as the chain-argument (*sorites*). Other examples follow.

2. Later Cicero does not commit himself so definitely on this point (p. 93).

name to the whole heap. The same applies to happiness – its components are of the same material as itself; in other words, they are all good things – that is to say morally good. They cannot be a mixture of various different elements, because no such mixture would add up to a total of moral goodness: and that is the total that you have got to have, since otherwise you have not got happiness.

For everything that is good is desirable: what is desirable deserves approval: what deserves approval is acceptable and welcome: and what is acceptable and welcome must be regarded as possessing excellence. But if it is excellent, it must necessarily be praiseworthy: and from this it again follows that there is no good but moral good.

Unless we adhere firmly to this conclusion, the things we have to call good form a very heterogeneous collection. We can disregard wealth, which I do not include in the category of good things because anyone, however unworthy, can get hold of it – and that could never be true of things that are really good. I will likewise leave renown and popularity out of the list, since all that is needed to acquire them is for a stupid or mischievous crowd to shout loud enough. But consider, instead, certain things of trifling significance which people are accustomed to describe as good, such as nice white teeth or attractive eyes or an agreeable complexion or the attributes praised by Anticlea when she was washing the feet of Ulysses, 'a pleasant way of talking, and softness of skin'.[1] If we are really prepared to allow the term 'good' to be used in that sort of context, I cannot see how our supposedly serious philosophers are likely to produce anything more significant and elevated than emerges from the foolish sentiments of the common herd.

*

1. From the *Niptra* of Pacuvius of Brundusium (c.220–130 BC). In the *Odyssey* it was Euryclea, the nurse of Odysseus (Ulysses), who washed his feet, not his mother Anticlea.

But wait a minute. Although the Peripatetics include these things among the 'good', the Stoics prefer to describe them as *advantageous* or *preferable.*

Yes, and as the latter terms imply, these Stoics carefully avoid suggesting that the possessions in question are an indispensable element in happiness. The Peripatetics on the other hand declare that the happy, or at any rate the supremely happy, life cannot possibly exist without them. But I maintain exactly the opposite: supreme happiness does not need them at all.

I have Socrates's well-known demonstration to support me. For according to that prince of philosophers the disposition of a man's soul indicates the man: the man indicates his speech: his speech indicates his actions: his actions indicate his life. Since, then, the disposition of a good man's soul is laudable, the same applies to his life. His life is therefore morally good. And so, once again, we come to the conclusion that the good people are happy.

For, heaven knows, unless we were talking merely to amuse ourselves and pass the time, our previous discussions ought to have convinced us by now that the wise man is free from all those disturbances of the soul which I describe as passions; his heart is full of tranquil calm for ever. And anyone who is self-controlled, unwavering, fearless, undistressed, the victim of no cravings or desires, must inevitably be happy. But that is precisely the description of a wise man: which is the same thing, therefore, as saying 'a happy man'. Again, a person who is good cannot fail to measure everything he does and feels by the standard he regards as praiseworthy. But he also measures everything by happiness: so the happy life is praiseworthy: but nothing is praiseworthy unless it is morally good: on which, therefore, happiness entirely depends.

You can reach the same conclusion by another route as well. A life that is unhappy, or one that is neither unhappy nor happy, does not contain anything deserving of praise or commendation. Yet some people's lives do contain achievements which merit such commendation and glorification. Think of Epaminondas, who was able to declare, 'My counsels sheared the renown of the Spartans', and the elder Scipio Africanus: 'From the place where the sun rises above the Maeotian marsh to farthest west, there is no man on earth who can match my deeds.'[1] If such claims were justified, lives such as theirs, which earn fame and renown, are happy lives: for the only thing worth praising and glorifying is happiness. And you see the implications of this. Suppose that happiness were *not* absolutely synonymous with moral goodness. And yet the people I am arguing against will surely, at the very least, have to concede that moral goodness is the best thing that there is – that it ranks above everything else. If therefore, happiness and moral goodness are not identical, it would be necessary to suppose that there is something morally *better* than the happy life – which would be an utterly nonsensical conclusion.

Now, my opponents admit that moral badness is enough to make life miserable. So must it not also be admitted that moral goodness has just as much power to make it happy? For from opposites follow opposite conclusions.

*

At this point, I would ask you to consider the significance of those famous scales of Critolaus.[2] If the good things of the spirit, the morally good things, are placed in one of the scales,

1. The former quotation is the first of the lines inscribed on the statue of the Theban commander and statesman Epaminondas (d.362 BC). The epitaph of Scipio the elder was written by Ennius of Rudiae (239–169 BC), the epic and tragic poet and 'father of Latin poetry', whom Cicero selected as the model (to be improved upon) for the poetry that he himself wrote.

2. Critolaus of Phaselis was a Peripatetic who may have succeeded Aristo of Ceos as head of the school. He was a member of a famous delegation of philosophers to Rome in 155 BC (p. 29).

and what he regards as the good things of the body *plus* accidental, external good things in the other, he maintains that the first scale sinks so much lower than the second that the whole earth and all the oceans together would not be enough to redress the balance.

Well, in that case why ever did the philosopher who tells us this, and the eminent Xenocrates who attaches the same immense importance to moral goodness – so much so that he depreciates and disregards everything else in the world – fight shy of basing not just the happy life, but the *supremely* happy life, on moral goodness and moral goodness only?

Because if you do take any other line it is going to mean, in effect, that you are wiping out moral standards altogether. Consider, for example, a man who is morally imperfect enough to feel distress. Then he is also certain to feel fear as well: since fear is the anxious anticipation of distress to come. And if he is likely to feel fear, that is the same as admitting that he is susceptible to every sort of panic, faint-heartedness, hysteria and cowardice. In other words, he will be the sort of person who gets the worst of things. Not for him the saying of Atreus: 'In life let men be vigilant never to know defeat.'[1] On the contrary, as I say, the man we have in mind *will* be defeated; he is bound to be reduced to a state of slavery. Whereas moral goodness, according to my interpretation, is essentially something free and undefeated: the whole point of morality is its independence.

And here is something else. If moral goodness is sufficient to guarantee a good life, it follows that the same quality is also sufficient to guarantee a happy one. Now, one aspect of moral goodness, quite evidently, is courage; and courage is merely another word for the superiority of character which makes it impossible for a person to feel afraid or be worsted by setbacks. No one, then, who possesses these qualities will ever

1. From the *Atreus* of Accius of Pisaurum (c.170–85 BC).

have any regrets about anything, or feel the absence of anything, or find anything getting in his way. Instead, his entire life will be rich, complete, successful – in other words happy.

Folly, even after it has attained what it was seeking for, is still never satisfied. But wisdom is invariably contented with what it has got. It never has anything to feel sorry about.

*

How would you compare Gaius Laelius, who was elected to one consulship and one only, and even that after an initial rebuff (though when a wise and good man, as he was, fails to win an election, it is the electors rather than himself who have really had the setback) – but what I am saying is this: would you prefer, given the choice, to be consul once, like Laelius, or four times, like Cinna?[1]

I am sure I can guess what *you* would answer, because I know the man I am talking to. But it is not a question I would confidently put to everybody. Someone else might well reply that he would certainly prefer four consulships to one, and, what is more, he might rank one single day of Cinna's existence above many famous citizens' entire lives put together. A person who held that sort of view would make it his business to ensure that Laelius, if he had so much as laid a finger on any single individual, would have to answer for it in no uncertain fashion. Whereas Cinna, on the other hand, was the man who actually gave orders that his own consular colleague Cnaeus Octavius should have his head cut off, and not only Octavius but Publius Crassus and Lucius Caesar too, men of proved distinction in peace and war alike, as well as Marcus Antonius who was the greatest orator I have ever heard, and Gaius Caesar who seemed to me a paragon of

1. Laelius the Wise (see *On Friendship*) became consul in 140 BC after being defeated in the elections for 141. The democratic leader Lucius Cornelius Cinna was consul from 87 to 84.

enlightenment, wit, agreeableness and charm.[1] How can the creature who killed men of that stature be described as happy? To my mind, on the contrary, he seems wretched, partly because of what he did, and partly because it was he who was responsible for causing this state of affairs, which allowed him to do such things, to develop in the first place. I say 'which allowed him', but when we talk of people being 'allowed' to do things, meaning that they have got the power to do them, we are using inaccurate language, because, strictly speaking, if something is wrong no one is *allowed* to do it at all.

Was Gaius Marius happier on the day when he shared the glory of conquering the Cimbri with his colleague Catulus, who was almost a second Laelius (because I feel the two men were really very much alike), or when, rabid victor over his own fellow-citizens, he received an appeal for mercy from the relatives of Catulus and replied, not just once but over and over again, 'Let him die'?[2] In that situation, the victim of such impious words was happier than the man who gave the criminal command. For it is better to suffer an injury than to commit one. And it is also better to move forward a little, as Catulus did, to encounter a death that is anyway not far off, than to act like Marius and put a great man to death! It was a deed that obliterated the glory of six consulships and defiled the last days of his life.

*

Consider the case of Dionysius. He became tyrant of Syracuse

1. Cnaeus Octavius, consul with Cinna in 87 BC, fell in the siege of Rome by Cinna and Marius. Publius Licinius Crassus (consul 97, the father of the triumvir) committed suicide. Lucius Julius Caesar Strabo (consul 90) was murdered by Cinna's associate Fimbria, with his younger brother Gaius Julius Caesar Vopiscus Strabo, orator and tragic poet. For Marcus Antonius see *On the Orator*.

2. Gaius Marius and Quintus Lutatius Catulus (consul 107 BC) defeated the Cimbri near Vercellae (Vercelli) in 101. Proscribed by the Marians in 87, Catulus committed suicide.

at the age of twenty-five and remained in power for thirty-eight years.[1] It was a superb and immensely wealthy city, and he held it down in slavery. It is true that he lived a temperate enough life, as we are told by reliable writers, and that he was an efficient and hardworking administrator. But his character was evil and malevolent: and for this reason it is impossible for anyone with a clear eye for the truth to avoid regarding him as a supremely unhappy man. For even at a time when he believed that nothing in the world was beyond his powers he failed to get what he wanted.

Although historians disagree on the point, it appears that his origins were respectable, indeed excellent.[2] Moreover, in addition to extensive family connexions, he possessed many friends among his contemporaries. He also had amorous relationships with young men, in the manner of the Greeks. But he did not feel able to trust a single one of his associates. Instead he placed his personal security in the care of slaves, whom he had picked out of the households of wealthy citizens and set free; and he also enrolled in his bodyguard fugitives on the run and uncouth savages.

In other words, Dionysius's determination to maintain his tyrannical rule virtually caused him to shut himself up in a prison. He even refused to entrust his throat to the mercy of a barber, ordering his daughters to shave him instead. So these young princesses had to perform the humble and menial job of trimming their father's beard and head as if they were hair-dressers' assistants. However, when the girls grew up, he felt unhappy about letting them have the use of iron instruments, and instead got them to singe his beard and hair with heated walnut shells.

Dionysius had two wives, Aristomache who was a Syra-

1. Dionysius I, born c.430 BC, ruled the city from 405 until his death in 367.

2. According to other reports he was the son of a clerk or donkey-driver.

cusan like himself, and Doris from Locri. Whenever he visited either of these ladies at night, he first had a thorough inspection and search made of their rooms. Round his own bedroom he arranged for a wide trench to be dug; it could only be crossed by a wooden gangway, which he himself drew inside the door every time he wanted to shut himself in. As for his official appearances, he did not dare to appear on the public platform, but used to climb up a high tower whenever he wanted to address his subjects. He was very fond of playing ball-games, and the story goes that once, when he was about to take off his tunic for a game, he handed his sword to a youth whom he loved very dearly. One of his friends said as a joke, 'Here at least is someone you're prepared to trust your life to!' And the young man smiled. But Dionysius ordered both of them to be executed, the man who had made the remark because he had pointed out a way in which the king could be assassinated, and the youth because, by smiling, he had implied approval of what the other had said. This action caused Dionysius greater sorrow than anything else that happened throughout his entire life: because he had ordered the death of a person whom he deeply loved. The story illustrates the contradictory nature of a tyrant's urges. You can only satisfy one at the expense of another.

Indeed, Dionysius himself pronounced judgement on whether he was happy or not. He was talking to one of his flatterers, a man called Damocles, who enlarged on the monarch's wealth and power, the splendours of his despotic régime, the immensity of his resources, and the magnificence of his palace. Never, he declared, had there been a happier man. 'Very well, Damocles,' replied the ruler, 'since my life strikes you as so attractive, would you care to have a taste of it yourself and see what my way of living is really like?' Damocles agreed with pleasure. And so Dionysius had him installed on a golden couch covered with a superb woven coverlet embroidered with beautiful designs, and beside the couch was placed an array of sideboards loaded with chased gold and silver plate. He ordered that boys, chosen for their exceptional beauty, should stand by and wait on Damocles at table, and they were instructed to keep their eyes fastened attentively upon his every sign. There were perfumes and garlands and incense, and the tables were heaped up with a most elaborate feast. Damocles thought himself a truly fortunate person. But in the midst of all this splendour, directly above the neck of the happy man, Dionysius arranged that a gleaming sword should be suspended from the ceiling, to which it was attached by a horsehair. And so Damocles had no eye for those lovely waiters, or for all the artistic plate. Indeed, he did not even feel like reaching out his hand towards the food. Presently the garlands, of their own accord, just slipped down from his brow. In the end he begged the tyrant to let him go, declaring that his desire to be happy had quite evaporated.

Dionysius was indicating clearly enough that happiness is out of the question if you are perpetually menaced by some terror. And as for himself, the possibility of returning to lawful courses and restoring to his fellow citizens their freedom and their rights was no longer open to him: because during the thoughtless days of his youth he had entangled himself in such terrible crimes and committed so many guilty acts that he could only return to sanity at the cost of his own destruction.

Although Dionysius was so deeply suspicious of disloyalty, he showed how much he missed having friends by the incident of the two disciples of Pythagoras.[1] One of these youths had been condemned to death, and the other was allowed to stand surety for his appearance. But the first young man turned up punctually at the hour fixed for his own execution and released his friend from his pledge. Dionysius's comment was

1. Damon and Phintias.

this: 'I should give a great deal to be enrolled as the third partner in your friendship.'

And, indeed, to be without the company of friends, without the pleasures of social life, without anybody to talk to privately, was a truly deplorable fate, especially for someone who had received an excellent education since his earliest years and was a thoroughly cultivated person. For Dionysius was an extremely keen musician, we are informed, and even a tragic poet (how good he may have been is beside the point, for in that art, more than any other, everyone seems entirely satisfied with his own efforts: I have never known a poet – and Aquinius was a friend of mine[1] – who was not absolutely first class in his own eyes: that is how it is: you like your work, I like mine). However, to go back to Dionysius, he was a man who denied himself every single one of the amenities of civilized life. He lived with runaways and criminals and barbarians: no one who deserved or wanted freedom could possibly be a friend of Dionysius.

*

I can imagine nothing more ghastly and wretched and horrible than an existence of such a kind. It would be pointless to compare it with the lives of men famous for their wisdom and learning like Plato and Archytas.[2] But from Dionysius's own city of Syracuse I will summon up from the dust – where his measuring rod once traced its lines – an obscure little man who lived many years later, Archimedes.[3] When I was quaestor in Sicily I managed to track down his grave. The Syracusans

1. Unknown except for a similar reference by the poet Catullus, who calls him Aquinus.

2. Archytas of Tarentum, whom Plato visited, was a Pythagorean and an eminent mathematician, said to have been the founder of the science of mechanics.

3. The greatest mathematician of antiquity, killed in the sack of Syracuse by Marcus Claudius Marcellus in 212 BC. Cicero was quaestor at Lilybaeum (Marsala) in 75.

knew nothing about it, and indeed denied that any such thing existed. But there it was, completely surrounded and hidden by bushes of brambles and thorns. I remembered having heard of some simple lines of verse which had been inscribed on his tomb, referring to a sphere and cylinder modelled in stone on top of the grave. And so I took a good look round all the numerous tombs that stand beside the Agrigentine Gate. Finally I noticed a little column just visible above the scrub: it was surmounted by a sphere and a cylinder. I immediately said to the Syracusans, some of whose leading citizens were with me at the time, that I believed this was the very object I had been looking for. Men were sent in with sickles to clear the site, and when a path to the monument had been opened we walked right up to it. And the verses were still visible, though approximately the second half of each line had been worn away.

So one of the most famous cities in the Greek world, and in former days a great centre of learning as well, would have remained in total ignorance of the tomb of the most brilliant citizen it had ever produced, had a man from Arpinum not come and pointed it out!

*

But now to return to the point where I started that digression. Surely anyone who has even the slightest connexion with the Muses, that is to say with civilization and learning, would rather be the mathematician Archimedes than the tyrant Dionysius. If we weigh up the two men's ways of life and behaviour, we find that one of them fed his brain on scientific research and discovery, with all the satisfaction that comes from intense intellectual exercise – which is the most wonderful spiritual nourishment in the world – while the thoughts of the other dwelt on murder and oppression, and fear was his companion day and night. Compare Dionysius with Democritus, Pythagoras, Anaxagoras: what thrones or possessions on all the earth could you rank higher than their philosophical achievements, and the satisfaction they derived from them?

For since the best part of a man is his mind, that, surely, must be where the 'best', the supreme good you are looking for, is located. An acute first-class brain is the finest asset anyone can have – and, if we want to be happy, it is an asset we must exploit to the uttermost. But a good brain, mental excellence, is identical with moral excellence: so we have to conclude that moral excellence is what guarantees happiness. I have said this before, but I feel I must say it again in rather more extended terms – everything that is morally good, and fine, and distinguished, is infinitely productive of joy. Now, continuous fullness of joy is evidently what happiness means; and so moral goodness, we conclude once again, is what constitutes the happy life.

*

But I appreciate that this verbal sort of argument may not be enough to provide the conclusive proof we are after. Perhaps illustrations taken from life will make it easier to grasp and appreciate the point. Let us imagine a man pre-eminently endowed with the very highest qualities: and let us just think what sort of a person he will be. For one thing, he has got to be highly intelligent, because sluggish minds are not readily capable of achieving the highest sort of conduct. And then again he must have a passionate enthusiasm for trying to discover the truth.

And this leads to that famous threefold division of intellectual study.[1] One part constitutes the knowledge of the universe, the understanding of nature. The second consists of distinguishing between the things we ought to aim at and the things we ought to avoid – in other words, this is the art of the

1. According to the Stoics there were three parts of philosophy, Physics, Ethics and Dialectic. The Epicureans only recognized the first two.

good life. The third subdivision comprises the assessment of logical consequences and incompatibilities, which is the basic requirement for accurate discussion and analysis.

When these are the themes a wise man spends his days and nights contemplating, what exaltation they will bring to his heart! He will be able to discern the movements and revolutions of the entire universe. He will gaze at the numberless stars which stud the sky and revolve in unison with its revolutions, each in its appointed place; while seven others, far distant from one another in their highest and lowest positions alike, maintain their own special orbits and follow their own different courses, each with exact and well-defined precision. No wonder this varied spectacle excited the men of old and inspired them to extend their explorations ever further afield!

From these researches, too, sprang their investigation into the sources and elements from which every existing object was propagated and came into being and grew to maturity; and inquiry started into the beginnings of everything there is, whether inanimate or animate, vocal or mute, and into the meaning of life and death, and into the changes and transmutations of one thing into another, and the origins of the earth, and the forces that maintain its equilibrium, and the abysses through which the waters of the oceans rush upon their courses; and into the force which weighs all things down towards the centre of the universe, the lowest point of the sphere.[1]

To men immersed day and night in these meditations comes understanding of the truth pronounced by the god at Delphi, that the mind should know itself; and there comes also the perception of its union with the divine mind, the source of its inexhaustible joy.[2] For contemplation of the

1. Since nature always guides weights to the lowest point.

2. 'Know thyself' was inscribed in the vestibule of the temple of Apollo at Delphi. The link between the human and divine mind was Stoic doctrine (p. 26).

power and nature of the gods spontaneously kindles in human beings a passion to attain immortality like theirs; and the soul, when it discerns how all things in the universe are linked one with another by a chain of interlocked destined causes, a process which is governed by reason and intelligence and renews itself to all eternity, begins to nourish the conviction that it could not be true that its own life is just limited to this brief span upon earth. As a man contemplates this spectacle, and gazes upwards and round about upon every part and region of the universe, how serenely, then, he can look back again at our own mere mental activities, close beside where he is standing!

That is the point where the second branch of study begins – the comprehension of moral goodness. The virtues blossom forth in their various forms and manifestations, and it is revealed to us what nature has ordained as the ultimate good and evil, the principles on which human obligations ought to be based, and the rules we must adopt for the conduct of our lives. And it is the exploration of these and similar questions which brings us to the conclusion which our present discussion has been seeking to establish, that moral goodness is enough by itself to create a happy life.

The third subdivision of intellectual activity is one which extends widely over all aspects of knowledge. This is the branch of learning that defines and classifies, draws logical consequences, formulates conclusions, and distinguishes the true from the false. In other words, it is the art and science of reasoning: which is not only supremely useful for evaluating arguments of all kinds but also offers its devotees a noble satisfaction which merits the name of wisdom.

*

But these are occupations for a man's private life. And now let our wise man turn his attention to public affairs instead. In this field his qualifications are admirable. His intelligence will enable him to identify the path where the advantage of his fellow-citizens truly lies; his integrity forbids him to divert any of their property to his own pocket; and he has a great array of virtues to rely upon. Moreover, they can receive additional sustenance from the benefit he derives from his friendships. To a civilized man these provide not only the keen satisfaction of intimate association from day to day, but also a treasure of sympathetic counsel and communion which will enrich every aspect of his life.

Equipped with such blessings, what more could a life need to make it happy? Indeed, the enjoyment of these advantages is happiness itself. And yet all wise men have the power to enjoy them; that is why we are bound to recognize that all wise men must be happy.

FRIEND: Even if they are undergoing torture, stretched on the rack?

CICERO: Do you imagine I was supposing that they just reclined on beds of violets and roses? Consider what Epicurus says on this subject. Now he, I must remind you, is no genuine philosopher; he just calls himself one. And yet we have to listen to him, even to him, declaring like the rest of them that the wise man, at any time you like to mention, even when he is being burnt and racked and cut to pieces, will never cease to assure us: 'It means nothing to me at all.' Certainly, Epicurus deserves praise for making such a statement. But what inconsistency his works reveal. For here is a man who actually identifies evil with pain and good with pleasure, thus making a mockery of all our attempts to establish moral standards, a man who declares we are just wasting our time and uttering mere meaningless sounds, since nothing is really of the slightest significance *except pleasant or unpleasant physical sensations*. Taking this attitude, Epicurus scarcely differs from an animal; and yet, I repeat, it seems that we have to put up with him suddenly forgetting himself and minimizing the role of chance just at the very moment he has given it complete control over all the good and all the evil that exists! For he is perfectly prepared to assert that he is happy at the height of torture and torment in spite of the fact that, just before, he had offered the pronouncement that the worst of all evils, and indeed the only evil, is pain.

The real remedies for pain – moral force, distaste for wrongdoing, constant practice in endurance, manly toughness – these are all things that Epicurus has not bothered to acquire. All he troubles to say is that he derives satisfaction from recollecting the pleasures of the past. It is as though a man who was feeling extremely, unbearably, hot chose to comfort himself by remembering a bathe he once had in one of our cool streams back home at Arpinum! It is quite impossible to agree with his suggestion that past pleasures can alleviate present ills.

*

And yet Epicurus affirms that the wise man is always happy. If he had any desire to be consistent, it would be out of the question for him to say any such thing. But since he does say it, since *even he* says it, that is all the more reason why we have every right to expect equally praiseworthy declarations from those who insist that nothing at all is worth having, nothing is fit to be classified as 'good', if moral goodness is lacking. It is high time, I submit, for the Peripatetics and Old Academy to put a stop to all their hesitant stammerings, and summon up the courage to admit openly and loudly that it is still possible to be happy even when you are being roasted alive inside Phalaris's bull![1]

I am prepared to agree with them, if need be, that we may enlarge our idea of what is good to include three categories: because I do want to get away from Stoic hyper-subtleties,

1. Phalaris, tyrant of Acragas (Agrigentum) (c.570–554 BC), used to roast his victims alive in a hollow bull made of bronze. For this latest 'Old' Academy, see pp. 30, 96.

and I realize I have made more use of such refinements than I usually do. Let us accept, then, the possibility of this threefold division. But on this condition only: that two of the three categories, the good things of the body and the good things which are external and accidental, are kept nailed right down on the ground and only allowed to be classified as good at all because they are 'preferable', whereas the third type of good, the morally good, is of a higher status altogether, something truly divine which knows no limits and reaches right up to the heavens: so that I swear to you that anyone who has attained it has found not only happiness, but happiness that is complete and supreme.

*

Now will the wise man be seriously afraid of pain? For pain is the chief objection to the view I have been putting forward. Against death, the deaths of ourselves and those near to us, and against distresses and disturbances of the spirit, we have surely been sufficiently armed and equipped by our discussions on the previous days. But the most formidable obstacle to adopting a moral standard seems to be pain. When its fiery torches intimidate us they threaten the complete destruction of all the courage, character, and endurance that we can muster.

So does this mean that moral goodness is forced to succumb to pain? When pain comes, does the wise and steadfast man's happiness just have to bow down before it?

God, what a shameful suggestion!

A Spartan boy, even when his body is mangled by agonizing blows, refuses to utter a sound. At Sparta I myself have seen gangs of young men fighting one another with inconceivable stubbornness, using fists and feet and nails and even teeth, ready to die rather than admit defeat. And in India, which I suppose is the wildest and most savage land of barbarians in the world, the men they call sages live naked every day of their lives, enduring all the snows and fierce winters of the Caucasus[1] without showing the smallest sign of pain; and then at the last they hurl themselves voluntarily into the flames, and burn to death without uttering a sound. And Indian women, too, when the husband of one of them dies, compete with one another to decide which of their number he loved the best (because each man usually has more than one wife). Whereupon the woman who is proclaimed the winner, escorted by her relations, joyfully joins her husband on the funeral pyre, and the loser goes sadly away.

To suppose that these are cases in which custom has conquered nature, so that the Indians no longer feel frost and fire, would be an erroneous conclusion because nature can never be overcome. But what their customs have achieved is to give them the power to face pain. Whereas our customs, on the other hand, have infected our characters with escapism and luxury and inactivity and idleness and inertia. Our false beliefs and dangerous habits have softened and enervated us.

The Egyptians, too, have a well-known tradition which provides an excellent illustration of the endurance that they possess. An irrational superstition, of which they have many, forbids them ever to do any injury to an ibis or an asp or a cat or a dog or a crocodile. And indeed, rather than harm those beasts, they would submit to the most fearful tortures; indeed, even if they had hurt one of them by mistake there is no penalty on earth these people would not submit to. So much for human beings. And what about even animals? Do they not endure cold and hunger, and spend their lives roaming over mountain crags and ranging among the trees of the forests? To defend their young, are they not prepared to suffer terrible wounds, do they not face the most violent assaults and blows without shrinking?

I could also point out all the sufferings men are prepared to

1. The Hindu Kush (Paropamisus), which Alexander the Great had mistaken for a continuation of the Caucasus.

endure from other motives as well: because they are ambitious and want to further their careers, or because they long for praise and popularity, or because they are in love and hanker to gratify their passion. Life is full of examples of all these things.

*

But let me call a halt and return to the point where I digressed from. Happiness, I say again, will not tremble, however much it is tortured. Clinging steadfastly to its integrity, its self-control and above all its courage, with all the strength of character and endurance that the word implies, happiness will not flinch even when the countenance of the executioner himself is revealed. While the virtues, one and all, move fearlessly onwards to suffer the torments of the rack, happiness, I repeat, will scorn to linger behind outside the prison gates. For to be abandoned there alone and in isolation, separated from all that glorious company, would be the most disgraceful and degrading thing in the world.

However, such a thing could not possibly happen. For virtues can have no existence at all without happiness, and conversely, happiness cannot exist without the virtues either. Consequently, they will never allow happiness to give them the slip. On the contrary, they will hustle it along with themselves. Whatever agony, whatever torment, lies ahead, they will endure it together.

*

This is the sort of person a truly wise man has to be. He will never do anything he might regret – or anything he does not want to do. Every action he performs will always be dignified, consistent, serious, upright. He will not succumb to the belief that this or that future event is predestined to happen; and no event, therefore, will cause him surprise, or strike him as unexpected or strange. Whatever comes up, he will continue to apply his own standards; and when he has made a decision, he will abide by it. A happier condition than that I am unable to conceive.

The belief of the Stoics on this subject is simple. The supreme good, according to them, is to live according to nature, and in harmony with nature.[1] That, they declare, is the wise man's duty; and it is also something that lies within his own capacity to achieve. From this follows the deduction that the man who has the supreme good within his power also possesses the power to live happily. Consequently, the wise man's life is happy.

Well, now I have told you the doctrines about happiness which seem to me to command the most respect, and, as far as we can tell at present, look nearer the truth than any other suggestions. Or have you something better to propose?

FRIEND: No, I cannot improve on these ideas in any way. But I should like to ask you a favour, if it is not too much trouble; and I feel able to do this because, not being hampered by belonging to any one philosophical school, you are in the habit of picking up from this one and that whatever point you regard as closest to the truth.

A short while back you appeared to be urging the Peripatetics and Old Academy to have the courage to state openly, without reservations, that wise men are always supremely happy. But what I should like to hear from you is this: how do you imagine they could do any such thing without being open to attack for inconsistency? Because, as you yourself indicated – criticizing them from the Stoic viewpoint – what they actually said was precisely the opposite.[2]

CICERO: All right, I will exploit my freedom! Unlike anyone else, the people I support positively encourage it. For

1. See p. 26.

2. i.e. that the wise man is happy but not supremely happy. For this confusingly named 'Old' Academy – the school which Cicero is now going to tell us that he supports – see above, p. 30.

what we like is to refrain from positive pronouncements, preferring to discuss whatever question is being considered from every angle, so as to enable our audiences to judge each question on its own merits, without feeling compelled to accept any particular solution as authoritative.

Presumably what you want to establish is this: that the philosophers' numerous disagreements about ultimate good and evil should not be allowed to disturb the conclusion that moral goodness in itself sufficiently guarantees a happy life. This, we are told, is a proposition which Carneades frequently debated. But his discussions often turned into attacks on the Stoics, whose doctrines he was always most eager to refute, working up a good deal of excitement in the process. I, on the other hand, propose to look at the matter in a calmer fashion.

If the Stoics are right in their definition of the ultimate good, then the question is settled: for it inevitably follows that the wise man is always happy. But let us inquire also into the views of the other schools, one by one, and see how this splendid pronouncement about the happy life can be harmonized with the various attitudes and systems of each individual sect.

*

It seems to me that the propositions about the ultimate good which still have supporters and defenders today may be listed as follows. First of all, there are four simple points of view. There is the Stoic contention that nothing is good except what is morally right. There is the attitude of Epicurus that nothing is good except pleasure. There is the idea of Hieronymus that the only thing which is good is the absence of pain.[1] And then there is the opinion which Carneades maintained against the Stoics, that nothing can be good except the

1. Hieronymus of Rhodes, a Peripatetic, lived at Athens c.290–230 BC.

enjoyment of the 'first goods of nature' (one's bodily and mental gifts), either the whole lot of them or the principal ones.

So much, then, for the straightforward answers. There are also the more complex attempts to reach a conclusion. First comes the Peripatetic division of goodness into three parts, the highest being of the soul, the second highest of the body and the third comprising things that come from outside. The Old Academy says much the same. Dinomachus and Callipho bracket moral goodness with pleasure. Finally the Peripatetic Diodorus identifies it with freedom from pain. Those are the only systems which can be described as at all coherent. (As for the theories of Aristo of Chios, Pyrrho, Herillus and others, they have evaporated into thin air.)[1]

So let us see what these doctrines have to offer us – leaving aside the Stoics whose thesis I feel I have sufficiently defended already. Indeed much the same applies to the main Peripatetic case, for that, too, is virtually settled. Apart from Theophrastus and any who chose to share his excessively timid and abject terror of pain, the attitude of the rest of them is acceptable enough, since they do the best they can to exalt the dignity and grandeur of moral goodness. And when they have duly praised this virtue to the skies – which they do very frequently, with the brilliance that comes easily to such eloquent orators – it is easy to go on from there and spurn and despise everything else. For people who claim that glory must be pursued even at the cost of pain are no longer in a position, after making that concession, to deny that those who have won such glory are happy men: even if 'evil' (according to their interpretation) may not be altogether absent, still the

1. Dinomachus and Callipho belonged to the Cyrenaic school founded by Aristippus which became the pioneer of Epicureanism. Diodorus was a pupil of the Peripatetic Critolaus. Pyrrho of Elis (c.360–270 BC) was the founder of Scepticism. Herillus of Carthage, a pupil of Zeno, founded a separate branch of Stoicism.

word 'happiness' has a sufficiently wide and far-reaching application to warrant its use in this context.

Consider the analogies of commerce and agriculture. Trading can be regarded as profitable, and farming as productive, even when the former is not totally free of loss, and the latter has not wholly escaped damage from the weather. For the pursuits in question are held to deserve these favourable descriptions if things have gone prosperously by and large. The same applies to human affairs in general. In order to deserve the designation 'happy', life need not consist wholly and entirely of good things of every sort and kind; if on the whole, and for the most part, such things predominate, that is enough to warrant the assertion that happiness has been achieved. This is the approach of the Peripatetics and Old Academy. And so they feel able to go on to argue – on the authority of Aristotle and Xenocrates and Speusippus and Polemo – that when moral goodness is tortured and roasted in the bull of Phalaris, happiness will still remain its companion all the same, and no threats or cajoleries will succeed in keeping it away. Callipho and Diodorus speak in similar terms, to the extent that they attach such great importance to morality that everything which lacks it ranks far behind.

The others seem to have got themselves into a bit of trouble: Epicurus, that is to say, and Hieronymus, and any who care to defend the discredited arguments of Carneades. But they manage, all the same, to swim out of the dangers they have got themselves into, because even they, like the rest, unanimously elevate the human soul to be arbiter of all that is good and bad; indeed they are eager to instruct it how to reject the alleged goods and evils that are fictitious and illusory. For Epicurus takes up basically the same position as Hieronymus and Carneades and indeed the whole lot of them: their defences against death and pain are impregnable.

Let us begin, if we may, with Epicurus. We call him an effeminate pleasure-lover. However, it would, as I have said, be impossible to accuse him of being afraid of death or pain. He even goes so far as to assert that the day of his death is an occasion of happiness; and at the very moment, he tells us, when he is afflicted with the most grievous pain he suppresses the agony by thinking about all the philosophical discoveries he has made. And when he assures us of that, he is not just indulging in casual talk. On the contrary, he is convinced that death means the disintegration of every living creature, that all sensation is extinguished, and that with sensation gone nothing has any significance for us at all. His attitude to pain, too, is guided by precise rules. They enable him to console us by pointing out that if the pain is intense it will not last long, if it lasts long it will not be intense. In dealing, therefore, with these two principal causes of anguish, death and pain, Epicurus seems to me every bit as sound as your fine Stoic talkers.

And Epicurus and the rest of them are equally well equipped to handle all the other things that are generally regarded as evil. For example, there is a universal fear of poverty. But none of the philosophers allows himself to share this fear; and Epicurus himself is content with very little indeed to live on. No one has used more emphatic language than he has about the desirability of plain living. Other men are keen to make money to enable them to pay for their love affairs and their careers and their day-to-day living; but since none of these activities has the slightest importance for Epicurus, he has no reason to feel any great desire for money; indeed he does not need to trouble about it at all.

Anacharsis displayed the same disregard for money,[1] and since he, a Scythian, was able to take this attitude, it is scarcely surprising that philosophers of our own country have contrived to do the same. We have a letter written by Anacharsis

1. Anacharsis (c.600 BC) was a Hellenized Scythian (from southern Russia), who came in the fourth century BC to be regarded as one of the Seven Wise Men, in the capacity of a 'noble savage'. The letter quoted is a forgery influenced by the Cynic school of Diogenes (see next note).

in these terms. 'Greetings from Anacharsis to Hanno. My clothing is a Scythian mantle, my shoes are the hard soles of my feet, my bed is the earth, my food is only seasoned by hunger – and I eat nothing but milk and cheese and meat. Come and visit me, and you will find me at peace. You want to give me something. But give it to your fellow-citizens instead, or let the immortal gods have it.'

And indeed nearly all philosophers of any and every school, when they avoid being misled by private perversities of their own, have managed to display the same spirit. On one occasion Socrates, when he saw a great quantity of gold and silver being carried in a procession, remarked: 'What a lot of things there are that I don't feel any need for!' As for Xenocrates, envoys from Alexander once brought him fifty talents, a very large sum for those days, especially at Athens. Xenocrates took the envoys to dine with him in the Academy and set before them a sufficient quantity of food, but without any luxury trimmings. Next day, they asked him the name of the representative he wanted them to hand the money over to. 'What!' he replied, 'didn't yesterday's frugal dinner show you I don't need any money?'

Diogenes, being a Cynic,[1] was even more frank when Alexander urged him to say if there was anything he needed. 'Yes,' he answered, 'stop getting between me and the sun.' And indeed Diogenes used to argue that his way of life was much superior to that of the Great King of Persia himself. For whereas nothing would ever be enough for that monarch, he himself, he pointed out, had no needs at all: consequently he never felt the lack of the pleasures the king could never have enough of, while the king, on the other hand, was quite incapable of enjoying *his* pleasures.

I expect you know how Epicurus classified the different types of desire. His classification may not have been particularly exact, but all the same it has proved useful. Some desires,

1. Diogenes of Sinope (c.400–325 BC), founder of the Cynic school.

he said, are both natural and necessary, some are natural but not necessary, some are neither the one thing nor the other. As for the first category, these are the desires which scarcely anything is required to satisfy, since the resources of nature are at everyone's disposal. The second sort of desire he regards as easy to satisfy, and easy to do without. But the third subdivision, according to him, should be wholly rejected, because desires of this kind, being unnatural as well as unnecessary, are quite superfluous. At this juncture, however, the Epicureans embark on prolonged disputations. Although they dismiss as insignificant the individual pleasures belonging to the categories they despise, all the same they try to obtain a plentiful supply of them! On sexual pleasures they dwell at length. These, they point out, are easily satisfied, habitual, and readily available. So if there is a natural demand for these pleasures, well and good, provided that the standard we apply is not birth or position or rank but looks and age and figure. But if, on the other hand, considerations of health or duty or reputation require abstinence, no great hardship is involved. In general, maintain the Epicureans, pleasures in this category may be welcomed, unless there happens to be some particular objection; but they can never be of any positive advantage.

Epicurus's whole theory of pleasure is based on the idea that the reason why this is always attractive and desirable is precisely because it *is* pleasure, and the reason why pain cannot fail to be undesirable is because it is pain. This means that if a man has any sense he will take care to weigh the pros and cons, avoiding pleasure if the pain it involves seems likely to predominate, and accepting pain if the inherent pleasure is going to outweigh the disadvantages. And another of Epicurus's doctrines goes as follows. Although the sensations of the body are what provide the means of judging whether a thing is pleasant or not, the pleasure is then passed on by the body and communicated to the mind. Granted that it is the body that feels delight during the actual sensation of a pleasure, the mind derives its own enjoyment as well. Furthermore, the mind possesses the additional function of anticipating pleasures to come and keeping past pleasures alive in the memory. In this way, it is argued, the wise man will always have a continuous, unbroken succession of enjoyable experiences, since his anticipation of those he is looking forward to in the future will merge with his recollection of those he has enjoyed in the past.

Applying the same arguments to food, Epicurus and the others belittle expensive and sumptuous banquets, on the grounds that nature's needs are modest. And need, anyone can see, is what provides the seasoning for any and every appetite. When Darius was fleeing from Alexander, he managed to get a drink of some muddy water, polluted by corpses.[1] However, he declared he had never drunk anything better – since whenever he drank before, he said, he had never known what it was to be thirsty. Similarly, Ptolemy had never felt hungry when he ate;[2] and so when, in the course of a tour round Egypt, he got separated from his escort and was given some coarse bread in a cottage, he said he had never enjoyed anything so much in all his life. There is also a tradition about Socrates. He liked walking, it is recorded, until a late hour of the evening, and when someone asked him why he did this he said he was trying to work up an appetite for his dinner.

And we have all heard about the food the Spartans eat at their public meals. Once when the tyrant Dionysius was dining with them he remarked that he did not care for that famous black broth which was their principal dish. 'No wonder you don't,' said the cook, 'because you haven't got the seasoning.' 'What's that?' asked Dionysius. 'Hard hunting, sweating, a sprint down to the river Eurotas, hunger,

1. Darius III Codomannus of Persia, in his flight after the battle of Gaugamela (331 BC).

2. Perhaps Ptolemy I of Egypt (323–284 BC).

thirst. Those are the things Spartans employ to season their banquets.' And the same lesson can be learnt from animals as well. They are satisfied with any food you fling at them provided their instincts do not reject it; and then they do not bother to look any further.

Sparta, which I mentioned just now, is only one of a number of communities which have collectively trained and habituated themselves to enjoy frugal living. For the Persians, too, according to Xenophon's description of their eating habits, will eat nothing but cress on their bread. And yet, if they had an inclination for something more inviting, they have the whole earth and everything that grows in it to provide them with the most savoury flavours in any variety and quantity they could desire. However, they are content with a moderate diet; and it means a sound body[1] and unimpaired health. What a contrast between such people and the sweating, belching individuals who stuff themselves with food like fatted oxen! And what the contrast demonstrates is that the true satisfaction to be derived from food comes not from repletion but from appetite – the people who run hardest after pleasure are the least likely to catch what they are after.

The story goes that Timotheus, the famous Athenian statesman,[2] once had dinner with Plato. Timotheus greatly enjoyed the party; and when he met his host on the following day he complimented him in the following terms: 'Your dinners are enjoyable not only when one is eating them but on the morning after as well!' For the point is that, when our stomachs are filled with a great deal of food and drink, we cannot possibly make proper use of our minds. There is an excellent letter which Plato wrote to the relatives of Dion,

1. Literally 'dryness', of the four properties natural to the human body (the others are warmth, coldness and moistness) the one which was believed to make it healthiest and strongest.

2. He held generalships between 378 and 356 BC and died in 354.

containing a passage which goes something like this. 'When I got here, I was not at all attracted by the so-called happy life, crammed with Italian and Syracusan banquets and involving two heavy meals a day, with never a night spent alone, and all the other things that go with such a life – things which will never make anyone wise, much less temperate. For no one's equipped with the ability to cope with such a mixture of opposites!'[1]

Indeed, a life so wholly lacking in reason and moderation must of necessity be highly unattractive. That was the mistake of Sardanapalus, the enormously wealthy king of Syria,[2] who had these lines engraved on his tomb: 'Everything that I have eaten, everything I have consumed to satisfy my appetites, is still within my power: all my other great riches I have left behind me, and they are gone.' That, remarked Aristotle, is an epitaph fit for an ox, not a king. For Sardanapalus claims, in death, to control things which even when he was alive he only possessed at the very moment of enjoyment.

So why should people hanker to be rich? In what respects does poverty prevent people from being happy? All right, you like statues, or pictures. But if you should happen to have such tastes, people of modest means are actually better placed to indulge them than men of substance. For, in our city, there are huge quantities of all these things, exhibited at every public place: whereas people who own such objects privately do not have so many specimens to look at, and, what is more, only see them on the rare occasions when they are visiting their country mansions: and even then they feel a prick of

1. *Letters*, VII, 326 B. Dion, tyrant of Syracuse 'in spite of himself', was murdered by another Platonist in 354.

2. Sardanapalus, more generally regarded as the last great king of Assyria, is the same name as Ashurbanipal, but the holocaust in which he was believed to have burnt himself and his wives to death was actually the fate into which Ashurbanipal frightened his half-brother (648 BC).

remorse, when they remember how they got them in the first place.[1] However, if I once started arguing in favour of poverty, I could go on for ever! And in any case the matter is self-evident, seeing that nature herself teaches us every day how few, and how small, and how inexpensive, her requirements are.

*

Then will insignificance or obscurity or unpopularity prevent a wise man from being happy? No! And, besides, we ought to ask ourselves whether the popular affection and glory we so greatly long to win are not more of a burden than a pleasure. Our Demosthenes once showed rather a petty side. When he heard a poor woman, carrying water as Greek women do, whisper to her friend: 'Look, here comes the great Demosthenes', he expressed pleasure. Yes, that was petty. He was a marvellous orator, no doubt. But evidently, while learning admirably how to speak before an audience, he had not made so much progress in communing with his own self. For it is imperative to understand that popular glory is not worth coveting for its own sake; and there is nothing very frightening about obscurity. 'I came to Athens,' said Democritus,[2] 'and no one there took any notice of me.' Now that really is high-minded and dignified: to glory in not having any glory!

Flutists and harpists do not adjust their melody or rhythm according to the taste of the multitude, they base it on what suits themselves. Why, then, should the wise man, who is the practitioner of a far greater art, follow the pleasure of the crowd, instead of pursuing the truth without regard to popular pressures? Surely it is the height of foolishness to

1. Cicero, in 70 BC, charged Gaius Verres with stealing them from Sicily (see *Cicero: Selected Works*, op. cit., p. 42).

2. Democritus of Abdera (c.460–370 BC) adopted the atomic theory of Leucippus of Miletus.

attach great importance to people in the mass, when in their individual capacities you look down on them as mere uneducated labourers.[1] The truly wise thing is to despise all our trivial ambitions, all our honours bestowed by the crowd – even if these distinctions come when you have not asked for them. Our trouble is that we never do manage to look down on such honours until it is too late – until we have reason to lament that we had not looked down on them before!

The natural philosopher Heraclitus[2] tells a story about Hermodorus, a leading man of Ephesus. The fellow-citizens of Hermodorus expelled him from the city: and the philosopher declares that the entire Ephesian population ought to have been deprived of their lives, because the occasion prompted them to make the following thoroughly deplorable pronouncement: 'No single individual among us,' they said, 'must ever be allowed to rise above the rest. Anyone who aspires to such a thing must go and live in another place, among other people.' You get that feeling in every community. People always hate anyone who is a better man than themselves. Take Aristides[3] (for I prefer to choose my examples from Greece rather than Rome!). Was that not the reason why he was banished from his country – because they could not bear him being such a just man?

What a lot of trouble one avoids if one refuses to have anything to do with the common herd! To have no job, to devote one's time to literature, is the most wonderful thing in the world. And by literature, I mean the works which give us an opportunity to understand the universe and nature in all its

1. Cicero is echoing a remark which Socrates was said to have made to Alcibiades.

2. Heraclitus of Ephesus, c.500 BC. The Romans believed that their laws of the Twelve Tables (attributed to 451–450 BC) were partly derived from Hermodorus, while he was in exile in Italy.

3. The Athenian statesman, exiled by ostracism in 483–482 BC.

infinity, and the world in which we ourselves live, its sky, land and sea.

*

All right, then, one views honour and wealth with proper contempt. So what is there left to be frightened of? Banishment, I suppose, which is held to be one of the worst of evils.[1] If, however, banishment is regarded in that light because its victim has incurred unpopularity and hatred among the crowd, then that, as I explained just now, is a matter of no importance. If it is a miserable fate to be separated from one's country, then our provinces are full of miserable people – very few of whom ever return to their original homelands. Yes, but exiles also have their property confiscated. Yet what of that? Surely we do not need to enlarge any further on the advantages of being poor.

And when, in fact, one takes a closer look at the condition of an exile – his real condition, leaving aside any disgrace people may choose to attach to the designation – surely in the last resort it amounts to exactly the same thing as permanent residence abroad. And that was how many of the very greatest philosophers spent their lives, Xenocrates, Crantor, Arcesilaus, Lacydes, Aristotle, Theophrastus, Zeno, Cleanthes, Chrysippus, Antipater of Tarsus, Carneades, Clitomachus, Philo, Antiochus, Panaetius, Posidonius and countless others.[2] Once they had gone away, not one of them ever returned home. They were not in disgrace, it is true. But can disgrace really have any affect on a wise man? Because he is the person

1. Cicero's banishment in 58–57 BC caused him misery, and Brutus later described him as highly unphilosophical, in practice, about death, exile and poverty.

2. Those not mentioned elsewhere in this book are Lacydes of Cyrene, who succeeded Arcesilaus as head of the Middle Academy in 241–240 BC, and Antipater of Tarsus, who in the following century succeeded Diogenes of Babylon as head of the Stoic school.

we are talking about all this time, and that such a person should deserve to be exiled is a contradiction in terms (if a man has been exiled and deserved it, then it is not our business to comfort him). And, incidentally, exile is one of the happenings of life which fits in very well with the school of thought that refers everything to the standard of pleasure: because if that is the view you hold, what is to stop you from living happily in any place you like, provided that you can get pleasure there?

So the pronouncement of Teucer, 'One's country is wherever one fares well', is acceptable to any philosophical sect you like to name.[1] When Socrates was asked which country he belonged to, he replied, 'The world'; for he regarded himself as an inhabitant and citizen of every part of it. And then there was Titus Albucius; after he had been banished, he studied philosophy at Athens in perfect serenity.[2] However, he would have been spared banishment altogether if he had obeyed the maxim of Epicurus and detached himself completely from public affairs. As for Epicurus himself (to go back to what Teucer said), it is hard to see how he was any happier living in Athens, which was his homeland, than Metrodorus, who had been born elsewhere; or how Plato was better off, as far as happiness was concerned, than Xenocrates, or Polemo than Arcesilaus.[3]

Besides, one cannot attach much importance to the opinion of a community which drives good and wise men away. Damaratus, the father of our king Tarquinius Priscus, fled from Corinth because he could not endure the tyrant Cypselus;[4] he settled in Tarquinii and founded a family there. His

1. From the *Teucer* of Pacuvius.

2. Titus Albucius was accused of misuse of funds in Sardinia in 103 BC.

3. Arcesilaus was founder of the sceptical Middle Academy (p. 28).

4. Tarquinius Priscus was traditionally the fifth king of Rome (615–579 BC). Cypselus was tyrant of Corinth c.655–625 BC.

preference for freedom in exile to slavery in his own home cannot, surely, be condemned as an act of stupidity.

Another point is this. When people devote their thoughts to pleasure, forgetfulness alleviates their anxieties and distresses. That was the point of Epicurus's bold assertion that good always predominates in the wise man because he never has any lack of pleasures. And that, again, is how Epicurus, like the rest, reaches the conclusion we are after, that the wise man is always happy.

*

Even, you may ask, if deprived of the senses of sight and hearing? Yes, even then, because he regards such things as entirely insignificant. Take blindness. What pleasures, in fact, does this dreaded condition deprive you of? Whereas all the other pleasures are actually located in the organs of sensation, it has been pointed out that the contrary applies to visual perception, which does not cause any direct pleasure to the eyes themselves in the same way as taste, smell, touch and hearing gratify the appropriate organs in which each of those senses is localized. In the case of the eyes, however, the situation is different, because our visual impressions are not destined for them at all, but for the mind.

And the mind is capable of receiving a wide and varied range of satisfactions in which sight is not involved in any way whatever. I am speaking of educated, cultivated people, the sort of person for whom life means thought: and a wise man rarely needs the support of his eyes in order to think. Happiness does not come to an end at the conclusion of every day, when night falls; so why should it cease when blindness turns day into night? On this subject Antipater the Cyrenaic[1] made an apt remark, though it is admittedly a trifle coarse. When he heard his womenfolk moaning because he was blind, his answer was this: 'What's the matter? Don't you think

1. For the Cyrenaics, see p. 25n.

one can have a good time in the night?' The famous Appius Claudius, the early personage of that name,[1] was likewise blind for many years. But the offices of state he held and the deeds he performed make it abundantly clear that his disability did not in the slightest degree disqualify him either as a private citizen or a statesman. Gaius Drusus,[2] too, we are told, always had his house thronged with people who had come to seek his advice. They could not see for themselves, with their own eyes, how their own affairs ought to be handled; and so they appealed to a blind man to be their guide.

When I was a boy, the blind Cnaeus Aufidius, a former praetor, frequently expressed his views in the Senate and helped his friends in their deliberations. Indeed, he also wrote a Greek history: in literary matters his vision was clear enough. And the Stoic Diodotus, another man who lost his sight, lived for many years in my house.[3] It seems hard to believe, but after he became blind he devoted himself more strenuously to philosophy than he ever had before. He also played the lyre, like a Pythagorean, and had books read to him day and night; he had no need of eyes to get on with his work. He also did something which seems scarcely credible for a man who could not see: he continued giving lectures on geometry, giving his pupils verbal indications of the points where they should begin and end the lines they had to draw.

We are told that Asclepiades, the eminent philosopher of the Eretrian school,[4] was once asked by someone to explain how blindness had affected him. He replied that it had enlarged his retinue by one boy! For just as even the depths of

1. Appius Claudius Caecus, who built the Appian Way (312 BC) and the Aqua Appia aqueduct.

2. Gaius Livius Drusus was brother of the more famous Marcus, tribune 122 and consul 112 BC.

3. He taught Cicero in c.85 BC, and made him his heir (60 BC).

4. Asclepiades of Phlius, a pupil of Menedemus (c.319–265 BC) who established an Eretrian school, based on the Megarian school (founded by Socrates's companian Euclides) and concentrating on dialectic.

poverty would be tolerable if we could do what we see certain Greeks doing every day,[1] blindness, too, can perfectly well be endured if we are supplied with the necessary aids. When Democritus lost his sight, it is true that he could no longer distinguish black from white. Yet he could still distinguish good from bad, just from unjust, right from wrong, expedient from inexpedient, important from unimportant.

In other words he did not need to see different colours in order to live happily; whereas if it had been the comprehension of ideas that he lacked, a happy life would have been out of the question. But here was a man who believed that eyesight is actually a hindrance to the vision of the soul. While other people were constantly failing to see what lay at their very feet, he was able to range freely throughout the infinities of space; and he never found a boundary which could stop him.

Homer, too, is traditionally said to have been blind. But when we read what he wrote, it seems more than poetry; it is as distinct as if he had painted the whole thing. So vividly, indeed, has he depicted every region and sea-coast and locality in Greece, every shape and form of warfare and battle, every manoeuvre which a ship can possibly make, every possible activity of men or beasts, that he gives us the most brilliantly clear vision of all the things his blindness prevented him from seeing himself. Surely, then, we are not going to suppose that Homer lacked pleasure or enjoyment! Or, for that matter, any other man of learning. Had that been so, we cannot imagine that Anaxagoras,[2] or Democritus whom I was speaking about just now, would have been willing to throw away their own lands and inheritances, and devote themselves with all their hearts to research and discovery – quests that bring truly

1. i.e. acting as parasites and beggars – though Cicero avoids saying so explicitly.

2. Anaxagoras of Clazomenae (c.428 BC) was the first philosopher to reside in Athens.

divine satisfaction. And for the same reason the prophet Tiresias[1] is never shown lamenting his blindness; for he too, as the poets tell us, was a man of real wisdom.

It is true that Homer, depicting the Cyclops Polyphemus as a barbarous savage, makes him talk to a ram and assure the animal how lucky it is to be able to see, so that it can stray wherever it wants to and get at everything it needs.[2] But the poet was right to let Polyphemus talk like that: his whole point is that the Cyclops is just as senseless as the ram.

*

And what about deafness? Is that really such a misfortune? Marcus Crassus[3] used to hear pretty badly. But what he suffered from worst was something different: he had to hear himself being spoken ill of, although at the time I did not think he deserved these unfriendly comments.

But consider the fact that our compatriots do not generally know Greek, and Greeks have no knowledge of Latin. In other words, we are deaf to their language and they to ours; and indeed every one of us is deaf to all the innumerable tongues we do not understand. You may say that deaf men miss the pleasure of hearing a lyre-player's songs. Yes, but they also miss the squeaking of a saw being sharpened, the noise a pig makes when its throat is being cut, the roaring thunder of the sea which prevents other people from sleeping. And if they happen to like singing, they should reflect, first, that many wise men lived happily before the art was ever invented, and, secondly, that reading poetry silently gives far more pleasure than listening to it aloud.

Just then I was trying to comfort blind people by reminding

1. The legendary seer of Thebes.

2. cf. Homer, *Odyssey*, IX. 447. But Cicero's recollection of the passage is not accurate.

3. Marcus Licinius Crassus, member of the first Triumvirate (killed at Carrhae 53 BC).

them of the pleasures of the ear – and now I hope to console the deaf by reminding them of the pleasures of seeing! Besides, there is this point too. A man who has the ability to commune with himself does not feel the slightest need for anyone else's conversation.

*

Well, let us now imagine that all these afflictions are simultaneously heaped on one and the same individual, so that he loses his sight, loses his hearing, and is simultaneously gripped by the acutest physical pains. Often these, by themselves, are enough to finish a man off completely. But suppose, instead, that they are greatly prolonged, and inflict agonies more severe than he can be expected to endure. In that case, why, for God's sake, should we continue to suffer? After all, there is a haven close at hand. I refer to the eternal refuge of death – where nothing is felt any longer.

When Lysimachus threatened to kill Theodorus, the philosopher replied, 'What a really superb achievement – to have acquired as much power as a poisonous beetle!' And the defeated king Perseus begged Paullus not to make him march in his triumph. But the general's answer was, 'That's up to you.'[1]

We talked a lot about death on the first day of these discussions; indeed we went into the whole subject carefully. And then we returned to it on the second day, when what we were discussing was pain. Anyone who recalls the points we made cannot surely be in any danger of regarding death as undesirable or terrible.

1. Lysimachus (c.360–281 BC) was one of the companions and successors of Alexander. Theodorus was a philosopher who came from Cyrene or belonged to the Cyrenaic school (p. 25n.). The beetle referred to is the 'Spanish fly', from which cantharidin is extracted. Perseus, king of Macedonia from 179 BC, was defeated at Pydna by Lucius Aemilius Paullus Macedonicus (p. 344) in 168.

My own opinion is that we ought to model our lives on the rule which the Greeks follow at their banquets: *let him drink, or let him go.* That is fair enough. For either you should be content to keep on drinking with the others, or else, in order to avoid the predicament of the sober man surrounded by noisy drinkers, you had better leave. The same applies to whatever assaults fortune may launch against you. If you are unable to face them, there is nothing to prevent you from running away. That is what Epicurus suggests; and Hieronymus specifically offers the same advice.

*

Now, there are men who hold that moral goodness, by itself, is ineffective. Everything we call right and praiseworthy seems to *them* mere meaningless and empty verbiage. And yet even they manage to conclude that the wise man is always happy! If even people with views such as theirs manage to come to such a conclusion, are we not, surely, entitled to expect that philosophers who claim descent from Socrates and Plato ought to be able to do the same?

Well, it is true that some of them do take the line that spiritual, moral good is so pre-eminent that it completely eclipses all goodness of a physical or accidental, external, nature. Others, however, as we know, do not even regard the last two categories as coming under the heading of good at all, declaring that the moral sort of goodness is the only sort. When Carneades tried to adjudicate this dispute, since the two parties had chosen him to act as umpire, he pointed out that there was no difference between the things the Peripatetics called 'good' and those the Stoics described as 'advantageous'. The Stoics, he said, in spite of this different way of expressing the matter, attached as much weight to riches and good health and all other such things as the Peripatetics did; and so there were no real grounds for disagreement – the substance is more important than the form.

As for the other schools, they, too, would be well advised to try to reach the same conclusion. Meanwhile I am glad to record that they have at least made one pronouncement that is fully in keeping with the dignity of the philosophical profession! I refer to their acceptance of the doctrine that the wise man invariably has the power to lead a happy life.

*

However, we have got to leave here tomorrow morning. So let us try to fix in our minds all the things we have been talking about during these five days. Later, I intend to write them down; for now that I have free time at my disposal (without commenting on the reasons for such a state of affairs!) I can think of no conceivable way in which this time could be better employed.

Consequently I propose to describe these discussions in a second series of five volumes. These I shall send, as I did before, to my friend Brutus, for it was he who pressed me to write about philosophy in the first place, and indeed challenged me to do so.

Whether my efforts in this direction will be useful to anyone else, I have no idea. But I do know this. The work gives me a chance, the only chance I have, to obtain relief from my own cruel sorrows and the many troubles that press in on me from every side.

## ON DUTIES

*On Duties*, or *On Obligations*, has generally been the most popular of Cicero's writings, and has perhaps exercised more influence on the thought and standards of the western world than any other secular work ever written.[1] And even now, as will be seen, the study possesses certain marked advantages over other guides to conduct. The first two books had been mainly written, and the third begun, during the months September to November 44, the period in which Cicero achieved the last and bravest of his political triumphs – though it was all too shortlived. This achievement was represented by his *Second Philippic*, a violent denunciation of the autocratic Marcus Antonius (Mark Antony) which was composed in October and published after Antonius had left Rome on 25 November.[2] The important period in the composition of the present study was this same time, leading to the final break with Antonius.

The treatise *On Duties* is prompted partly by the immediate circumstances of the crisis. It contains strong criticism of the recent dictatorship of Caesar (p. 15), a blueprint for many subsequent denunciations of despotism. The work has been described as an attempt to provide a moral code for the aristocracy liberated from Caesar's tyranny, and even as 'a last farewell to family and country'.[3] This reference to Cicero's family alludes to the book's dedication to his son Marcus, who was studying in Athens (and had shown signs of going to the bad earlier in the summer). But although *On*

1. See pp. 31ff. For the title see p. 21.

2. For a translation of the *Second Philippic* see *Cicero: Selected Works*, op. cit., pp. 101ff.

3. H. A. Holden, *Cicero: De Officiis*, Book III, Cambridge University Press, 1927, p. ix.

*Duties* did, in fact, prove to be something like a last farewell since Cicero was killed in the following year, it was not meant to be. On the contrary Cicero, with his *Philippics*, was right back in politics again, and had consequently, as we can see in these pages, become a good deal less interested in the higher flights of philosophy.

Nevertheless in *On Duties* this emphasis on practicality is not particularly directed towards the problems of the moment, since in a wider sense the work is designed to represent a further step in the fulfilment of a great programme. After the *Tusculans* and other works, here is a new attempt, this time from a more concrete point of view, to tackle the problems involved in trying to live up to the highest moral standards. *On Duties* has been called 'a theoretical treatment of the obligations which a citizen should render to the Commonwealth, that is, a manual of civic virtue'.[1] It was a manual which provided a system of applied ethics, and, in the process, sought to justify Cicero's own standards of behaviour and his career.

The first volume discusses the duties or obligations arising from Moral Right, the second those arising from Advantage or Expediency,[2] and the third considers what is to be done when right and advantage seem to clash. I have translated Book III elsewhere;[3] here we have the second book. It tends, I have noticed, to irritate some people, first because there is (as there inevitably is in real life) a calculating element in its assessments, and secondly, because Cicero so ardently accepts institutions such as private property. However this acceptance

1. R. Syme, *The Roman Revolution*, Oxford University Press, 1939, p. 145.

2. Seen generally in this book (though with some wavering) not as an inferior morality conflicting with the good, but as comprising actions appropriate for the full development of human beings. Moreover, as Cicero shows, it is even worth discussing problems of expediency that have little or no moral implication at all.

3. *Cicero: Selected Works*, op. cit., pp. 157ff.

can also be seen, not as something reactionary, but as a proper insistence on a fundamental right of the individual against the demands of the state. The discussion strikes a realistic, practical note – illustrating Aristotle's assertion that moral philosophy is a study best suited to people who are really grown up (p. 44).

This is the only one of the writings included in this volume which is not cast, superficially, in the form of a discussion. Much of its content, especially in the first and second volumes, is based on Panaetius of Rhodes, who adapted Stoicism to the requirements and conditions of Roman society (p. 27). Cicero's own experiences, and observations of life, are more completely reflected in this work than in any other of his treatises. Written in haste, it is almost as self-revealing as his private letters; and for all its literary sources and trappings, it is sincere and written from the heart.

# ON DUTIES (II)

If, my son, we firmly adopt moral goodness as our guide – in each and every one of its forms – it will follow automatically what our practical duties or obligations must be. I believe I have said enough in the previous volume to make this clear. The next step is to go into the various kinds of obligation which have a direct bearing on people's daily lives and needs, such as personal possessions and property and other resources. That is what I am going to discuss now.

But first I want to offer certain general observations about what I am aiming at, since this will give me a chance to explain the approach I am proposing to follow. My earlier writings have, I believe, encouraged people to read more about these themes, and indeed to write about them as well. All the same, I sometimes suspect that certain excellent persons find the whole idea of philosophy distasteful and cannot understand why I devote to it such a very great deal of my energy and time. My answer is this. As long as our country was still governed by men it had voluntarily elected as its rulers, I was delighted to dedicate all my efforts and thoughts to national affairs. But when the entire government lay under the domination of a single individual, no one else but he any longer had the slightest opportunity to exert statesmanlike influence in any way whatever. Besides, I had lost the friends who had worked with me in the service of the State; and great men they were.[1] When they were gone, I refused to give way to my distress – if I had not resisted by every possible means it would have overwhelmed me. Nor, on the other hand, did I

1. Cnaeus Pompeius Magnus, Cato the Younger, and other victims of the Civil War against Caesar, the 'single individual' who became dictator.

just abandon myself to a life of pleasure; to do that would have been unworthy of an educated man.

If only the government had stood firm on the lines it was starting to follow! Instead of succumbing to creatures who were not seeking its reform at all, but its total obliteration. If things had gone better I should never have been devoting my attention to writing, as I am now. No, I would have been delivering public addresses, as I used to in the days when we still had a government: and if I wrote anything it would have been those speeches – just as I always wrote down and published my speeches after I had delivered them – it would not have been these essays I am engaged in now. Every scrap of my energy, attention and care used to go to politics. So when there was no such thing as politics any more, it was inevitable that my voice should be heard in the Forum and Senate no longer.

Yet how could I let my mind become completely idle? And, besides, philosophical study was something I had gone in for from a very early age. So I decided that the most honourable way of forgetting my sorrows was to revert to the same occupation once again. When I was a boy I used to give a great deal of time to this pursuit. But thereafter, once I started my official career and began to concentrate entirely on public duties, the only time I had left for philosophy was what remained over from the affairs of my friends and the nation. And that bit of time, such as it was, I spent entirely in reading; the leisure needed to write was not forthcoming.

So the terrible calamities that have descended on us nowadays have at least made it possible to extract one advantage from the situation. That is to say, they have given me the opportunity to prepare written accounts of certain extremely worthwhile subjects which our compatriots have never known enough about before.

*

For surely *to be wise* is the most desirable thing in all the world. It is quite impossible to imagine anything better, or more becoming for a human being, or more appropriate to his essential nature. That is why the people who try to reach this goal are called philosophers, because that is precisely what philosophy means, the love of wisdom. And wisdom, according to the definition offered by early philosophers, signifies the knowledge of all things, divine and human, and of the causes which lie behind them. If anyone is prepared to disparage so noble a study as that, I cannot imagine anything he would find himself able to approve of!

If we are trying to achieve mental enjoyment, for example, or relief from trouble, the findings of philosophy are of incomparable value, because the people who practise this study are perpetually searching for the things that produce a good and happy life. Or suppose what we are after is strength and excellence of character; if any means of acquiring such qualities exists, philosophy surely must be that means. To say, when one is thinking about supremely important objectives like these, that there is *no* special method for attaining them, although methods and systems exist for getting hold of other requirements even of the most trivial nature, would show that the man who uttered such a remark does not think before he speaks, and must not, therefore, be employed as a guide in any matter of importance whatever. For it is necessary to assume that a method for learning how to behave well *does* exist – and that the place to find it is philosophy and nowhere else.

When I advocate attention to this sort of learning, I usually go into a lot of careful detail. In another of my books, that is just what I have done.[1] At the present juncture, however, all I wanted to do was to explain why I have devoted myself so wholeheartedly to this occupation during a time when I am excluded from public duties.

1. In his lost *Hortensius*.

Some people protest that the line I am following is not as consistent as it ought to be; and the objectors include men of culture and learning. What they object to is the fact that, whereas the philosophical school I support[1] maintains that nothing can be known for certain, here I am all the same, in this work, not only presenting views on all manner of subjects but actually trying to lay down rules indicating what our obligations are. But I must ask those critics to make a greater effort to understand our position. For in spite of our negative attitude towards the certainty of knowledge we are very far from being just intellectual drifters who flounder about without any idea what we are looking for. To be quite without any sort of principles to base our discussions and our lives upon would totally rule out any intellectual life, or indeed any life at all. Other schools of philosophy maintain that some things are certain, and others uncertain. We adopt a special view of our own. What we say is that some things are probable, and others improbable.

I cannot see what there is to prevent me from accepting what seems to be probable, and rejecting what does not. Such an approach avoids the presumption of dogmatism, and keeps clear of irrationality, which is the negation of all accurate thinking. On the other hand our people always argue against all categorical assertions. Their reason for so doing is that you can only get a clear view of what is probable by setting out, comparing and weighing up the arguments on both sides of every question.

But I think I explained all this sufficiently in my *Academics*.[2] As for yourself, Marcus, you are attached to another very ancient and distinguished school, represented by your professor Cratippus, who deserves to be ranked with the founders

1. The Academy (p. 29).

2. Cicero's explanation, in dialogue form, of the tenets of the Academy.

of his illustrious movement.[1] All the same, I did not want you to be unaware of the opinions of my own school; nor, after all, are they so very far from the doctrines of yours.

But now I must get on with my task.

*

To govern the performance of our obligations, five principles have been laid down. Two are concerned with what is right and proper, two with the external advantages of life – means, resources, influence – and the fifth with the correct way of making a choice in case there is a conflict between the other categories. The first two headings, relating to what is morally right, I have already dealt with, and I hope you will make yourself thoroughly familiar with this branch of the subject.[2] The next two headings bring us to the range of matters covered by Expediency. In the course of time the word has changed its sense, and a distinction has gradually sprung up between what is expedient and what is right. But the implication that something can be right without being expedient, or expedient without being right, is the most pernicious error that could possibly be introduced into human life.

It is true that extremely reputable philosophers, reasoning with all the rigour and fairness they can command, claim to see three quite separate hypotheses here.[3] In fact, however, the three themes are all indissolubly linked together. Some students of the subject fail to appreciate this point, because they get dazzled by the sheer cleverness of the thinkers in question, and consequently mistake ingenuity for wisdom. In fact, the triple division is a complete misapprehension, which has got to be rooted out. It is necessary for us to revise the whole way of thinking of these people, and make them understand that

1. Cratippus of Mytilene, a leading Peripatetic (p. 24).
2. *On Duties*, Book I.
3. (1) moral right that is expedient, 2) moral right that appears to be inexpedient, 3) expediency that appears not to be morally right.

they will only attain the objects of their desires, not by tricky and misleading arguments, but by moral goodness, both in thought and in action.

The things that go towards the maintenance of human life can be classified as follows. Certain of them are inanimate, for example gold and silver and the products of the earth and other objects of the same kind. Others are animate, endowed with their own impulses and appetites. Some of these animate objects are rational, others irrational. The irrational subdivision includes horses, oxen and other animals which labour for the service and subsistence of mankind. The rational category is divided into two sections, gods and men. The gods will be satisfied if one lives a devout and pure life. Next to the gods, and after them, the greatest contribution to the lives of mankind is made by men themselves. And if we then turn to things of the opposite type, those which can hurt and damage human beings, and if we attempt a similar classification here, we have to record our belief that the gods are not capable of doing harm to mortals. They, therefore, must be left out of account in this connexion; and it has to be concluded that the greatest source of harm to man is man.

Going back to the inanimate range of objects, we find that it is again man, that is to say human labour, which has mobilized the greater part of these things. For unless men had exercised their efforts and skill, we should not have the use of the objects in question at all; it is human intervention that has made them available to us. Equally, had it not been for man and his endeavours, we should have no medical care, no sailing on the sea, no cultivation of the land, no harvest or storage of the crops. Exports of our surplus products, too, and imports of the things we need for ourselves, are only possible because of the work that human beings put into these tasks. And then again, without the labour of man's hands, the stones we need for building would never have been quarried from inside the earth, and the

iron, copper, gold and silver, hidden deep
within[1]

would never have been brought out of the mines.

Consider also the houses we need to keep out the rigours of the cold and mitigate the severity of the heat. How do you suppose these dwellings could have been provided in the first place, or repaired later on after storms or earthquakes or the passage of time had destroyed them, unless human beings, amalgamating in communities, had learnt to look to one another for mutual help in such matters? Or think of our aqueducts, canals, irrigation channels, breakwaters, artificial harbours. How could we have been able to enjoy any one of these achievements without human effort? Such examples – and one could add many others – illustrate the obvious fact that it is only the labour of man's hands that places the profits and advantages from inanimate objects at our disposal.

And exactly the same applies to our employment of animals. Without human intervention they would be of no value or benefit to us at all. It was man who first discovered the uses to which the different sorts of animal could be put. And today, still, human labour is what enables us to feed them, and tame them, and look after them, and, in due season, exploit all that they produce. It is man, once again, who kills dangerous animals, and captures useful ones.

To make a list of all the multitude of human skills, without which life would be impossible, is not what I am concerned to do here. But it should just be said that, if mankind did not possess these skills, there would be no healing of the sick, no pleasure for the healthy, no food, no comforts at all. And these are just the things that make a human being's civilized life different from the existence of a beast.

1. The quotation (a translation of Aeschylus, *Prometheus Vinctus*, 502) is probably from the *Prometheus* of Accius.

Besides, if men had not gathered together in the first place, no cities could have been built, and no inhabitants found to live in them. It was the life men led in these cities which led to the creation of laws and customs, to the equitable distribution of rights, to an established social system. And these developments, in their turn, gave rise to a spirit of humanity and mutual consideration. The result was that life became more stable, and by mutual giving and receiving, by placing our resources at one another's disposal, we succeeded in ensuring that all our needs were met.

*

I did not really need to go into all this at such length, because the point which Panaetius describes in such detail must be self-evident to everyone:[1] no leader, either in war or in peace, could ever have performed important or beneficial actions unless he had gained the cooperation of his fellow men. Panaetius cited Themistocles, Pericles, Cyrus, Agesilaus and Alexander, none of whom, he pointed out, could have achieved their great successes if they had failed to enlist supporters. He mobilized witnesses to this assertion, but they could have been dispensed with because it is a conclusion no one could question.

And that is not the end of the story. Certainly, the fact that people join together and collaborate has brought us great benefits. But it is equally true that the worst calamities in the world are likewise those which man inflicts upon man. The eminent and prolific Peripatetic Dicaearchus dealt with this point in his book *On the Ways in which Men Die*. First of all he collected together all the non-human causes of death such as floods, and plagues, and natural disasters, and sudden onslaughts by wild animals – which, he assures us, have wiped out

1. Panaetius of Rhodes was the leading figure of the middle period of Stoicism (p. 27).

whole nations at a time.[1] But then he went on to compare the number of people who have been destroyed by the action of other human beings, that is to say by wars and revolutions; and his conclusion was that the aggregate of such casualties has greatly exceeded the victims of all other sorts of catastrophe put together.

That is to say, there is not a shadow of doubt that man has the power to be the greatest agent both of benefit and of harm towards his fellow-men. Consequently it must be regarded as a vitally important quality to be able to win over human hearts and attach them to one's own cause. The advantages that our life derives from inanimate objects and from its exploitation of animals may be classed under the heading of mere functional activities. But to gain the goodwill of our fellow human beings, to convert them to a state of active readiness to further our own interests, is a task worthy of the wisdom and excellence of a superman.

*

This brings me back to moral goodness. It may be held to fall into three subdivisions. The first is the ability to distinguish the truth from falsity, and to understand the relationships between one phenomenon and another and the causes and consequences of each one. The second category is the ability to restrain the passions (*pathe* in Greek) and to make the appetites (*hormai*) amenable to reason. The third, which is relevant here, is the capacity to behave considerately and understandingly in our associations with other people.[2] By doing so we shall secure their cooperation; and that is how we shall guarantee ourselves a generous sufficiency of all our natural wants. The adoption of this cooperative attitude will also make it possible for us to ward off any danger that may im-

1. Dicaearchus of Messana in Sicily was Aristotle's most important pupil next to Theophrastus.

2. These three qualities are wisdom, temperance and justice.

pend, and to retaliate against anyone who tries to harm us, punishing them as severely as considerations of justice and humanity permit.

In due course I shall go on to say something about the ways in which we can acquire this power to win and retain other people's support. But first let me make a few preliminary observations.

Everybody appreciates the enormous role of fortune in determining whether we succeed or fail. Hers are the favourable breezes that waft us to the haven we have been longing for; and if she should happen to veer against us, we are ruined. When we come to list the various sorts of calamity which Fortune is capable of bringing down on us, first we have to mention two categories which are not found very often. One of these types of disaster is produced by inanimate causes, and consists of storms, and hurricanes, and shipwrecks, and the collapse of buildings, and conflagrations. Another variety of mishap, likewise not very usual, comes from the wounds and bites and charges of animals. But much more frequent are catastrophes such as the annihilation of human beings by one another, formed up in armies. This has happened on countless occasions – and there have been no less than three instances in the immediate past.[1] Think of all the times when commanders have died violent deaths: recently we, ourselves, have lost a leader of exceptional distinction. Think, too, of the outbursts of popular hatred that have often caused the banishment, downfall and flight of men whose services to their states have been outstanding. And then consider, on the other hand, history's examples of success, and promotion to high civil and military office, and victory in the field. These, too, contain an element of chance. Nevertheless, whether for good or ill, no man on earth could ever have

1. Caesar's victories over Cnaeus Pompeius Magnus at Pharsalus (48 BC), over Metellus Scipio at Thapsus (46), and over the sons of Pompeius at Munda (45).

achieved them without the cooperation and resources contributed by other human beings.

Now that this point has been emphasized, I want to go on to explain how we can attract and stimulate this collaboration to our own advantage. And if my discussion may seem too long, compare its length with the vastness of the benefits the theme involves – and then what I have to say will perhaps appear after all to be not long enough.

When people take some step to enlarge a fellow citizen's property, or advance his career, there are several different motives from which they may have acted. It could be sheer goodwill – because for some reason or other, they like the man. It could be respect, because they admire his character and think he deserves success. Or he may inspire their confidence in such a way that it seems to be in their own interests to support him. Or perhaps they fear his power. Alternatively, they may be hoping for some future profit for themselves – such as the presents, for example, which a king or a demagogue is accustomed to distribute. Or they may actually have been promised a payment in reward for their services. This is the meanest and most squalid of all reasons for taking action, both for the people who succumb to such offers and those who have offered the remuneration. For things are in a bad way when people use bribery for something they ought to rely upon their own merits to get for themselves. Nevertheless, there are occasions when recourse to these financial inducements is impossible to avoid. I shall therefore, in due course, indicate my views as to the uses that may be made of this method.

But first I propose to speak about aspects of the subject which bear more directly upon the good life.

*

There are a number of reasons why people may, on occasion be willing not merely to help some individual, but actually to subordinate themselves to his authority and power. The motives which induce them to do this include goodwill; gratitude for favours conferred; the other person's eminence; the calculation that submission may prove a source of profit; the fear that if they do not subject themselves voluntarily their subjection may in any case be imposed by force; the reliance on promises given by the other party; or finally – as we have so often seen in our own country – the actual receipt of a bribe, about which I said something just now.

However, the best of all means of looking after one's own interests is by winning affection. I mentioned fear: but to make people frightened is the way not to maintain one's position but to lose it. Ennius wrote: 'People hate the man they fear; and the man they hate they want to see dead.'[1] And he was perfectly right. Only recently we had occasion to learn, if we did not know it already, that no amount of power, however enormous, can stand up against widespread unpopularity. That tyrant of ours, when he was alive, had to be endured by the State, since he had suppressed its operations by brute force. Now that he is dead, it is true, Rome has become more his slave even than it was in his lifetime; all the same, his death is an excellent illustration of the disastrous results of getting oneself generally hated. And the same lesson is taught by the similar fates of all other despots, scarcely any of whom have ever escaped the same sort of end. For fear is a very poor guarantee that power will last. The only possible way to keep it is by mobilizing goodwill.

Rulers who keep the populations down by force will obviously have to employ brutal methods, like masters who feel compelled to treat their servants harshly because they cannot keep them in order in any other way. But to make oneself feared deliberately, in a free state, is a lunatic procedure. For however drastically a man may have suppressed the free operation of the law and intimidated the spirit of liberty, sooner or later these submerged blessings will be brought up

1. Possibly from the *Thyestes* of Ennius.

to the surface again, either by inarticulate public feeling or through the secret ballots which elect officers of state. And freedom suppressed and then regained bites more sharply than if it had never been in peril. So here is a principle which has the widest possible application, a principle that ensures not only a man's safety but his prosperity and power: it is better to win affection than fear. That is the right recipe for getting what we want and achieving success, both in our private and our public lives.

Men who are eager to terrorize others will inevitably become frightened of the very people they are intimidating. Think of the excruciating anxieties of the elder Dionysius, who was so terrified by his barber's razor that he preferred to singe his own hair with burning coal. And what do you imagine was the state of mind of Alexander of Pherae? History tells us that he loved his wife Thebe very much. All the same, whenever he wanted to visit her bedroom after dinner we are told that he ordered a barbarian, some creature covered with Thracian tattoos, to walk in front of him brandishing a drawn sword. He also sent members of his bodyguard ahead with instructions to search the lady's jewel-cases and make sure no weapons were hidden among her clothes. What an unhappy man he must have been, if he believed a barbarous branded slave was more likely to be loyal than his own wife! However, he turned out to be perfectly right. For in the end Thebe, suspecting he had a mistress, did actually assassinate him.

No power on earth, if it labours beneath the burden of fear, can possibly be strong enough to survive. Witness Phalaris, who became notorious for his unequalled cruelty. He was not, it is true, the victim of domestic treachery, like Alexander of Pherae whose fate I was speaking of. Nor was he murdered by a small group of conspirators, like our man here in Rome. Phalaris's end was different: the whole population of Agrigentum rose up in revolt and went for him. And remember the case of Demetrius, whom the Macedonians abandoned in a body to go over to Pyrrhus. Consider what happened to the Spartans, too. When they exercised their supremacy oppressively, almost the entire body of their allies deserted them and stood as passive spectators watching the disastrous Spartan defeat at Leuctra.[1]

You will see that I prefer to prove my point by examples taken from foreign history rather than from our own. But I do also want to say this. As long as the Roman people governed its empire by goodwill and not injustice, our wars were fought either to protect our subject allies or to defend our own territory. When the wars were over, their after-effects were merciful – or at least no more severe than they had to be. In those days the Roman Senate was a haven of refuge for foreign kings, for whole peoples and nations. The one ambition of our officials and commanders was to gain glory by loyally and justly upholding the safety of our provinces and allies. And so it could truthfully be said that we were not so much the rulers of the world as its protectors.

Even before Sulla's time these traditional high standards were already on the wane. Since the time of his triumph, we have abandoned such ideals altogether. When we treated our own fellow-citizens with such brutality, it could no longer seem wrong to inflict even the most frightful oppressions on our allies. Sulla's cause, it is true, was a just one; but his victory proved appalling. Planting his spear in the Forum he proceeded to auction the possessions of men who were patriots and people of substance – or, at the very least, every one of them was a Roman citizen.[2] Yet he had the effrontery

1. Alexander of Pherae in Thessaly reigned from 369 to 358. The army of Demetrius Poliorcetes (336–283 BC), son of Antigonus I of Macedonia, deserted in 288 to King Pyrrhus of Epirus. The Spartans were defeated by the Thebans at Leuctra in 371.

2. Sulla occupied Rome in 82 BC and became dictator in the following year. The Romans used to set up a spear as a sign of an auction-sale; the custom was derived from the sale of booty taken in war.

to declare that the objects he was selling were spoils he had won from an enemy in war. After him came a man whose cause was not right but evil; and his success was even more horrible than Sulla's.[1] Mere confiscations of the property of individual citizens were far from enough to satisfy him. Whole provinces and countries succumbed to his onslaught, in one comprehensive universal catastrophe. Entire foreign nations were given over to ruin and destruction.

Lately the world has been given a specific illustration of the sort of commonwealth that has vanished. For we have seen, with our own eyes, a model of the vanquished city of Massilia carried in a Roman triumphal procession.[2] And yet it was only by the staunch support of this community, now the victim of conquest and triumph, that our generals in the past were able to win their own Triumphs, returning victorious from Transalpine wars. That is by no means the only injury to our allies that I could mention. But I have singled it out, because there has never been a greater crime under the sun.

Surely, then, our present sufferings are all too well deserved. For had we not allowed outrages to go unpunished on all sides, it would never have been possible for a single individual to seize tyrannical power. As heirs of his personal estate only a few names were listed; but to take over his ambitions a whole host of vile characters was ready. The seeds and causes of civil wars will always be with us for as long as people remember that blood-soaked spear in the Forum – and as long as they hope to see it come again. Publius Sulla was the man who brandished it, when his kinsman was dictator, and it was the same Publius Sulla again, thirty-six years later, who had the effrontery to stand beside another spear, set up for an even

1. Caesar.

2. Massilia (Marseille), besieged and taken in 49 BC by Caesar. Cicero is referring to the multiple Triumph he celebrated in 46, and to the earlier alliance with Massilia which had enabled Rome to annex the province of Gallia Narbonensis (southern France) in 121 BC.

more abominable auction.[1] And there was yet another Sulla too: a clerk under the first dictator, he was city treasurer under the second. Such are the proofs that, while there are such vastly lucrative rewards, civil war will never end.

Here in the city nothing is left – only the lifeless walls of houses. And even they look afraid that some further terrifying attack may be imminent. The real Rome has gone for ever.

*

But to return to my subject. The reason why these disasters have descended upon us is because we chose to make ourselves feared rather than liked and loved. And if this could happen to the entire Roman community, because of its unjust imperialism, what lesson should individuals draw for themselves? We already know that goodwill possesses enormous power to get us what we want, whereas fear can achieve very little. What we have to do next is to discuss the ways of directing this goodwill towards ourselves. How can we win affection – based on loyalty and honour?

The number of people in whom this sentiment has to be instilled will inevitably vary according to the individual who is trying to instil it. Does he want numerous devotees, or will just a few suffice? The answer depends on the sort of life he leads. But we do have to lay down one primary and fundamental requirement: when we are selecting friends to trust, let us at least choose people who are genuinely fond of us and honestly prepared to take our side. As far as this point is concerned, it is of little significance whether the man looking for friends is important or unimportant. Whatever his position, he needs friendship just as pressingly as anyone else.

Some people are keener to win honour, reputation and popu-

1. Under Caesar. Publius Cornelius Sulla was the nephew of Lucius Cornelius Sulla the dictator. Nevertheless, Cicero spoke in Publius's defence in 62 BC (the *Pro Sulla*). The third Sulla mentioned was a freedman of the dictator.

larity than others. But it must be admitted that, if you possess these advantages, it does become easier to win friends. As regards friendship itself, I have already discussed the subject in my essay entitled *Laelius*.[1] So now I shall, instead, say something about how to obtain this other asset we have now begun to discuss, an impressive reputation. It is true that this, again, is a theme I have written two volumes about.[2] Nevertheless, I want to revert to the subject here, since we are now talking of practical obligations, and a reputation of this kind is a great help towards an important official career.

Now the truest, loftiest sort of reputation can be obtained by inspiring three feelings in the public: (i) goodwill, (ii) confidence, (iii) respect of the kind which gets one promoted to high office. To put it briefly and simply, these sentiments are aroused in the population as a mass by the same methods which produce them in single individuals (although there is a further technique for getting at the masses, which has the special advantage of commending us to all their collective hearts at one and the same time).

Let me go over these three headings one by one. The first concerns the question of winning goodwill. The most important way to achieve this is by doing someone a service.[3] A second method is to show that one would *like* to perform such a service, even if one's resources do not actually permit one to do so. For popular favour is profoundly influenced by a name and reputation for generosity, beneficence, fair dealing, loyalty and all the other good qualities which are associated with an attractive and agreeable character. These virtues owe

1. Cicero's *Laelius: On Friendship* is translated elsewhere in this volume.

2. Cicero's two books *On Glory* were known to Petrarch but are now lost.

3. Cicero is thinking particularly of a defence in the courts – 'a service' because the speaker was not allowed to accept a fee, though he could be rewarded in other ways.

their influence to the fact that we approve of right and proper conduct, and admire not only its intrinsic excellence but its external manifestations as well. Now, the qualities I have just enumerated are particularly well adapted to making a brilliant display of such behaviour, and that is why Nature itself impels us to love the people who appear to possess these assets. So much, then, for the principal factors that induce people to feel goodwill. There may be others as well, but if so they are less important.

The second method of gaining a reputation, then, is by winning confidence. There are two requirements for this. A man must be considered intelligent; and he must be regarded as just. We feel confidence in people we believe to be wiser than ourselves, and better judges of the future – people who seem capable of dealing with critical situations and making whatever decisions circumstances require. For that is the sort of useful intelligence that people reckon to be the real thing. And as to the second requirement for gaining confidence, that one should have a name for justice – justice is the same thing as goodness, and the designation of a just man is bestowed upon the person whose character is untouched by any suspicion of dishonesty or unfair dealing – the sort of man to whom we should consider it safe to entrust our lives, our fortunes and our children.

Goodness or justice is more effective than intelligence in inspiring trust. And indeed, even when intelligence is conspicuous by its absence, justice still carries great weight; whereas intelligence without justice creates no confidence at all. If a man is not regarded as honest, the more shrewd and sharp he is the more he will be disliked and distrusted. To sum up, then, a combination of justice and intelligence is best of all – and capable of winning all the confidence that could be desired. Justice without intelligence will also be able to achieve a great deal. But intelligence without justice is useless.

It may cause surprise to hear me distinguishing between one

virtue and another in this way. After all, it is a commonplace among philosophers that the person who possesses one virtue possesses the others as well; and I myself have often argued to the same effect. There is no question, that is to say, of anyone being a just man unless he is endowed with intelligence as well. The reason for my apparent inconsistency is that the exact kind of language we employ in philosophical analyses of abstract truth is one thing, and the language used in attempts to popularize the subject is another. In my present study, when I call one man brave, another good, and another intelligent, I am speaking in terms suited to this wider circulation. In dealing with popular conceptions, it is right to use common and familiar words – as Panaetius for example did.

But let me get back to what I was discussing.

The third prerequisite for a glorious reputation is that people should admire us and deem us worthy of high honours. In general, men admire everything which strikes them as fine, or finer than they had expected; and in their fellow human beings too, they admire qualities that exceed their expectations. And so they heap praises and respect upon any individual in whom they claim to discern remarkable and exceptional features; whereas anyone who shows neither character nor spirit nor vigour earns their scorn and contempt. If, however, they disapprove of somebody, this does not invariably mean that they despise him. A person, for example, whom they regard as dishonest and abusive and fraudulent and malevolent incurs their disapproval, but not necessarily their contempt. The objects of contempt, as I have indicated elsewhere, are those who, as the saying goes, profit neither their neighbours nor themselves: the idle, sluggish and indifferent.

Admiration, on the other hand, goes to individuals who seem finer than the rest of the community because they are free from any taint of disrepute and lack the vices which so many others find it hard to resist. Sensuality, for example, is an alluring mistress which succeeds in seducing the greater part of mankind from the path of integrity. Pain too, when its scorching brand makes itself felt, terrifies most people immeasurably. Life and death, wealth and want, exercise an overwhelming effect on the entire human race. It is only when men become capable of displaying high-minded detachment and disregarding such outward circumstances, whether good or bad – when they get totally absorbed and immersed in some noble, honourable purpose – that we cannot help admiring their splendid and imposing qualities.

The ability to rise above outward circumstances, then, wins special admiration; and that is why justice, which is the peculiar mark of a good man, is universally regarded as marvellous. And quite right too. For if someone possesses this virtue, it means that he has emancipated himself from the fear of death and pain and exile and poverty: that is to say, he does not regard it as more important to achieve the reverses of these conditions than to behave like a decent person. And most of all people admire someone who refuses to be influenced by money. To prove oneself in that particular direction is the equivalent of emerging triumphantly from a fiery ordeal.

If, that is to say, one can claim to be a just man, all the three requirements for a glorious reputation will already be at hand: goodwill, because the favourable effects of one's just dealings have conferred widespread benefits; confidence, for the same reason; and admiration, because the just man is admired for disregarding and scorning the very things most people are spurred on by greed to try to lay their hands on.

*

Now no one at all, whatever his way and manner of life, can in my opinion dispense with the help of his fellow-men. In the first place, he has to have friends to speak to. But if you are not looked upon as a good man, no one will have the slightest desire to talk to you. Even someone who shuns company and spends his life out of town still has great need to possess a reputation for goodness and justice, because even he has to have associates of some kind. For without them, isolated as he is, he will have no one to support him – in which case he may easily become the victim of every sort of persecution. And so he needs a name for justice more than anyone else.

And people who buy and sell or let and hire, the members of the business world generally, depend on justice every bit as much. Indeed, its power is so far-reaching that even people who live on wrong doing and crime cannot get along without a modicum of the same quality. For if a thief steals or seizes something from another thief, he loses his status even in that community. If the boss of the gang divides the spoils unfairly, his comrades will desert him or even murder him. Indeed, robbers supposedly have a code of their own, which they are under an obligation to obey. Impartial division of the loot was what brought power to the Illyrian bandit Bardylis, whom we read about in Theopompus; and Viriathus the Lusitanian won an even greater position by precisely the same means. Roman armies, Roman generals, fell away before him, until in the end he was broken and crushed by the praetor Gaius Laelius, known as the Wise, who checked his ferocious activities so sternly that Laelius's successors easily finished off the war.[1]

Since, then, the influence of justice is great enough to strengthen and increase even a bandit's power, think of the

1. Bardylis, ruler of the Illyrians, overran much of western Macedonia before he was repelled by King Philip II in 358. The contemporary historian Theopompus of Chios wrote a history of Philip's reign. In Spain and Portugal, Viriathus (d. 139) maintained a revolt of the Lusitanians, and then the Celtiberians too, against Rome for eleven years. Laelius (see *On Friendship*) was praetor in 145.

effect the same quality will exert upon a well-ordered government properly furnished with laws and courts.

Herodotus tells us that the Medes always chose a good man to be their king, because they wanted to make sure they would receive just treatment.[1] And our own ancestors, I believe, felt the same. For when the Roman populace began to be oppressed by certain dominant individuals, they themselves chose another citizen, a man of outstanding character, to be their monarch and their protector. His job was to defend the weaker members of the community against tyranny and to establish equitable conditions which guaranteed equal rights to the grand and the humble alike. And laws were created for the same reason as kings. People have always wanted equal rights before the law; for otherwise whatever rights they might happen to possess would not be worthy of the name. And if some single person, a just and upright man, enabled them to fulfil this aim, then that was good enough for them. But when this did not work, laws were invented, to speak to everybody the whole time in one and the same language.

So there is no doubt that the men chosen to rule in ancient times were those who enjoyed a great popular reputation for justice; and if they were believed to be intelligent as well, there was no limit to the advantages people expected to obtain under their leadership. But the main thing the leaders had to provide was justice. Indeed it is a quality that must be cultivated and maintained by every possible means. This must be done for its own sake – for that is what justice means, its very essence. But it is also true that just dealings add honour and glory to one's reputation.

In some ways winning a reputation is like making money. To take the latter pursuit, we are able to demonstrate the methods not only of acquiring money but also of investing it so as to provide an income which will meet our recurrent expenses and supply the necessities and amenities of life. The

1. Herodotus, *Histories*, I, 96.

same applies to a reputation; first you must acquire it, and then you have to invest what you have acquired. As to the process of acquisition, Socrates was perfectly right when he declared that there is a direct short-cut to winning a reputation: 'Make yourself the sort of man you want people to think you are.'[1] For to suppose that any permanent reputation can be won by pretence, or empty display, or hypocritical talk, or by putting on an insincere facial expression, would be a serious misapprehension. A genuine, glorious reputation strikes deep roots and has wide ramifications, but pretences of every kind wither away like wilting blooms; nothing counterfeit has any staying power. I could quote many examples both of the real thing and the fake, but for brevity's sake I shall confine myself to a single family. Tiberius Gracchus the elder, the son of Publius, will be honoured as long as the memory of Rome endures. But his sons, while they lived, did not gain the approval of right-minded people, and after they died they rank among the men whom it was justifiable to put to death.[2]

So anyone who wants to enjoy a genuine reputation is obliged to fulfil the obligations demanded by justice. What they are, I described in the previous volume of this work.

Although the essence of the situation, as Socrates indicated, is that we really should *be* what we want our fellow human beings to think we are, there are certain methods of ensuring that people do in fact discover what we are like, and I will now suggest what these methods are. Now it is true that if someone begins life as the bearer of a famous name, either because he has inherited the name from his father (which might be said of yourself, Marcus!) or through some other chance turn of events, the eyes of the world will be fastened upon him.

1. Xenophon, *Memorabilia*, II, 6, 39.

2. Tiberius Gracchus senior (the father of the famous tribunes Tiberius and Gaius whose reforming methods are frequently deplored by Cicero, p. 161, etc.) was consul in 177 and 163 BC and censor in 169. See Genealogical Table (II), p. 361.

Everything he does, and his entire way of life, will come under careful scrutiny; it is as though he were bathed in some glaring light, illuminating every one of his words or actions. Others, however, remain quite unknown to the world at large throughout their youth because their origins were humble and obscure; and these have to make special determined efforts, as soon as they reach adult years, to aim at the heights and try to scale them. And they can feel a measure of special confidence in dedicating themselves to this task, because the fact that they are young will win them encouragement instead of jealousy.

The first way for a young man to set himself on the road towards a glorious reputation is to win renown, if he can, upon the field of battle. Many of our ancestors succeeded in doing this, because in those times there was always a war being fought. Your own youthful years also coincided with a war. But it was a war in which one side was loaded with all the guilt, and the other with all the bad luck. Nevertheless, when Pompeius, in that campaign, entrusted you with the command of a cavalry squadron, your horsemanship and javelin-throwing, and the way you endured the hardships of army life, earned you high praise both from the great man himself as well as from all your fellow-soldiers. Yet the reputation you had gained proved useless after all, because when the Republic vanished your reputation came to nothing too.

*

However, your own personal case is not what I am discussing; my theme is a more general one. So let me proceed to the next stage of the argument.

There is a general rule that a man's character is more important than his body; and this applies fully to the subject we are considering here. The achievements in public life which come from spiritual strength are more impressive than those which are merely manifestations of physical force. Bearing this in mind, a youth will find he can best win himself praise if he behaves with moderation, if he displays loyalty to his parents, and if he shows devotion to the rest of his family. Young men also find it easier to gain ready and favourable recognition if they select some wise, famous and patriotic statesman, and attach themselves to him as his companions. If they associate continually with an individual of that calibre, the public forms the impression that they, too, are going to turn out like the man they have chosen to imitate. For example, the young Publius Rutilius Rufus owed much of his renown for integrity and legal brilliance to his constant attendance at the home of Publius Scaevola. Lucius Crassus, on the other hand, adopted a different method. Even when he was little more than a boy he looked to no one else for assistance, but acting completely on his own account won enormous prestige from that extremely important and glorious prosecution he undertook in the courts. He was of an age when the only sort of praise most boys get is for the exercises they have been doing at school. But Crassus repeated the achievement that is credited to Demosthenes. That is to say, in spite of his tender years, he accomplished in open court what would have been impressive enough if it had just been a practice essay done in the privacy of his own home.[1]

Oratory, it is true, is only one kind of speech; there is conversation as well. An affable, pleasant conversational manner certainly plays some part in gaining friends. But it is hard to say exactly how much; and it is perfectly clear that oratory,

1. Publius Rutilius Rufus (consul 105 BC). This Publius Mucius Scaevola, the first of his family to win distinction as a jurist, was consul in 133, father of Quintus Mucius Scaevola the Priest, and uncle of Quintus Mucius Scaevola the Augur (see *On Friendship* and *On the Orator* and Genealogical Table (I), p. 360). Publius Scaevola's son-in-law Lucius Licinius Crassus (see the latter treatise) is here compared with the Athenian Demosthenes. At the age of twenty-one Crassus successfully prosecuted Gaius Papirius Carbo, who had supported the Gracchi (p. 99), and compelled him to commit suicide.

by which I mean eloquent public speaking, is an immeasurably greater help towards securing a reputation than any private chatting could be. The value of such eloquence is illustrated by three letters written by fathers to their sons – by Philip of Macedonia to Alexander, by Antipater to Cassander, and by Antigonus to his young son Philip.[1] These three writers, we understand, were among the wisest men in all history, and in their letters, which still survive, each one of them advises his son to win over the hearts of his people by amiable speech-making, and counsels him to keep his soldiers loyal, too, by persuasive exhortations. But the most effective of all, very often, is a speech delivered in a public debate, because when there is a large audience such an address has the power to enlist enormous numbers of people on one's side. A fluent and perceptive oration will earn a speaker intense admiration, and his hearers will be convinced that he is wiser and more intelligent than anyone else. If he manages to make his speech sound both impressive and sensible, people will admire him very much indeed, particularly if he is young.

There are several different avenues for eloquence. The law-courts, Assembly and Senate are all places in which many young Romans have won distinction by public speaking. But it is in the courts that the possibilities for winning approval are the greatest.

Speeches in the courts fall into two categories, those for the prosecution and those for the defence. To defend someone is the more honourable course; but reputations have often been won by speeches for the prosecution as well. I mentioned Crassus just now; Marcus Antonius the Orator enjoyed a similar success in the days of his youth. And it was again the

1. These letters were forgeries. Philip II (359–336 BC) was the father of Alexander the Great. Alexander's general Antipater (d. 319) was the father of Cassander (d. 297) who founded Thessalonica. Antigonus I, one of Alexander's successors (d. 301), had two sons, Philip and Demetrius Poliorcetes.

role of accuser which made Publius Sulpicius Rufus a famous speaker, when he brought an action against that bad, subversive character Gaius Norbanus. But nobody ought to act as a prosecutor regularly. Indeed, one never really ought to do it at all, except in the national interest (which was involved in the cases I mentioned), or to avenge personal wrongs (which was the motive of the two Luculli), or to protect provincial clients (as I myself did when I conducted a prosecution to help the Sicilians, and Julius when he brought a charge against Albucius at the request of the people of Sardinia). The hard work Lucius Fufius put into his impeachment of Manius Aquilius is equally well known.[1]

Once, then; or at any rate not at all often. But if anyone should have to conduct prosecutions with greater frequency, he will be well advised to concentrate on cases which render a service to his country. For there could never be any disgrace in bringing retribution upon the enemies of Rome. And yet, even so, there should still be a limit. To make repeated accusations of the sort which involve defendants in the loss of their civil rights looks heartless, one might almost say inhuman. Consequently, a reputation for specializing in prosecutions puts a man in a precarious situation, and has an adverse effect on his good name. That is what happened to that member of a great family, Marcus Brutus, whose father was an outstanding authority on the law.[2]

1. For Marcus Antonius the Orator and Publius Sulpicius Rufus see *On the Orator*. Gaius Norbanus, tribune in 104 BC, was charged by Rufus with treason in c.98 but was defended by Antonius and acquitted. Cicero also refers to prosecutions by the brothers Lucius Licinius Lucullus and his brother Marcus Terentius Varro Lucullus (consuls 74, 73 BC), to his own prosecution of Verres in 70 (p. 106), and to the prosecutions of the Epicurean Titus Albucius by Gaius Julius Vopiscus Caesar Strabo (aedile 90 BC), and of Manius Aquilius (consul 101 BC) by Lucius Fufius for corrupt maladministration in Sicily.

2. The father (praetor c. 150 BC) was known as one of the three 'founders' of the *ius civile*; his son was known as the Accuser.

Another rule, which must be observed meticulously, is never to bring a charge involving the loss of civil rights against someone who is innocent. For this could not fail to be a criminal act. Nature bestowed eloquence on human beings for their safety and preservation; and it is therefore the height of inhumanity to divert such a gift to the ruin and destruction of honest men. So this must never be done. There is no need, on the other hand, to have any scruples about occasionally defending a person who is guilty – provided that he is not really a depraved or wicked character. For popular sentiment requires this; it is sanctioned by custom, and conforms with human decency.

The judge's business, in every trial, is to discover the truth. As for counsel, however, he may on occasion have to base his advocacy on points which *look like* the truth, even if they do not correspond with it exactly. But I must confess I should not have the nerve to be saying such things, especially in a philosophical treatise, unless Panaetius, the most authoritative of Stoics, had spoken to the same effect!

The greatest renown, the profoundest gratitude, is won by speeches defending people. These considerations particularly apply when, as sometimes happens, the defendant is evidently the victim of oppression and persecution at the hands of some powerful and formidable personage. That is the sort of case I have often taken on. For example, when I was young, I spoke up for Sextus Roscius of Ameria against the tyrannical might of the dictator Sulla. As you know, the speech has been published.[1]

*

So much, then, for the obligations a young man has to fulfil in order to win himself a reputation. The next subjects that have to be discussed are kindness and liberality.

1. *Pro Sexto Roscio Amerino* (80 BC).

There are two ways of displaying these qualities, and helping those who are in need: either by personal services, or by money. The second way is the easier of the two, especially if you happen to be rich. But the first way is the finer and nobler, and more appropriate for a man of character and distinction. Both methods show the same generous desire to do a favour. But the former is merely a draft on one's financial capital, whereas the latter means drawing on one's own personal energies. Besides, drafts on capital tend to mean that the source of the generosity will in due course dry up. Generosity of this kind, in other words, is self-destructive: the more people you have given money to, the smaller the number you will be able to assist in the future. But if someone is kind and generous with actions involving his own personal abilities and efforts, the more individuals he assists the more helpers he can mobilize for further acts of assistance hereafter. Besides, he will have got into a habit of kindness, which will make him more prepared and better trained for performing similar services on a wider scale in the future.

In one of his letters to his son Alexander, Philip rightly remonstrated with him for courting popularity with the Macedonians by gifts of cash. 'Whatever gave you the disastrous idea,' the monarch wrote, 'that men you had corrupted by money would remain your loyal supporters? Do you want the people of Macedonia to think of you as a sort of steward and purveyor, instead of as their king?'

Well, that is what Philip said to his son. And his advice is relevant to every one of us.

The form of liberality, then, which consists of offering one's own services and endeavours is certainly more honourable than the other kind. It also has a wider application, and can assist a larger number of people. Nevertheless, gifts of money *do* sometimes have to be made. This sort of liberality cannot be ruled out altogether. There are occasions, quite often, when we have to draw on our private means in order to assist fellow-citizens who are poor but deserving. But we must do so with discretion and moderation. There have been many cases when indiscriminate benefactions have dissipated entire inheritances; and even if you want to give help in such a way, it is surely the height of stupidity to indulge your taste so unrestrainedly that you run out of the means to keep the practice up. Besides, lavish hand-outs lead to stealing – when someone has given away so much that he is beginning to go short himself, he finds himself obliged to lay hands on other people's property.[1] Although his purpose was to secure goodwill by displaying generosity, the goodwill he succeeds in extracting from his recipients is outweighed by the detestation he earns from the men he has robbed.

In other words, whereas one's purse must not be tightly closed against every generous inclination, it must also not be opened so wide that its contents are available to everybody and anybody. There has to be a limit, and the determining factor is our means. We must remember the saying – repeated in Rome so often that it has become proverbial: bounty is a bottomless pit. For how can it be anything else, when those who have got accustomed to being subsidized are bound to want more, and persons who have never been at the receiving end want to get there?

Large-scale givers fall into two classes, the extravagant and the generous. The extravagant ones are those who squander money on public banquets, and free distributions of meat, and gladiatorial shows, and expensive Games or wild-beast hunts – things which are remembered for a short time or not at all. Those, on the other hand, who really deserve to be described as generous are the people who pay to ransom prisoners from gangsters, or who assume responsibility for the debts of a friend, or help him to provide dowries for his daughters or to

1. Cicero is no doubt thinking of Catilina (whose conspiracy he put down in 63), Sulla, Caesar and Marcus Antonius (the future triumvir).

acquire a piece of property he wants or to enlarge the land he already possesses.

So I cannot understand what Theophrastus was thinking about when he wrote his book *On Wealth*. Much of what he said is excellent, but one point is quite absurd. For he devotes a great deal of praise to sumptuous arrangements for public Games – even going so far as to say that he regards the capacity to indulge in this sort of extravagant expenditure as the finest privilege of wealth! I maintain, on the other hand, that the display of real generosity, of which I have offered a few illustrations, is a far more significant and productive way of spending one's money.

What Aristotle said on the same subject is much more acceptable than Theophrastus's opinion, and more to the point. [1] For he took exactly the opposite view, blaming us for not being scandalized by all this outpouring of money to win popular favour. 'Imagine that the city was besieged,' he said, 'and that people were compelled to pay a *mina* a pint for their water; at first we should find this unbelievable, and everyone would be amazed, even if later, after reflection, they would be prepared to concede that the price was justified by necessity. And yet our gigantic, endless, wasteful expenditure on popular spectacles does not strike us as particularly surprising, although it satisfies no urgent need at all, and brings honour to no one. Indeed, it does not even gratify the public for more than the briefest and most transitory passage of time; and even then only its most fatuous members, who just gorge themselves on the immediate pleasure and then forget all about the whole thing in a moment.' And Aristotle goes on, quite correctly, to reach the following conclusion. 'Entertainments of this kind amuse children and silly women and slaves

1. Since the view quoted here is not found in Aristotle, and is indeed contrary to an opinion he expressed in the *Nicomachean Ethics*, IV, 1, 11 some prefer to regard the correct reading as 'Aristo' (Aristo of Ceos, head of the Peripatetic school, 230 BC).

and creatures with slavish mentalities. But serious men, capable of weighing things sensibly, could not possibly approve of such performances.'

And yet I do realize that in our own country, even in the good old times, even the most high-minded citizens were generally expected to produce grandiose displays during the year when they were serving as aediles. Publius Crassus for example, known as 'the Rich' – which he certainly was – gave magnificent Games during his aedileship, and shortly afterwards Lucius Crassus, in association with Quintus Mucius Scaevola the Priest (a thoroughly unpretentious man), behaved in the most sumptuous fashion when he held the same post. Next came Gaius Claudius the son of Appius, and afterwards many others – the Luculli, Hortensius and Silanus. And then, during the year when I was consul, Publius Lentulus outdid every single one of his predecessors, and later on Scaurus rivalled his achievement. But the most splendid shows of all were those given by my friend Pompeius during his second tenure of the consulship.[1]

*

Well now, I have given you some idea of what I feel about this aspect of the matter.

All the same, it is essential to avoid any suspicion of meanness. Mamercus, for example, was a very wealthy man, but his refusal to seek office as aedile, on grounds of the expense involved, meant that later on he was rejected for the consul-

1. Publius Licinius Crassus Dives, consul 97 BC, was father of Marcus Crassus the triumvir. Lucius Crassus and Quintus Mucius Scaevola the Priest were aediles in 103. Gaius Claudius Pulcher staged duels between elephants (99), and the Lucullus brothers between elephants and bulls (79). Quintus Hortensius Hortalus (75) was Cicero's rival. Decimus Junius Silanus, Publius Cornelius Lentulus Spinther and Marcus Aemilius Scaurus (stepson of Sulla) were aediles in 70, 63 and 58, and Cnaeus Pompeius Magnus was consul for the second time in the last of these years.

ship.[1] In other words, since there is a popular demand for these displays, a sensible man is obliged to submit; even if he cannot summon up any enthusiasm for the idea, he has got to do what is required of him. But even so, he must keep within his means – as I myself did. Another reason why he has to comply is that there are occasions when generosity of this kind towards the public will help him to achieve some more truly significant and useful purposes at a future date. Orestes, for instance, gained valuable goodwill owing to the public banquets he recently gave in the streets of Rome, ostensibly as a religious tithe-offering. And nobody held it against Marcus Seius when he supplied the public with grain at the extremely low price of one *as* a peck at a time when prices were rocketing. For this enabled him to put an end to the unpopularity which had long been a handicap to him, and considering that he was aedile at the time the cost was neither excessive nor discreditable.

But the greatest renown of all went to my friend Milo. This was at a time when the whole destiny of our country depended upon whether my own banishment could be rescinded. For this reason, acting in the national interest, Milo purchased a band of gladiators, and used them to put down the hostile terrorism of Publius Clodius.[2]

*

The distribution of money, then, can be justified on grounds of necessity or utility. But even when one of these conditions is present, moderation still remains the wisest policy. Lucius

1. Mamercus Aemilius Lepidus Livianus in fact became consul in 77 BC.

2. Cnaeus Aufidius Orestes Aurelianus was consul in 71 BC. Marcus Seius's price was so cheap that he was practically giving the grain away. When Cicero was exiled in 58 through the agency of his enemy Publius Clodius Pulcher, Titus Annius Milo, tribune in 57, helped to secure his recall (Milo murdered Clodius in 52).

Philippus, Quintus's very able and eminent son, used to boast that without paying for any entertainments at all he had succeeded in reaching every one of the highest positions in the official career. Cotta used to say the same, and Curio as well. I, too, can make a similar claim – or at least to some extent. I was unanimously elected to the successive offices of state at the earliest permissible age – a thing which none of the other people I have just been speaking about had ever achieved. And in proportion to the magnitude of these distinctions, my outlay when I was aedile had been far from extravagant.[1]

There is a special justification for disbursements of money when these sums are devoted to the defrayal of constructions of national importance – walls, dockyards, harbours, aqueducts and so on. It is true that greater immediate pleasure is provided by actual cash hand-outs. But the other sort of outlay produces more abundant gratitude in the long run. As for theatres, porticoes, new temples, and other buildings of that kind, I feel some diffidence about criticizing such projects out of respect for Pompeius, who was so active in this respect. All the same, the most distinguished philosophers do not approve of public works of such a kind. Panaetius, for example, did not care for them, and he is the man whom I have followed a good deal in this work (short of actually translating what he says). Demetrius of Phalerum, too, felt the same, because he censured the most important of all Greeks, Pericles, for throwing away such huge sums of money on the famous Propylaea. But this is a subject which I have discussed exhaustively in my work *On the State*.[2]

1. Lucius Marcius Philippus was tribune in 104 and consul in 91 BC. For Gaius Aurelius Cotta see *On the Orator*. Gaius Scribonius Curio was tribune in 90 and consul in 76. Minimum ages were laid down by the Lex Villia Annalis, later modified by Sulla. Cicero, as aedile in 69, had in fact staged three sets of public Games.

2. Demetrius of Phalerum (born c. 350 BC) was an Athenian writer and politician who was made governor of Athens by the Macedonian Cassander. The monumental roofed gateway to the Acropolis known as

One might sum up by concluding that all expenditure under this heading is intrinsically undesirable – but that there are times when it is necessary all the same. In such circumstances, however, the outlay should always be adjusted according to the means of the donor; and the principle of moderation should never be lost sight of.

*

Let us now turn to the second category of largess, the kind which is prompted by a desire to be generous.

Here again we have to examine different recipients on their merits. The case of a man who is overwhelmed by disaster must be distinguished from the position of someone who has suffered no calamity but merely desires to better himself. Liberality should prefer to direct itself towards the former category, the victims of misfortune – unless they should happen to have deserved their troubles. As for the others, the men who are looking for assistance not as a relief for hardship but to further their own careers, I am not saying that we should withold our support from them altogether. But we must exercise careful judgement in choosing whom we are going to help. Ennius was absolutely right when he said: 'Good deeds, if badly placed, become bad deeds.'

The man who grants a favour will be rewarded not only by the recipient's goodwill – provided he is both deserving and suitably grateful – but by other people's as well. Nothing wins so much gratitude and enthusiasm as generosity (applied with discrimination), because kindness in a leading man seems like a sort of sanctuary – to which everyone feels he himself may eventually want to turn! Every effort must therefore be made to include as many people as possible among our beneficiaries;

---

the Propylaea was designed by Mnesicles (c. 435). Presumably Cicero's discussion was contained in the lost portions of the fifth book of his *De Republica.*

and then the memory of what we have done will be handed down to their children and children's children, so that even they are still going to remember the donor appreciatively. For ingratitude is hated by everyone: and indeed it is taken as a personal injury by all and sundry, because it suggests that one is not going to be generously treated oneself. A person who behaves ungratefully, that is to say, is regarded as the common foe of all who are in need.

Another form of assistance that one may be called upon to furnish is the provision of a ransom for prisoners of war. This is not only a kindness to the prisoners themselves, but a patriotic service as well. And the same applies to improving the financial situation of people below the poverty line. One of the speeches of Lucius Crassus gave details of the help that Roman senators were at one time accustomed to give to the poor. In my opinion, private charity of this type is greatly preferable to lavish expenditure on public entertainments. Gifts of the former kind are what one would expect from serious-minded, high-principled men, whereas extravagant shows are typical of the sort of people who make a practice of flattering the public and like to tickle their frivolous instincts by holding out tempting allurements.

But there are other praiseworthy causes of action besides generous giving. For example, it is important to be lenient in the demands one makes upon others. In any and every business transaction, whether it be buying and selling, or hiring and letting, or relationships between neighbours, or matters relating to the boundaries between properties, a man must be fair and reasonable, prepared to concede his own rights to a substantial extent, ready to avoid litigation as far as he feels he justifiably can – and even a little more. Indeed, there are times when concessions of this kind are not only generous to others but actually, in the long run, profitable to oneself. We should care for our own property, certainly: it is discreditable to let it slip through our fingers. But we must take these measures in such a way that not the slightest suspicion of meanness or greed enters into the matter. For although the very best possible way to use one's money is to spend it on generous actions, it is necessary to stop short of actually giving one's paternal estate away free of charge!

Another virtue which Theophrastus commended was hospitality. I agree with him entirely. It is an admirable thing that eminent men should throw their homes open to eminent guests; and it is to the national advantage when visitors from abroad receive this form of generosity in our city. Besides, any man pursuing reputable ambitions is well advised to seek influence and goodwill among foreign communities by extending hospitality to their citizens who are visiting Rome. Theophrastus writes of the special case of Cimon[1] who used to provide this kind of entertainment for the Laciads, the people of his own constituency. If any Laciad should happen to call at his country home, he directed that every facility should be extended to him, and the bailiffs were given instructions accordingly.

*

Generous actions consisting not of cash gifts but of personal services are again of value not only to individuals but to one's country. But as a means of improving one's own position and popularity, it remains true that there is nothing so effective as to defend someone in the courts, and provide assistance in that field generally. One of the many excellent customs of our ancestors was their invariably respectful treatment of experts in the interpretation of our excellent law. Until the present time of confusion, leading statesmen concentrated this activity exclusively in their own hands. But now the glory of the profession has been obliterated – like all the other glories of a Roman official career. And this is all the more lamentable because it happened during the lifetime of a man who

1. The Athenian statesman and soldier (c.512–449 BC).

equalled any one of his predecessors in rank, and exceeded the whole lot of them in legal erudition.[1]

This sort of service, then, attracts widespread gratitude and performs the kind of good turn which places men under an obligation.

Closely related to legal ability is the gift of eloquence, which is a more elaborate art and wields an even greater power to attract goodwill. For eloquence is specifically adapted to winning the admiration of one's hearers; it awakens new hope in the destitute, and earns profound gratitude from the men whose causes you have pleaded. That is why our forefathers ranked oratory as the highest among all civilian professions. For if a man is a good speaker and prepared to take pains, if he follows the tradition of our ancestors by defending one client after another without the slightest show of reluctance or demand for compensation, he will have the widest possible opportunities to help his fellow men – and this will mean that he has hosts of beneficiaries indebted to him for his services.

The subject of oratory prompts me to repeat, at this juncture, an expression of the sorrow that has been caused me by the current interruption of the entire activity at Rome, or one might almost say its total extinction. And that is a theme which I should be very willing to enlarge upon were I not afraid that, if I did, people would suppose I was complaining about my own personal position. All the same, anyone can see how many orators have perished, how few of any promise remain, how those who possess the slightest talent are a good deal fewer still, and how even those practitioners who do exist include a large proportion whose only quality is aggressiveness. It is perfectly true, in the nature of things, that all men, indeed most men, cannot be expert lawyers or eloquent speakers. But, even so, it is open to anybody to place many of

1. The jurist Servius Sulpicius Rufus (d. 45 BC).

his fellow-citizens in his debt by canvassing when they are standing for offices of state, by testifying for them to juries and officials, by keeping a personal eye on their interests, by finding lawyers to advise and defend them. Men who perform services of this kind earn a very substantial amount of gratitude and reap exceedingly important rewards.

One further piece of advice is so obvious that it scarcely needs mentioning. When you want to help one group of persons, be careful not to offend another. Avoid the mistake, so frequently made, of acting to the detriment of any individual whom it is morally wrong (or highly inadvisable) to injure. To do such a thing by accident is careless; to do it deliberately is foolhardy. And if, inadvertently, you do contrive to offend somebody, you should excuse yourself as best you can by explaining why you could not help doing what you did, since there was no alternative. And you should try to make up for the apparent offence by rendering helpful services in the future.

*

In deciding whether to give a man help, we usually take either his character or his financial resources into account. It is easy to say, and most people do say, that in distributing favours the recipient's character ought to weigh more with donors than his resources. This sounds very good. But does anybody really find it more attractive to help someone who is poor but worthy rather than someone who is wealthy and influential?

It must be admitted that we are generally more inclined to offer our assistance to the person who will give us the prompter and speedier return. However, it is advisable to look into this aspect of the question with somewhat greater care. It is true that a man without possessions of his own cannot actually repay our favour in practical terms. But if he is a decent person, he can at least repay us in his heart. As someone aptly remarked, 'If a man still has money, he has not repaid it; if he has repaid it, he no longer has it.' But this does not apply to gratitude. For that is a sentiment which the beneficiary still continues to feel, even if he has repaid the favour itself; and indeed the very fact that he has the feeling means in itself, in a sense, that the favour has been repaid.

However, personages who like to think of themselves as rich and honoured and fortunate prefer not to be saddled with the obligation that the acceptance of a service would involve. Indeed, if someone has helped them, even on a considerable scale, they prefer to take the view that they have conferred a favour rather than accepted one! For they are very nervous of some claim being established against them, in case they might be expected to give something in return. They would die rather than have it thought that they were like some client beholden to his patron.

A poor man on the other hand, if someone has done him a good turn, is ready to believe this has been done on his own personal account and not because of any assessment of his financial resources. Consequently he makes every effort to show his gratitude, not merely to the particular person who has earned it but in general to anyone else from whom he may hope that a similar windfall may be forthcoming in the future: because he needs as many helpers as he can get. And if he does manage to perform a service in return, far from making the most of it he will actually minimize the importance of what he has done.

Another point that has to be considered in the same connexion is this. If you speak in defence of some prosperous favourite of fortune, the gratitude you receive will only come from himself, or possibly from his children as well. But if you defend a man who is poor but honest and worthy, every other citizen who is likewise poor and honest – and the population contains a great multitude of such persons – will look on you as a solid protection for themselves as well. My conclusion, therefore, is that decent beneficiaries are a better investment than rich ones.

Nevertheless, it remains true that the ideal course of action is to oblige people of any and every condition. But should conflict on this point arise, I feel we should do well to follow the advice of Themistocles.[1] Someone asked him whether he ought to give his daughter in marriage to a man who was honest but badly off or to one who was disreputable but rich. 'Personally,' he replied, 'I like a man without money better than money without a man.'

Today, on the other hand, our whole moral attitude is degraded and corrupted by the worship of wealth. Yet what does it really matter how rich someone is? Perhaps it is of advantage to himself at least. Sometimes it may not even be that: all the same, let us assume that it is. In other words, he will have more to spend. But does that make him in any way a better man? If his character is sound, certainly his wealth should not be held against him when there is a question of doing him a service. But it should also not be regarded as a special reason for helping him. Our decision should depend, not on the extent of his possessions, but purely and simply on what sort of man he is himself.

But the main rule in deciding when to offer your assistance is this. You should never agree to back a case which takes the wrong side against the right. For since the root of all lasting reputation and renown is justice, nothing from which justice is absent can conceivably deserve our support.

*

So much, then, for assistance to individuals. It now remains to discuss services which contribute to the national interest. Some acts in this category are directed towards the entire population, but others, although they may benefit the whole country, again take the form of help to this or that individual

1. The Athenian statesman (c. 528–462 BC).

person. Moreover the latter type of action produces a larger measure of gratitude than the former. If possible, we should contrive to give our attention to both these subdivisions.

But when we offer this sort of service to individuals, that is to say with an eye on the national interest, it is important that our intervention should be really and genuinely beneficial to the country as a whole – or at the very least that what we are doing should not oppose its interests. Take Gaius Gracchus, for instance. He benefited numerous individuals by massive distributions of free grain; yet in doing so he exhausted the national treasury. The modest distributions of Marcus Octavius, on the other hand, not only provided for the needs of the poorer sections of the population, but were useful to the State as well.[1]

*

It is also incumbent on everyone who holds a high governmental office to make absolutely sure that the private property of all citizens is safeguarded, and that the State does not encroach on these rights in any way whatever.

For example the attempt by Lucius Philippus to pass a bill providing for redistribution of land was outrageous.[2] It is true that when the measure was rejected he took the rebuff calmly enough, and to that extent he deserves credit for moderation. But while, previously, he had been agitating for popular support, he offered the malicious comment that the entire total of property-owners in the whole country did not add up to more than two thousand. For that remark he deserved to lose his rights as a Roman citizen, because his words implied that he was supporting the equal distribution of all property – which would be the greatest imaginable disaster. Indeed, the

1. The reference is to the first tribunate of Gaius Sempronius Gracchus in 123 BC. The corn-laws of Marcus Octavius, tribune in 120, were superseded by a more conservative measure.

2. During his tribunate in 104 BC.

principal reason why, in the first place, states and cities were ever organized at all was to defend private property. It is true that people had come together into communities spontaneously, by a natural instinct. But the reason why they sought the shelter of cities was because they wanted to safeguard their own personal possessions.

When constant wars made the Roman treasury run short, our forefathers often used to levy a property tax. Every effort must be made to prevent a repetition of this; and all possible precautions must be taken to ensure that such a step will never be needed. What I am going to say now will refer to the world in general and not specifically to Rome, because when I am making ominous forecasts I would rather that they were directed towards other countries and not our own. But if *any* government should find itself under the necessity of levying a tax on property, the utmost care has to be devoted to making it clear to the entire population that this simply has to be done because no alternative exists short of complete national collapse.

Obviously, too, it is incumbent on all those who are in charge of a nation's affairs to make certain that its people possess an abundant supply of the necessities of life. How this is normally done, and how it ought to be done, I do not need to explain. The duty is an obvious one; it just needed, for the sake of completeness, to be mentioned.

*

The essential thing, in all public business and service, is to avoid incurring even the smallest suspicion of greed. Gaius Pontius the Samnite[1] once declared, 'If only Fortune had postponed my birth until an epoch in which the Romans would begin to accept bribes! For then I should have been able to stop their empire from surviving for one single day

1. Gaius (Gavius) Pontius, victor over the Romans in the battle of the Caudine Forks (321 BC).

longer.' Yes; and he would have had to wait for many centuries, too. For it is only recently that this curse has begun to plague our national affairs. So, if Pontius was as formidable a man as he seems to have been, I am greatly relieved that he lived then rather than now. Less than a hundred and ten years have passed since Lucius Piso passed his law to punish illicit gains;[1] previously no such enactment had existed. From that time onwards there has been a multitude of similar measures, each stricter than the last. A whole host of people have been put on trial and condemned. Because of the fear of what the courts would do next, a horrible Italian war has been fought.[2] And then the lawcourts were suppressed, and the laws with them; and our subject allies were pillaged and plundered, one and all. The result of this whole series of events is that any strength we may still possess is no longer owed to any merits of our own. We owe it to the weakness of others.

Panaetius praises the younger Africanus because he was not grasping in public life. And the praise is fully justified. Nevertheless, one could think of even greater personal virtues to attribute to Africanus, for the credit for this particular quality, his self-restraint, belongs not to himself but to the age he lived in. When Lucius Paullus, for example, gained possession of the entire great wealth of Macedonia,[3] he brought so much money into our treasury that his spoils, the spoils of one single general alone, made it possible to do away with the property tax for evermore. Into his own home, on the other hand, Paullus brought no new possession at all – except everlasting renown. His son, the younger Africanus, copied his example; when he overthrew Carthage, there was no personal profit for himself. As for his fellow-censor, Lucius

1. The Lex Calpurnia de Repetundis (149 BC) had set up a permanent court to try cases of bribery and extortion.

2. The Marsian (Social) War (91–87 BC).

3. After he had crushed King Perseus of Macedonia at Pydna in 168 BC.

Mummius, he, too, after totally destroying the richest city upon earth, emerged not a penny the richer.[1] He was ambitious to adorn, not his own house, but Italy. And by this very attitude, so it seems to me, he did, in fact, adorn his own house in the most glorious way conceivable.

As I was saying before, the nastiest vice in the whole world is greed, and when this occurs in prominent citizens and leaders of the government it is nastiest of all. To use affairs of state for one's personal gain is not only immoral, it is a sin and a crime. Apollo declared through his Pythian oracle that the only thing that could bring down Sparta's power was greed, and his prophecy applies to all other successful nations as well. The best way for their rulers to win goodwill is by exercising self-restraint and self-denial.

*

When politicians, enthusiastic to pose as the people's friends, bring forward bills providing for the distribution of land, they intend that the existing owners shall be driven from their homes. Or they propose to excuse borrowers from paying back their debts.

Men with those views undermine the very foundations on which our commonwealth depends. In the first place, they are shattering the harmony between one element in the State and another, a relationship which cannot possibly survive if debtors are excused from paying their creditor back the sums of money he is entitled to. Furthermore, all politicians who harbour such intentions are aiming a fatal blow at the whole principle of justice; for once rights of property are infringed, this principle is totally undermined. It is, I repeat, the special function of every state and every city to guarantee that each of its citizens shall be allowed the free and unassailed enjoyment of his own property.

1. Lucius Mummius Achaicus suppressed the Achaean League and destroyed Corinth in 146.

Besides, politicians who propose a measure of this kind, with all its disastrous national implications, do not even succeed in winning the popularity they had hoped for. For anyone who has been deprived of his property automatically becomes their enemy; and the person who has taken the land over pretends he never wanted any such thing. Or, if his debt has been cancelled, he takes elaborate steps to conceal his satisfaction, so that people will not realize he had been insolvent. The injured party, on the other hand, not only remembers the injury, but displays his resentment for all to see. So even if the beneficiaries of the iniquitous measure outnumber the victims, that does not mean that they will be more influential; for in such matters numbers count less than determination. However, leaving all that aside, it is utterly unfair that estates which have been in a family's possession for many years and indeed centuries should be handed over to someone who has never owned any property at all, and that the rightful owner should be deprived of them.

*

This was precisely the sort of injustice which caused the Spartans to send their ephor Lysander into exile, and made them put King Agis to death, an action without precedent in their whole history.[1] And those were the men whose policies plunged their city into the dissensions that have racked its whole existence ever since. Tyrants sprang up, nobles were driven into exile, and the entire community, which had been admirably governed hitherto, collapsed in ruins. Nor was Sparta the only nation to fall. For the evils which had originated there spread far and wide, and the effects of their contamination involved the whole of Greece in disaster. And let us not forget our own Gracchi, the sons of the eminent

1. The reference is to Lysander the son of Libys (not the famous Lysander) who supported the land reforms of Agis IV in 242 BC.

Tiberius Gracchus and grandsons of the elder Africanus.[1] Strife over the redistribution of land was what caused their downfall too.

Aratus of Sicyon, on the other hand, wins much praise, and rightly so. After Sicyon had been dominated by tyrants for fifty years, he moved back there from Argos, entered the city secretly and seized control.[2] Striking down the tyrant Nicocles unawares, he recalled six hundred exiles, who had formerly been the richest men in the state. The coming of Aratus liberated Sicyon. But the question of property ownership involved him in grave difficulties. For, on the one hand, he regarded it as entirely unfair that the men he himself had brought back from banishment, men whose lands had previously been occupied by other people, should be left in want. On the other hand it also seemed by no means just to disturb tenures that were already fifty years old. Besides, during the course of that long period, many estates had been transferred quite innocently into other hands, through inheritance or purchase or dowry. Aratus therefore decided that, whereas it would be wrong for the present occupants to be deprived of their estates, the former owners must receive something in exchange.

However, to deal with this situation, money was obviously required. So Aratus announced that he was going to make a journey to Alexandria, and gave orders that the whole matter should be left in suspense until he returned. Then he sailed off forthwith to his friend Ptolemy, who was the second king of Egypt after the foundation of Alexandria.[3] Aratus explained to the monarch that he wanted to restore free constitutional government in Sicyon, and described how he was proposing to act. Ptolemy, whose resources were enormous, readily agreed to give him the substantial subsidy he wanted. With

1. For the family, see Genealogical Table (II), p. 361.
2. Aratus (d. 213 BC) gained control of Sicyon in 251.
3. Ptolemy II Philadelphus (283–246 BC).

this in his hands, Aratus returned home, and set up a commission consisting of fifteen leading men of the city. With their assistance he examined the cases of both types of person, those who were occupying property that rightly belonged to someone else, and those who had been deprived of their possessions. Aratus ordered that valuations should be made of all the estates concerned, and finally managed to persuade some of the occupants to leave their lands, and accept compensation instead. At the same time he convinced a number of his own followers that it was in their own interest to accept a good cash sum rather than receive their original holdings back. And so everyone concerned was satisfied, and harmony had been successfully re-established.

Aratus was a great statesman; he deserved to have been a Roman! That is the way to deal with one's fellow-citizens: the very antithesis to what we have now seen here on two occasions, when the auctioneer's spear was planted in the Forum,[1] and the possessions of Roman citizens were disposed of at the mercy of his cry. Aratus the Greek on the other hand, like the wise and admirable man he was, considered it his duty to work for the interests of *every* class in his community. And, indeed, that is the real sign of a right-minded citizen's statesmanship and wisdom – not to allow the special interests of different groups to be at variance with one another, but to unite the entire community without partisanship. Others might argue differently. 'Let people take over other people's estates,' they would say, 'and live on them – without paying a thing!' But why should they? When I have bought a property for myself, built on it, kept it up, spent money on it, why on earth should you then be allowed to occupy the place, in total disregard of my wishes? If you do, all that has happened is that one man has been robbed of what belongs to him, and it has been given instead to someone else who has not the slightest right to it. And the same applies to the repu-

1. Under Sulla and Caesar; see above, p. 134.

diation of debts. It means one thing and one thing only. It means you are buying your farm with my money. You have got the farm – and I have not got the money!

The real answer to the problem is that we must make absolutely certain that private debts do not ever reach proportions which will constitute a national peril. There are various ways of ensuring this. But just to take the money away from the rich creditors and give the debtors something that does not belong to them is no solution at all. For the firmest possible guarantee of a country's security is sound credit, and, once you cease to regard the repayment of debts as mandatory, soundness of credit is no more.

The most vigorous of all agitations to cancel debts took place while I was consul. Men of every sort and condition were involved, and they took up arms and enrolled themselves in whole armies. I stood up to them: and the result was that this pestilential business was wholly rooted out of our national life. Never have debts been more extensive than they were at that time. And yet they were paid off more fully, more easily, than ever before or since: because once all hopes of evading the obligation had been dispelled, repayment was recognized to be inevitable. But the individual who was thwarted on that occasion won in the end, since he subsequently managed to put his old plan into effect, though by that time it had ceased to be a matter of personal profit for himself. He was a man who had such a positive lust for criminal behaviour that he went on revelling in it just for its own sake, even after the personal motive had vanished.[1]

1. Cicero claimed that the cancellation of debts (*tabulae novae*) had been part of the programme of Catilina, whose conspiracy he suppressed when he was consul (63 BC), and that Caesar – whom Cicero believed to have had a hand in Catilina's schemes – 'won in the end' because of a series of laws (in fact, statesmanlike measures) that Caesar passed in 49 BC and subsequent years in order to deal with the extremely serious problem of debt.

So the men in charge of our national interests will do well to steer clear of the kind of liberality which involves robbing one man to give to another. Instead, they must make it their foremost concern to ensure that the just operation of the law and the lawcourts shall guarantee to each and every citizen the safe possession of his own property. They must ensure that poor men are not swindled because they are poor. But they must equally guarantee that rich men are not prevented, by envious prejudice, from keeping what is theirs or recovering what was once theirs but is now lost.

And it is the prime duty of our statesmen, by every means within their power, to increase the strength and the territory and the revenue of our country in war and peace alike. Such tasks demand greatness. Our ancestors successfully undertook them again and again. Anyone who tackles these noble tasks can rest assured that he will not only be rendering splendid services to the State, but will win enormous popularity and glory for himself as well.

*

With regard to these principles of expediency, Antipater of Tyre, the Stoic who recently died at Athens,[1] expressed the opinion that his predecessor Panaetius had left two topics out – the care of health, and the care of money. Certainly both these things are expedient, but I imagine the reason why the great philosopher omitted them was because he regarded both points as obvious.

The way to keep healthy is to know one's own constitution, to understand what is good for it and what is bad and to exercise moderation regarding all one's physical needs, holding sensual pleasures in check. It is also desirable to rely on the counsel of professional advisers.

As for one's financial affairs it is a duty to make money; but this must only be done by honest means. It is also a duty

1. Antipater introduced the younger Cato to the Stoic philosophy.

to save money, by care and thrift, and to increase what one has got by similar methods. An extremely apt survey of the questions involved was provided by Socrates's pupil Xenophon in his book *Estate Management*, which I translated from Greek into Latin when I was about your age.[1] However, this whole subject of making and investing money, and (I am inclined to add) spending it as well, is more appropriate for discussion by the worthy gentlemen who congregate round the Middle Janus, than by any philosophers, whatever school they may belong to.[2] All the same, we do have to remember that these things exist – because they come under the heading of expediency, which is what this volume is about.

*

I noted at the beginning that this subject has been divided into three parts.[3] But there is also a fourth division, relating to the problems that arise when one expediency has to be weighed against another. Panaetius said nothing about this type of issue either; yet assessments of such a kind frequently have to be attempted. To take one example, it is often necessary to measure expediencies or advantages of a physical nature against those of an external or accidental character, derived from outward circumstances. Furthermore, if you consider these two categories separately, each of them includes, within itself, potential advantages which have to be measured against others in one and the same category.

Let me consider these two points in turn. Here is one instance of the sort of way in which physical and external advantages need to be weighed one against the other: would

1. The *Oeconomicus* of Xenophon (c. 430–354 BC). The young Marcus was about twenty.

2. 'Middle Janus' was the exchange. It is probably identifiable with the Temple of Janus beside the Roman Forum; cf. M. Grant, *The Roman Forum*, Weidenfeld & Nicolson, 1970, p. 218.

3. See above, p. 124n.

you rather be healthy or rich? And then, to go on to the second point, if you consider physical advantages alone and attempt a relative estimate of one such physical advantage against another, the sort of question that arises is this: would you rather be strong or agile? Or, passing to advantages of an external nature, this is the sort of thing you will have to consider. Is glory more desirable than wealth? Would you regard it as preferable to have an income from city property or from a farm?

Incidentally, that was the sort of comparison which old Cato the Censor was dealing with when they asked him to indicate what he believed to be the most important activity on a country estate.[1] 'Raising cattle profitably,' he said. Asked what came next, he answered, 'Raising cattle fairly profitably.' His third priority was 'Raising cattle unsuccessfully.' Only then came 'raising crops'. Next, his questioner asked him what he thought of money-lending. But then he replied: 'You might as well ask me what I think about murder.'

This is just one of innumerable illustrations of the point that expediencies often have to be weighed against one another, so that when we are dealing with the question of obligations it is necessary to add this fourth subdivision.

And now let us pass on to the other questions.

1. Cato the elder (the Censor) of Tusculum wrote a treatise *De Agri Cultura* (c.160).

# LAELIUS: ON FRIENDSHIP

AFTER the death of Caesar his assassins, Brutus and Cassius, rapidly found that the Republic could not be restored as they had hoped. They left Rome and never returned, sailing east from Italy in August 44 BC; and Marcus Antonius rapidly assumed dictatorial control. On 17 July Cicero, disgusted with this state of affairs, set out by sea for Athens from Pompeii, incurring the disapproval of Atticus who reproached him for deserting his country. But on calling at the south Italian port of Velia (Elea), Cicero learnt that a meeting of the Roman Senate had been called for 1 September. And so he returned to the capital where, on the following day, he launched his great series of *Philippics* against Antonius.[1]

During the previous miserable months Cicero had been composing the essay *Laelius: On Friendship*. Dedicated, like its recently composed companion piece *Cato the Elder: On Old Age*,[2] to his friend, confidant, banker and publisher Atticus, the treatise takes the form of a discussion. Cicero dates the occasion to 129 BC, and claims to have heard the substance from Quintus Mucius Scaevola the Augur, whom he attended as a young student and made one of the participants in the debate *On the Orator*, of which a volume is translated elsewhere in this book (p. 236).

In *Laelius: On Friendship*, Scaevola takes one of the minor parts. Another figure who appears is Gaius Fannius Strabo, a Roman historian praised by Sallust for accuracy but criticized by Cicero for the roughness of his style. Both these men were sons-in-law of the famous Gaius Laelius Sapiens, whose exposition comprises far the greater part of the work. Born

1. For translations of the *First* and *Second Philippics* see *Cicero: Selected Political Speeches*, op. cit., pp. 295ff., and *Cicero: Selected Works*, op. cit., pp. 10ff.

2. Translated in *Cicero: Selected Works*, ibid., pp. 211ff.

in 186 BC, Laelius was a close friend of Scipio Africanus the younger (Scipio Aemilianus), who had died in mysterious circumstances a few days before the present discussion is supposed to have taken place (p. 182).[1] While praetor and governor of Nearer Spain (145), Laelius had served successfully against the Lusitanian rebel Viriathus, and became consul five years later. Next to Scipio, he was the most distinguished orator of his day, and a master of pure Latin – some believed him to be the author of Terence's gracefully written comedies. He owed his title Sapiens, the Wise, to his erudition – especially in philosophy, which he studied under the Stoics Diogenes of Babylon and Panaetius of Rhodes. Laelius's character was greatly praised in antiquity.

*Laelius: On Friendship*, in earlier times, was one of the greatest European best-sellers, and exerted a tremendous influence, notably on Dante.[2] But its interest lies not only in this importance through the ages but in the intrinsic qualities of the work itself. To us, who are supposed to be imbued with the Christian doctrine of brotherly love, the treatise may at times sound a little too calculating, or at least distinctly realistic. But to the Romans, for whom 'friendship' meant an intricate affair of practical tit-for-tat upon which their whole political life was based, it was clear that Cicero was striking a blow for a more idealistic approach than theirs. It is true, he says, that friendship is 'the regulation of the good of all by mutual service', but it is also based on something more elevated – on a community of feeling.[3] He had read Plato's *Lysis* and Aristotle's *Nicomachean Ethics* on the subject, and in particular he had studied a monograph on friendship written by Aristotle's chief pupil Theophrastus.[4] But Cicero is writing

1. For *The Dream of Scipio* see pp. 341ff. 2. See p. 36.

3. *For Cnaeus Plancius*, 2, 5.

4. Fragments of Theophrastus's essay survive. Cicero may also be influenced by Xenophon (on Socrates) and the Stoics Chrysippus and Panaetius (p. 27).

in relation to his own society and his own troubled times – and is considering (without some of the thornier points of Theophrastus's treatise) how far personal friendship is compatible with the political oppositions that were inevitable at such an epoch.

However, friendship is of universal concern, and to read such an intelligent man, and such a loyal friend, on this theme cannot fail to be of value at any place or time. Indeed no one else has ever dealt with the subject in so memorable a fashion.

To us the discussion possesses the curious disadvantage that it is restricted to relationships between men; and the same limitation had no doubt appeared in Cicero's main source, as in other Greek writings. For this was the social relation which really seemed to matter, and which affected the political life of the community. Concentration on this aspect does not mean that Cicero was homosexual, for he was not; on the contrary, the male relation was emphasized just because it was not physical (like hunger and thirst) but moral. Nor was he by any means lacking in a tender side; for instance he was very fond of children. But his relations with women were unsatisfactory. His marriage with Terentia had ended in failure, and the teenager Publilia whom he married next was sent away almost immediately, because she showed no grief at the death of his daughter.[1] In 46 Cicero had written to his friend Lucius Papirius Paetus that he met a famous high-class prostitute, Cytheris, at a party: 'As for myself,' he remarked, 'I was never tempted by anything of that sort, even when a young man, much less now that I am old.'[2] And then in the *Tusculans* he wrote quite violently against sexual love, which he described, with appropriate quotation, as utterly trivial, and the promoter of shame and inconstancy.[3]

1. In spite of the intercession of a literary woman friend of Cicero, Caerellia.

2. *Letters to his Friends*, IX, 26, 2.

3. *Tusculans*, IV, 32, 68.

# LAELIUS: ON FRIENDSHIP

QUINTUS MUCIUS SCAEVOLA the Augur used to call on his abundant memory to tell many excellent stories about his father-in-law Gaius Laelius. And whenever he mentioned him he invariably spoke of 'Laelius the Wise'.

After I had grown up[1] my father took me to Scaevola. His idea was that, as far as I could manage it – and as far as he would let me – I should never be out of the old man's company. Scaevola used to talk about a wide range of subjects, with great wisdom and a wealth of terse, apt comments. I made a practice of committing every one of them to memory, since I believed his legal learning would provide a very useful addition to my own knowledge. When he died, I transferred my attentions to Quintus Mucius Scaevola the Priest,[2] whom I would call the most able and upright man in the whole country. But I shall speak of him on another occasion. Now I want to return to Scaevola the Augur.

*

I remember a great many of the talks we had together. But clearest of all is my recollection of a day at his home. He was sitting in his garden, as he often used to do, in a semi-circular arbour. The only other people there besides myself were a few other close friends of his.

Scaevola hit upon a topic which at just about that time was on many people's lips. You yourself, Atticus, were seeing a

1. The reference is to the assumption of the *toga virilis*, which Romans of this time put on at the age of sixteen or seventeen.

2. This man was the younger cousin of Quintus Mucius Scaevola the Augur who appears in the dialogue. 'The Priest' was consul in 95 BC and Chief Priest from 90, and published the first systematic treatise on the *ius civile*. See Genealogical Table (I), p. 360.

good deal of Publius Sulpicius Rufus[1] in those days, and I am sure you recall what happened. Sulpicius, who was a tribune at the time, had become a deadly enemy of Quintus Pompeius Rufus,[2] after being his most intimate and affectionate friend; and everybody was surprised and sorry. On this occasion Scaevola happened to mention the matter, and then he went on to tell us of a discourse on the subject of friendship which Laelius had pronounced to himself and another man who, like Scaevola, was Laelius's son-in-law, Gaius Fannius the son of Marcus. This happened a few days after the death of Scipio Africanus the younger. I memorized the main points of what Laelius said, and now, after my own fashion, I have set them down in this book. I have done so by bringing the actors on to the stage to speak for themselves. My intention was to avoid constant interruptions of 'I said' and 'he said', since I wanted to make it seem as if they were actually in our company and talking to us themselves.

You have often asked me to write something about friendship, and the subject is one which appeals to me deeply. Friendship is something everyone ought to think about; and the theme is particularly appropriate to people who are such close friends as you and I are. For these reasons I warmly welcomed your suggestion. And I do venture to hope that this volume, which has emerged as a result, will be useful not only to yourself but to others as well.

*

When, at your request, I wrote my *Cato the Elder: On Old Age*,[3] I made Cato himself, as a very old man, the principal speaker. He seemed to me the most suitable person I could

1. For Publius Sulpicius Rufus, see *On the Orator*.

2. Quintus Pompeius Rufus, consul 88 BC, was the husband of Sulla's daughter Cornelia.

3. Translated in *Cicero: Selected Works*, op. cit.

think of to talk about that period of life, since it was years and years since he had been anything but old; and he had prospered more than anyone else of similar age.

As regards my present subject, however, we have heard from our elders that the friendship which Gaius Laelius enjoyed with the younger Scipio Africanus was outstandingly memorable. It therefore seemed to me that Laelius was the appropriate character to deliver his opinions about friendship; and indeed, according to the recollections of Scaevola, he actually had spoken on the subject. Somehow expositions of this kind seem to carry special conviction when they are placed in the mouths of personages of an earlier generation, especially when these were eminent men. For example, when I read my own treatise *On Old Age*, it sometimes affects me so profoundly that I actually feel it is Cato who is doing the talking and not myself!

In that book I was writing on the subject as one old man to another. And now, in accordance with the same procedure, I am writing about friendship as between friends. In my earlier work, as I said, the speaker was Cato, who lived to almost as great an age as anybody else of his time, and was inferior to none of them in talent. Laelius, my present spokesman, was another man of exceptional wisdom – indeed he was famous for this – but he also provided a conspicuous example of my present theme of friendship. So I ask you to dismiss myself altogether from your mind for the time being, and to imagine that it is Laelius who is speaking.

At the time we are thinking of, Africanus is just dead, and Gaius Fannius and Scaevola the Augur have come to see their father-in-law Laelius. The two visitors start a conversation, and Laelius is going to reply. He will devote the whole of his discourse to friendship. Read what he says, and you will recognize yourself.

*

FANNIUS: When you say, Laelius, that a finer and more illustrious man than Africanus never existed, you are perfectly right. All the same, you must realize that the person towards whom everyone's eyes are now turned is yourself. People call you 'the Wise', and they do so from profound conviction. Not long ago that is what they used to call Cato,[1] and we know that Lucius Acilius was similarly described in our father's time.[2] But they were awarded the title for rather different reasons. Acilius earned it because of his renown as an expert in the law, and Cato because of his wide-ranging experience and the shrewd foresight, resolution, and oratorical skill he had so conspicuously displayed in Senate-house and Forum alike. As a result, by the time he was an old man the designation 'Wise' had almost become part of his personal name.

When you are given the same title, on the other hand, it possesses a rather different significance. For in your case the compliment refers to a wide range of different qualities that you possess: natural talent, character, industriousness and learning all play a part. Besides, this term is not applied to you by any means loosely, in the way that ignorant people employ it, but in the accurate sense in which erudite scholars use the word. I am thinking of the strict type of definition maintained by authorities who are such severe critics that they are not even prepared to admit that the Seven Sages themselves deserve inclusion among truly wise men.[3] According to this view of the matter, there has never been a wise man in the whole history of Greece, with the single exception of that one

1. Cato the elder (Censor) had died in 149 BC, the year after the imaginary date of the discussion in Cicero's treatise *On Old Age*.

2. Unknown. An alternative reading is 'Atilius'.

3. The list often comprises Solon of Athens, Pittacus of Mytilene, Bias of Priene, Cleobulus of Rhodes, Chilon of Sparta and Myson of Chenae. Periander of Corinth sometimes replaces Myson. Anacharsis the Scythian (p. 100) also appears.

individual at Athens who was specifically declared to be the wisest of men by the oracle of Apollo himself.[1]

Nevertheless you, too, are generally believed to be wise. This is because of your firm belief that your entire well-being depends upon yourself and yourself alone, and that all human vicissitudes are insignificant: since the only thing that matters is whether a man is morally good or bad.

That is why I am always being asked, and the same inquiry, I understand, is addressed to Scaevola as well, how the death of Africanus is affecting you. The inquiries have become particularly insistent because on the Nones of last month, when we met at Decimus Brutus's country house for our usual discussion of matters concerning the augurs, you did not join us.[2] This attracted attention, because you have always been so very meticulous in your attendance on these occasions, as indeed in all your other augural duties.

SCAEVOLA: I too have noted that there has been curiosity about your reaction to Africanus's death. But when I am asked about this I always answer, Laelius, what I have seen with my own eyes – that, although you have lost a very great friend, who was also a very great man, you are enduring your grief with composure. It could not be expected, I go on to point out to them, that your loss would leave you unmoved – you have too warm a heart for that. But your absence from the meeting of our association on the Nones, I assure them, was due to the fact that you were unwell, and not because you were mourning.

LAELIUS: Quite right, Scaevola; what you told them was perfectly accurate. Whenever I am in good health I have always fulfilled the obligations you mentioned, and I would

1. Socrates.

2. The Board of Augurs regularly met on the Nones of each month (i.e. the 7th of March, May, July and October, the 5th of other months). Decimus Junius Brutus, consul in 138 BC, was surnamed Callaicus after his conquest of Callaecia (Galicia) and Lusitania (Portugal).

never have allowed any question of personal convenience to keep me away from them. Indeed, in my view, no man with the slightest sense of responsibility would allow himself to be deflected by considerations of such a kind from the performance of any of his duties whatsoever.

Now, Fannius, when you tell me that I am being paid these compliments, I feel quite unable to accept them, nor of course did I ask for them – though it is very kind of you. When you speak of Cato, however, I do not think your estimate does him justice. It may well be, certainly, that no such thing as a wise man has ever existed; and I am inclined to believe that this is the correct view. But if there ever has been one, Cato is the man.

Even if we leave all the other evidence to one side, think how he took the death of his son. I remember when Paullus suffered a similar loss, and I myself saw Galus when he, too, was bereaved.[1] But the sons they lost were only boys, whereas Cato's was a grown man who had already revealed his gifts. So I myself feel that Cato ought to be placed at the very top of all – not even after the personage whom Apollo, as you say, judged the wisest in the world. For, after all, the man who won Apollo's praise is only honoured for what he said; whereas we esteem Cato for what he did.

*

But now to turn to myself. Let me tell you both the position; and I assure you that what I shall be saying is accurate. If I were to tell you Scipio's death caused me no sorrow, the philosophers could advise us whether this was the appropriate reaction: but at all the events it would certainly not be the truth! Of course I am upset. I have lost a friend such as will

1. Lucius Aemilius Paullus Macedonicus was also the father of the younger Scipio Africanus (see Genealogical Table (II), p. 361) and a friend of Laelius. Gaius Sulpicius Galus (consul 166) was an orator, writer and astronomer.

never be seen again. Or so I must assume. For of this at least I am sure – there has never been a friend like him before.

Yet I am not without a remedy, all the same. For it is at least a comfort and consolation that I am spared the delusion which causes most people to grieve when their friends have died. For I do not believe Scipio himself has suffered any misfortune. If anyone has suffered a misfortune, it is myself. But if you let your sorrows at such a happening overwhelm you, this shows how much you love, not your friend, but yourself.

As for Scipio, on the other hand, surely everybody must agree that life treated him remarkably well. For unless he had conceived the idea of living for ever – a thought which surely must have occurred to him – he fulfilled every ambition that anyone could justly pray for. When he was no more than a boy his fellow-countrymen already expected great things of his career, and while he was still a mere youth his amazing gifts enabled him to satisfy these expectations and even exceed them. Although he never offered himself for the consulship, he was elected consul not once but twice; on the first occasion before the minimum legal age and on the second occasion at the proper time – proper, that is, as far as he himself was concerned, but none too early for the safety of our country. By overthrowing two cities, the two deadliest foes of this empire of ours,[1] he totally abolished war: not just now, but for the whole of time to come.

His engaging manners, his devotion to his mother, his generosity to his sisters, his kindness to his relations, his fairness to one and all, I do not need to mention, because both of you have full knowledge of all these things; and as for the great love his fellow-citizens bore for him, this was abundantly displayed by the lamentations at his funeral. So what could he have gained by living a few years longer? Even if old age is

1. Carthage in north Africa (146) and Numantia in Spain (133).

no burden, as I remember Cato arguing to Scipio and myself the year before he died, yet it does admittedly take away that vigorous freshness which Scipio never lost.

So rich, then, in fortune and fame was his life that there could have been no way of enriching it further. And so sudden was his death that he never felt its sting. About the way he died, it is difficult to speak. You know, both of you, what people suspect.[1] Yet one thing may be safely said. During his lifetime he enjoyed many days of brilliant popularity and happiness. But the most notable of them all was that final day on which, after the Senate had finished its meetings, he was escorted home towards evening by a vast concourse of his fellow senators, and the people of Rome, and our subject allies from all the regions of Italy, and the Latins.[2] So great a hero had he now become that, when he left us, his destination can surely not have been the shades below: he must have been on his way to the gods above.

For although some authorities have lately begun to argue that the soul perishes along with the body, so that everything is obliterated by death, I disagree with them. I prefer the more ancient view, which was held, among others, by our own ancestors. They used to pay meticulous reverence to the dead, which they would never have done had they believed that once a person is dead nothing affects him any more. And other beliefs to the same effect were held by those inhabitants of our peninsula whose principles and doctrines brought civilization to Greater Greece, a region which is ruined today

1. It was suspected, rightly or wrongly, that supporters of the Gracchi had murdered him (p. 198).

2. After a violent scene in the Senate, where he spoke against Carbo to check the work of the Gracchan Land Commission, the younger Scipio was found dead in bed the next morning (129 BC). Before the Social War (90 BC), 'allies and Latins' was the usual formula to describe Rome's Italian subjects or confederates, among whom the citizens of the old Latin towns and colonies held a pre-eminent place.

but was flourishing at that time.[1] Besides, there was that man we were speaking of who, according to Apollo's oracle, surpassed the whole of the rest of the world in wisdom. When most topics were discussed, he liked to argue first on one side and then on the other. But on one subject he maintained a consistent point of view: he declared that the human soul is divine. When it leaves the body, he believed, it has the power to take the road back to heaven; and the better and more decently it has behaved in life, the easier this road will be.

That was also Scipio's opinion. A conversation he took part in only a very few days before his death seemed to show a presentiment of what was about to happen to him. Philus was there, and Manilius, and a number of others,[2] and you and I, Scaevola, had gone together to join them. For three days Scipio spoke about the condition of our country. And then, near the very end of his discourse, he turned to the immortality of the soul, repeating what, as he declared, the elder Africanus had told him in a dream.[3]

If it is true that, when the best men die, their souls have a special opportunity to escape from the imprisoning confinement of the flesh, it would be impossible to think of anyone whose journey to heaven can have been easier than Scipio's. To utter lamentations, then, because of his death, would seem to me a proof of envy rather than friendship. If, on the other hand, the soul perishes at the same time as the body, and all sensation ceases to exist, then while it is true that there is nothing good in death, it is equally evident that it can have no bad results either. For if sensation has been lost, a man is exactly as if he had never been born – though the fact that

1. Greek south Italy. The allusion is to the Pythagorean school of philosophers (p. 22).

2. Lucius Furius Philus was consul in 136 BC and Manius Manilius in 149. Both were learned members of the younger Scipio's circle.

3. The *Dream of Scipio* is translated elsewhere in this book.

Scipio *was* born brings us joy, and will never cease to bring joy to this land of ours as long as it remains in existence.

*

And so I say once again that all has gone very well with him, but less well with myself. I entered life before he did, and it would have been more appropriate for me to depart from it first as well. Yet so happy are my recollections of our friendship that I feel convinced my life has been a good one – because I have spent it with Scipio. Both in our public and private lives he and I have shared all the same interests. We lived in the same home; we soldiered together in the field. Our tastes and aims and views were identical – and that is where the essence of a friendship must always lie. As for my reputation for wisdom, which Fannius just mentioned, it is quite undeserved, and in any case it satisfies me less than the hope that my friendship with Scipio will go down to posterity. This is a hope which I cherish all the more keenly because, throughout the whole course of history, the pairs of friends who have been lastingly remembered only amount to barely three, or four at the very most.[1] It is my greatest desire that future generations will add the friendship of Scipio and Laelius to this small number.

FANNIUS: That is a hope, Laelius, which will be fulfilled; there is no doubt about that. But you touched just now on the question of what friendship really means. Since we are free of public business at the moment, I am going to ask you to do me a favour – and I know I am speaking for Scaevola as well. When people seek your views, whatever the topic may be, they always find you most obligingly ready to answer their queries. Now will you please speak about friendship in the same way? Tell us how you would define it; and let us know the principles you consider it involves.

1. Theseus and Pirithous; Achilles and Patroclus; Orestes and Pylades; Damon and Phintias (p. 85).

SCAEVOLA: Yes, do please talk to us on this subject! If you will, I shall be quite as delighted as Fannius. Indeed, when he asked you, I was just about to make the same request myself. So you would be doing us both a very great favour.

LAELIUS: I should be willing enough to do as you say if I felt in the slightest degree confident of saying anything worth-while. The subject, certainly, is a splendid one, and, as Fannius remarked, we have the spare time. But who am I to do such a thing? And what are my qualifications? The people who offer discourses of this kind tend to be scholars, and Greeks at that – speakers who claim the ability to deal with any subject you care to set before them, without the slightest preparation.[1] But that is a formidable thing to attempt, and needs a lot of practice. So if you want a comprehensive discussion about friendship, I advise you to apply not to me but to the men who make a profession of such speeches. All I, myself, can do is to urge you to place friendship above every other human concern that can be imagined! Nothing else in the whole world is so completely in harmony with nature,[2] and nothing so utterly right, in prosperity and adversity alike.

But one point I particularly want to make is this. Friendship is only possible between good men. I do not propose to go into this aspect too meticulously, like the people who argue at length that no one is good unless he is wise. That is all very subtle, and may well be logically correct, but it possesses little relevance as a practical guide to living. Moreover, even if we concede that the people who put forward this view are right, the 'wisdom' they have in mind is something which no mortal man has ever achieved. What you and I want to do, on the other hand, is not to look at such purely theoretical, imagina-

1. The art of extempore discussion was practised by rhetoricians and sophists, and by the philosophers of the Academy.

2. This was the ideal of the Stoic Chrysippus. The founder of Stoicism, Zeno, had indicated the aim of living 'in harmony'. The Stoics also believed that virtue is based on knowledge (p. 26).

tive aims, but at the actual possibilities of everyday life. Our ancestors admitted Gaius Fabricius, Manius Curius and Titus Coruncanius into the category of wise men.[1] But one could not claim that even they were wise by any such perfectionist standard as that.

So much, then, for the name of Wise Man. It is an invidious and confusing definition anyway; the philosophers can keep it! All we shall ask them to concede is that those early Romans were *good* men. But even this they will refuse to admit – because of their insistence that no one can be good unless he is wise.

All we ourselves can do, therefore, is to get on as best we can, with the aid of our own dull wits. So let us take some individual whose life and behaviour have displayed proven loyalty, honesty, fairness and generosity – a man of unflinching integrity, like those whose names I just mentioned; someone whose character does not contain a trace of covetousness or violence or unscrupulousness. For such are the men who are generally described as 'good'. And we are obliged to agree that they are entitled to the designation.

They deserve it because, in so far as human beings can, they are acting in accordance with nature – which is the best possible guide to right living. For nature itself, I believe, was the creator of the ties that exist between one person and another. The closer the relationship, the more powerful the ties: thus they are stronger between fellow-citizens than between foreigners, stronger among relatives than among strangers. It is true that, even between people who are foreign and strange to one another, nature encourages the development of a friendly feeling. But in such cases the sentiment lacks a solid basis.

1. Gaius Fabricius Luscinus (consul 282, 278 BC) refused bribes from Pyrrhus, king of Epirus. Manius Curius Dentatus (consul 290, 275, 274) defeated the Samnites, the Lucanians and Pyrrhus. Titus Coruncanius (consul 280) was the first plebeian to become Chief Priest (254).

Real friendship is even more potent than kinship; for the latter may exist without goodwill, whereas friendship can do no such thing. You can see its unique power when you consider this point. The bonds which nature has established to link one member of the human race with another are innumerable; but friendship not only surpasses them all but is something so choice and selective that its manifestations are normally restricted to two persons and two persons only – or at most extremely few.

Friendship may be defined as a complete identity of feeling about all things in heaven and earth: an identity which is strengthened by mutual goodwill and affection. With the single exception of wisdom, I am inclined to regard it as the greatest of all the gifts the gods have bestowed upon mankind. Some people, I know, give preference to riches, or good health, or power, or public honours. And many rank sensuous pleasures highest of all. But feelings of that kind are something which any animal can experience; and the other items in that list, too, are throughly transient and uncertain. They do not hang on our own decisions at all, but are entirely at the mercy of fickle chance. Another school of thought believes that the supreme blessing is moral goodness; and this is the right view. Moreover, this is the quality to which friendship owes its entire origin and character. Without goodness, it cannot even exist.

*

Let us follow the procedure we adopted before, and define 'goodness' according to the usage of our daily life and speech. All those ideal measurements and grandiose phrases, which certain philosophers like to produce, can be left on one side altogether. If men are generally regarded as good, let us accept them as such: Paullus, and Cato, and Galus, and the younger Scipio, and Philus, and people like that. For all ordinary purposes they amply meet the case. But as to those other hypothetical personages who are not to be found anywhere in the world, we shall be well advised to forget all about them.

Among individuals of the kind we are considering, the benefits that friendship offers almost defy description, they are so great. To begin with, how can life be 'worth living' at all, to use the term of Ennius,[1] unless it reposes on the mutual goodwill of friends? It is the most satisfying experience in the world to have someone you can speak to as freely as your own self about any and every subject upon earth. If things are going well, you cannot possibly enjoy your prosperity to the full unless you have another person whose pleasure equals your own. Should things go wrong, your misfortunes will indeed be hard to bear without someone who suffers as badly as yourself, or even worse.

And so friendship is quite different from all the other things in the world on which we are accustomed to set our hearts. For each and every one of those other objectives is specifically adapted to some single purpose – riches, to be spent; power, to secure obedience; public office, to win praise; pleasure, to enjoy oneself; good health, to be free from pain and make full use of one's bodily endowments. Friendship, on the other hand, serves a great host of different purposes all at the same time. In whatever direction you turn, it still remains yours. No barrier can shut it out. It can never be untimely; it can never be in the way. We need friendship all the time, just as much as we need the proverbial prime necessities of life, fire and water. I am not speaking of ordinary commonplace friendships, delightful and valuable though they can be. What I have in mind instead is the authentic, truly admirable sort of relationship, the sort that was embodied in those rare pairs of famous friends.

Friendship, then, both adds a brighter glow to prosperity and relieves adversity by dividing and sharing the burden.

1. His expression *vita vitalis* is an attempt to translate a Greek phrase.

And another of its very many and remarkable advantages is this. It is unique because of the bright rays of hope it projects into the future: it never allows the spirit to falter or fall. When a man thinks of a true friend, he is looking at himself in the mirror. Even when a friend is absent, he is present all the same. However poor he is, he is rich: however weak, he is strong. And may I attempt to convey an even more difficult concept? Even when he is dead, he is still alive. He is alive because his friends still cherish him, and remember him, and long for him. This means that there is happiness even in his death – he ennobles the existences of those who are left behind.

Take away the bond of kindly feeling from the world, and no house or city can stand. Even the fields will no longer be cultivated. If that sounds an exaggeration, consider the converse situation: note the disasters that come from dissension and enmity. When there is internal hatred and division, no home or country in the world is strong enough to avoid destruction. That shows the value of the opposite situation – friendship.

A certain learned man of Agrigentum[1] is said to have composed an inspired Greek poem in which he sang that all things in nature and the universe, whether stationary or moving, are united by friendship – and discord is what pulls them apart. Here, at least, is something said by a philosopher which no one can fail to appreciate and approve!

That is why, when an instance arises of someone incurring or sharing danger on behalf of a friend, the act is welcomed by the rest of the world with superlative praise. For example, when my guest and friend Marcus Pacuvius produced his recent play, one incident earned loud applause from the entire audience. This was the scene in which the king was confronted by two men, and did not know which of them was Orestes. Pylades claimed that *he* was Orestes, in order that he should be the one to be put to death, in the place of his friend.

1. Empedocles (p. 313).

The real Orestes, however, continued to insist on his own true identity. The entire crowd stood and cheered, although it was only a play; you can imagine how they would have felt if it had happened in real life.[1] Here, then, was a case of nature asserting its power. People were applauding in others what they had not been given an opportunity to achieve for themselves.

Well, that is what I have to tell you about my views on friendship. If more remains to be said – and I have no doubt that it does – you had better ask the people who are used to conducting this sort of discussion.

FANNIUS: No, you are the person we want to ask! I have often had occasion to interrogate the professionals you mention, and it was pleasant enough to hear what they have to say. But your approach to the subject is quite different from theirs, and wholly distinctive.

SCAEVOLA: You would stress that point even more, Fannius, if you had been at Scipio's country house the other day when they were discussing state affairs. Laelius spoke magnificently in defence of the idea of justice, while Philus produced elaborate arguments to the contrary.

FANNIUS: Laelius cannot have found it very difficult to stand up for justice, since no one displays the quality better than himself.

SCAEVOLA: Yes, and that means he ought to find it easy to speak in favour of friendship as well, since that, too, is something he has put into practice with outstanding loyalty, perseverance and fairness, and we all know the great admiration he has earned by so doing.

1. Pacuvius's play, of unknown title, seems to have had the same plot as Euripides's *Iphigenia in Tauris;* and it was the king of Tauris (the Crimea) whom Pylades tried to deceive. The reference to 'standing and cheering' has been taken as evidence that, contrary to a widespread view, there were already seats in theatres at the supposed date of this dialogue.

LAELIUS: This really is coercion! Your tactful choice of weapons does not change the situation at all – whatever may be said about your methods, they are violent, and when one's sons-in-law really press one for something, especially in a worthwhile cause, it is by no means easy to resist them. Indeed, I suppose one ought not to try.

I have thought a lot about friendship. And the more I think about it, the stronger my feeling is that the important question one has to decide is this. Does the fact that people need friendship mean there is some weakness and deficiency in themselves? If so, this would mean that their main purpose in acquiring friends is to exchange services with another person, that is to say to give and receive benefits which it would be beyond their own individual powers to grant or obtain on their own account. But surely this giving and receiving constitutes merely *one* feature and consequence of friendship. As for its origins, do these not, rather, lie in something altogether more primeval and noble, something emanating more directly from the actual processes of nature?

For goodwill is established by love, quite independently of any calculation of profit: and it is from love, *amor*, that the word for friendship, *amicitia*, is derived. It is true that you do often find people extracting advantages from someone by pretending they are his friends – the reason they are courting him so deferentially is because they are after some immediate benefit. But when there is real friendship, no element of falsity or pretence can possibly enter into the matter. Friendship simply cannot help being genuine and sincere all through. And that is why one is obliged to conclude that it must be a product of nature rather than of any deficiency. It cannot under any circumstances be derived from any calculation of potential profit. It comes from a feeling of affection, an inclination of the heart.

The nature of this feeling can be deduced from the behaviour of certain types of animal. These, it is easy to see, love their offspring up to a certain age, and are loved by them in return. In the case of human beings the same process is far more evident still. It is demonstrated by the mutual love existing between parents and their children, which nothing except the most outrageous crimes can possibly destroy. And the same sort of affection sometimes arises when we find a person whose habits and character attract us so much that we look upon him as a shining light of goodness and excellence.

Goodness exercises an altogether exceptional appeal and incentive towards the establishment of affection. People who possess this quality can inspire love in us even if we have never set eyes on them. When we think of Gaius Fabricius and Manius Curius the hearts of all of us grow warm, although they lived long before our time. Equally, everyone detests Tarquinius Superbus and Spurius Cassius and Spurius Maelius. And then there were the two individuals against whom we fought for the supremacy of Italy, Pyrrhus and Hannibal.[1] Towards the former we do not feel particularly hostile, since he was a good man. The latter, on the other hand, will always be hated by Romans, because of his cruelty.

Goodness, then, is such a powerful thing that we love it even in people we have never seen, and, more remarkable still, even in those who have been our enemies in war. Since that is the situation, it is scarcely surprising that our spirits are stirred when we believe we discern virtue and excellence in people who are really available for us to form an intimate association with. These feelings are naturally intensified if we receive kind treatment from someone – for that means they like us. Another source of friendly feeling is to see a lot of

1. Tarquinius Superbus, who traditionally reigned from 534 to 510 BC, was believed to have been the last king of Rome. In the early Republic, Spurius Cassius Vecellinus (consul 502, 493, 486) and Spurius Maelius (c. 440) were accused of aiming to restore the monarchy. Pyrrhus of Epirus invaded Italy and Sicily in 280–275 and Hannibal in the Second Punic War (218–203). Hannibal's alleged cruelty was a tradition of Roman propaganda.

someone in one's daily life. Add all these factors to the original friendly impulse, and the result will be a truly splendid and substantial glow of affection.

Anyone of the opinion that this feeling emanates from mere inadequacy and is entirely concerned with getting hold of someone who will provide us with things that we should like to get is surely assigning friendship altogether too humble and ignoble an origin. For it really cannot just be the child of poverty and destitution. If it were, the less confidence a man felt in himself, the better his qualifications for friendship would have to be regarded. But that is far from being the case. Indeed, the contrary is true: the *more* confidence a person feels in himself, the stronger his equipment of moral and intellectual gifts will be. And although these are qualities that relieve him of dependence upon others and make him feel completely self-sufficient, they will actually strengthen his capacity for making and keeping friends.

Consider Africanus, for example. Did he *need* me? Of course he did not. Nor, for that matter, did I need him. I was attached to him because I admired his fine qualities; and he returned my feeling because he also, on his side, appeared not to have formed too bad an opinion of my own character. And as we got to know one another better, our mutual affection grew. Certainly, the association did bring practical advantages – and on a considerable scale. But in the formation of our friendship no expectations of such a kind played even the slightest part.

When a man shows kindness and generosity, his motive in doing so is not just to exact repayment. We do not hire out our favours, and charge interest for them: we behave kindly because that is the natural thing to do. The reason why we count friendship as a blessing is not because we are hoping for a material return. It is because the union is quite enough profit in itself.

These views will be vigorously repudiated by anyone who

prefers to measure everything in animal-like terms of pleasure. That is not surprising. For when people are prepared to debase their whole standard of thinking to such a lowly and degraded level as that, any kind of lofty vision reaching up to the skies is obviously beyond their powers. So let us not bother to think about that category of individual at all. We shall do better, I repeat, to conclude that our feelings of attachment and affection towards our fellow human beings represent a wholly natural phenomenon – and that they are stimulated by evidence of superior character in the other person.

And so, when two people have formed a taste for such qualities, this common inclination draws them together and unites them with one another. Next, association with the object of their love causes them to enjoy the company and character of the person in question, to reciprocate his devotion, and to desire to perform services on his behalf without demanding any for oneself in return. Two people in such a situation will become rivals, will compete with one another in the noblest way. That is how we can get the most out of a friendship. The fact that it has been founded on the processes of nature and does not rely on human defects will make it all the sounder and more genuine. If advantage were what kept friendships together, the removal of that advantage would mean that the friendship itself would cease to exist. But since, instead, nature is the originator, and since nature is everlasting, authentic friendship is permanent too.

That, then, is what I think about how friendships come into being. Do you want to make any comments?

FANNIUS: No, Laelius; do please go on. And since Scaevola is younger than myself I am entitled to speak for him as well; and so on both our accounts I ask you to continue.

SCAEVOLA: Fannius is quite right, Laelius; please let us hear everything else you have to say to us.

LAELIUS: In that case, my dear friends, I shall tell you the points that used to come up on the numerous occasions when

I was discussing this subject with Scipio. He maintained that it was the most difficult thing in the world for a friendship to last until the very end of life. Either it ceases to be mutually advantageous, or people's political views change and affect their relations with one another. And another thing that changes, he added, is a person's character; it gets altered, by the blows of misfortune or the increasing burdens of age.

He illustrated this point by comparing what happens to people in the early years of their lives. When boys discard the dress of childhood, at the same time they often throw off their friendships, however strong these may have been before. Or else, even if they manage to maintain these associations into early manhood, they frequently break them off at that point, because the two youths then find themselves competing for a wife, or some other acquisition, which can only go to one or the other partner but cannot go to both at the same time. Indeed, even if their friendship does succeed in lasting longer, it is likely to be ruined as soon as rivalry for public office begins. Among the majority of the population, on the other hand, friendship's worst destroyer is greed for money. But in men at the top competitive ambition for jobs and distinctions is what causes the deadliest enmities, even between those who have been the most intimate friends hitherto.

Scipio also expressed the view that many friendships are violently, and often quite rightly, broken when one party has asked the other to do something that is wrong – perhaps to help him gratify his vices, or to take part in some other equally deplorable act. When the demand, however justifiably, is rejected, the person who has been rebuffed claims that the laws of friendship have been flouted; and those other individuals who would be prepared to ask anything of a friend take the opportunity to hint that even if they themselves are importunate this is only a sign that *they* would be prepared to do anything whatsoever for a friend's sake. The recriminations which go on and on after an incident of this kind are very often apt to put a stop to friendships, and indeed they produce lasting enmities. Such, said Scipio, are the varied and perilous fates which hang over the relations between friends. To avoid every one of them requires the greatest wisdom – and a good deal of luck as well.

Evidently, then, it is necessary to consider just how far a man ought to be ready to go on behalf of his friend. If Coriolanus, for example, had friends, was it their duty to stay at his side even when he took up arms against his own country? Or should the friends of Spurius Cassius or Maelius have supported them in their attempts to become tyrants of Rome? As for Tiberius Gracchus, when he was disrupting the government, we saw how Quintus Tubero and other friends of his own age completely abandoned him.[1] On the other hand Gaius Blossius of Cumae, who enjoyed the hospitality of your family, Scaevola, came to me to plead for leniency (I was an adviser of the consuls Laenas and Rupilius). He justified this request on the grounds of his devotion to Tiberius Gracchus. He himself thought so highly of Gracchus, said Blossius, that he felt obliged to do whatever his friend required. 'Even,' I asked, 'if Gracchus had told you to set fire to the Capitol?' 'He would never have wanted any such thing. But if he *had* wanted it, I should have obeyed.' What an abominable thing to say! And, heaven knows, Blossius acted in accordance with his professions – and even worse. Not content with merely following Gracchus's outrageous schemes, he actually directed them: he was not just his comrade but took the lead in the whole frenzied enterprise. And when

1. i.e. when Tiberius Sempronius Gracchus, the tribune, sought to introduce the reforms which led to his death in 133 BC. His fellow-tribune Quintus Aelius Tubero, a Stoic philosopher, was a nephew of the younger Scipio (see Genealogical Table (II), p. 361). The consuls in 132 were Publius Popillius Laenas and Publius Rupilius. Cnaeus Marcius Coriolanus was a legendary figure who, after his enforced withdrawal from Rome (attributed to 491 BC; p. 200), was believed to have led a Volscian army against the city.

this lunacy resulted in the establishment of a court of inquiry, Blossius took fright and fled to the province of Asia, where he joined the enemies of our country and paid a heavy and richly deserved penalty for the crimes he had committed against the Roman State.[1]

To claim, then, that one did wrong for the sake of a friend is no excuse. After all, what had originally brought the two of you together was a mutual belief in each other's goodness. So if, subsequently, you stop being good, it is hard to see how the friendship can continue. If we decided it was right either to grant our friends everything they wanted or to extract from them everything we wanted ourselves, this could only be harmless if we were persons of supreme and flawless wisdom. But the friends I now have in mind are the ones whom we ourselves actually see before our eyes and come across or whom we at least know from hearsay: men, that is to say, who belong to the realities of everyday life. For after all, those are the people we are obliged to take our models from; perfect wisdom, of course, they have not attained, though we are entitled to select those who approach that ideal most closely.

Thus we see, for example, or rather we have learnt from our fathers, that Aemilius Papus enjoyed a great friendship with Gaius Fabricius, that they were twice colleagues in the consulship, and that they served together as censors. Manius Curius and Tiberius Coruncanius, too, according to tradition, were very closely associated, not only with the two I have just mentioned, but with each other as well.[2] Now when we think of men of that sort of calibre, it is surely quite impossible for us to suspect that any of them could possibly have asked a

1. In 132 BC Gaius Blossius fled to Aristonicus who was leading a rebellion against the Romans.

2. Quintus Aemilius Papus and Gaius Fabricius Luscinus were consuls together in 282 and 278 BC and censors in 275. For Curius and Coruncanius see above, p. 186.

friend for anything conflicting with his honour, or with an oath he had taken, or with the interests of the nation. And if they themselves had received such demands, to suggest in the case of persons like these that the demands would have met with refusal is so obvious as not to be worth mentioning. For they were all men of the utmost integrity, who would have regarded it as equally wrong to have granted such a request, if they had received it, or to have made the request themselves. Tiberius Gracchus, on the other hand, does not come into this category. He was perfectly well able to find people prepared to pursue his designs – men such as Gaius Carbo and Gaius Cato. And his own brother Gaius Gracchus, too, although he was by no means enthusiastic at the time, has become a fanatical supporter of the same policy now.[1]

So this is the rule we must lay down between friends: do not ask for anything that is wrong, and if *you* are asked for such a thing, turn the application down. To excuse oneself for committing a misdemeanour on the grounds that it was done for the sake of a friend is entirely unacceptable. Such an excuse is no justification for any offence whatever, and least of all for offences against our country. For, as both of you, Fannius and Scaevola, are well aware, our present situation requires us to keep the sharpest look-out for national crises that may be impending. The political traditions established by former generations of Romans have already been deflected quite strongly off their track and course. Tiberius Gracchus tried to give himself the power of a king: in fact for a few months he *was* virtually king. The people of Rome had never heard or seen anything like it before. Moreover, even after he was dead, his friends and relatives continued along the path on

1. After the death of Tiberius Sempronius Gracchus, Gaius Papirius Carbo (consul 131 BC) continued the opposition to the younger Scipio, of whose assassination he was suspected (p. 182). Gaius Porcius Cato was consul in 114. Gaius Gracchus renewed the reform movement as tribune in 123 and 122, and was killed.

which he had led the way. What they did to Publius Scipio it brings tears to my eyes even to mention.

As for Carbo, we have put up with him as best we can because, after all, his leader, Tiberius Gracchus, got his punishment, and not so long ago.[1] But what is to be expected when Gaius Gracchus becomes tribune in his turn I should not care to forecast. The trouble seeps down further every day, and once this sort of deterioration has started, it gains momentum rapidly, and soon there is a headlong rush to disaster. You can see how the decisions about the ballot taken even before the Gracchan disturbances ever began – first the Gabinian law, and then two years later the Cassian law – have had their ruinous consequences.[2] As I see it, the Assembly has now broken completely with the Senate, and major policy is settled by the whim of the masses. What we shall find before long is that more people understand how to become agitators than understand how to stop them.

The relevance of these happenings to our present discussion is this. No one goes in for such activities unless he has found associates. So every right-thinking man has to get this into his mind: if inadvertently, by any chance, he should have contrived to involve himself in friendships of such an extremely perilous nature, he must under no circumstances let that debar him from abandoning any of these friends once the man in question has committed some treasonable offence. Wrongdoers have to be punished, and the punishment will be just as severe for the followers as the leaders.

Let Themistocles be an object-lesson. He was the most famous and powerful man in the whole of Greece; and by

1. In 131 BC Gaius Papirius Carbo, as tribune, proposed that tribunes should be eligible for annual re-election. The murder of the tribune Tiberius Gracchus was too recent to have been forgotten by their supporters.

2. A law of the tribune Aulus Gabinius introduced voting by ballot (139 BC), and then a law of Lucius Cassius Ravilla extended the ballot to juries in criminal actions (137).

leading his fellow-countrymen in the Persian War he had saved them all from slavery. Subsequently, however, he became unpopular, and was driven into exile. He should have endured what his ungrateful compatriots were doing to him, unfair though it was; but that he refused to do. Instead he acted as Coriolanus had acted, here at Rome, twenty years earlier.[1] Both these individuals rose against their own compatriots. They were unable, however, to find anyone to help them; and so each in turn took his own life.

An alliance with malefactors, which is what Themistocles and Coriolanus had become, could not be excused by any plea of friendship. On the contrary, such an association has to be penalized with the greatest severity, so that no one may be misguided enough to imagine that he would be right to support a friend who is making war upon his own country. And yet, the way matters are going now at Rome, I am very much afraid that this is just the sort of thing which is likely to happen here once again one of these days. Already at this very moment the existing state of the Republic fills me with the deepest anxiety. But I also feel just as anxious, terribly anxious, about its fortunes in the future when I am dead and gone.

So among the rules of friendship this ought to come first of all. Never ask your friends for anything that is not right, and never do anything for them yourself unless it is right. But then do it without even waiting to be asked! Always be ready to help; never hang back. Offer advice, too, willingly and without hesitation, just as you yourself, if you have a friend whose advice is good, should always pay great attention to what he says. But when you yourself are the adviser, use your influence, as a friend, to speak frankly, and even, if the occasion

1. Themistocles the Athenian, who was chiefly responsible for the Greek victory over the Persians at Salamis (480), was ostracized and retired to Argos c. 470; then, after condemnation by Athens, he fled to the Persian empire. For Coriolanus see p. 196 above.

demands, severely. And if you are the recipient of equally stern advice, listen to it and act as you are advised.

*

I have heard of some strange views held in Greece by individuals who are respected over there as wise men, I understand, though this sort of character is generally inclined to be over-subtle. I refer to suggestions from certain quarters that intimate friendships ought not to be indulged in at all, so that no one will have the slightest need to trouble himself with any other person at all. Everyone, according to this hypothesis, has more than enough worries of his own, and it is tiresome to get too deeply involved in those of others: the best thing, therefore, is to keep the reins of friendship as loose as you can, – and then you can tighten them, or relax them further, as you please. For the essence of a happy life, the argument continues, is freedom from care, which no one can achieve if he has the worries of a lot of his fellow-citizens on his hands.

There is also, I am told, another view, which is even more heartless. I briefly touched on it just now.[1] This is the assertion that friendships should be cultivated not for the sake of kindly and affectionate feeling at all, but solely for purposes of mutual utility. This would mean that the people who would get the most out of friendship would be those whose wills and bodies are the weakest: helpless women would need its protection more than men, the poor more than the rich, the unfortunate more than those who are considered fortunate. What a peculiar philosophy! People who propound this sort of theory seem to me to be doing nothing less than tearing the very sun out of the heavens. For they are, in fact, depriving life of friendship, which is the noblest and most delightful of all the gifts the gods have given to mankind.

1. Here and in the previous paragraph Cicero is thinking of Epicurus and his precursor Aristippus of Cyrene and their followers (pp. 25, 91).

And in any case what does such 'freedom from care' really mean? Superficially it looks attractive, but in reality there are many circumstances in which this is the very last thing we want. For there could, in fact, be nothing more misguided then to refuse to perform a good act, or having embarked on it to stop in the middle, merely in order to keep out of trouble. Certainly, we may succeed in avoiding trouble. But at the same time we shall be avoiding decent behaviour, because *that* is always bound to produce a certain amount of trouble because of its determination to eliminate everything that is incompatible with itself – when kindness, for example, rejects unkindness, self-control spurns licence, courage throws out cowardice.

For obviously, the people who hate injustice more than anyone else are the just, the keenest opponents of cowardice are the brave, those most hostile to shameful behaviour are the virtuous. Naturally, every person whose mind works in the right way welcomes what is good and grieves at what is bad. In other words, a wise man cannot possibly escape having any feelings of distress whatsoever – unless every trace of humanity has first been rooted out from his heart. Consequently, to remove friendship from our lives, just because it might bring us worries, would be the biggest possible mistake. For if we eliminate all human emotions, there is no difference left, I will not say between men and animals because animals have their feelings, but even between men and tree-trunks, or stones, or any other inanimate object you like to mention.

And to anyone who maintains that the way to be good is to possess the hardness of iron we should turn a deaf ear. In many aspects of life, and particularly in matters of friendship, goodness is a sensitive and pliable thing. It is like a liquid reacting to heat and cold: when our friends are doing well, it expands with them, and when their affairs go badly it shrinks in sympathy. Friendship, as I have just admitted, will inevitably involve distress, and quite often at that. But we simply must not let this prospect banish friendship out of our lives altogether, any more than we should be justified in rejecting moral standards because they, too, entail worries and troubles.

Friendships, I repeat, are formed when an exemplar of shining goodness makes itself manifest, and when some congenial spirit feels the desire to fasten on to this model. Then the result will be affection. And if we allow ourselves, as we do, to be pleased by a whole host of meaningless things such as public office and fame and fine architecture and rich clothing and personal adornment, it would be ridiculous, when we encounter a noble living being who possesses a capacity for loving, not to be wholly delighted with what we have found, and to reciprocate his affection.

Certainly, it is very agreeable indeed to be able to perform the practical tasks of repaying kindness and exchanging friendly services. But it still remains true that the greatest of all possible incentives to friendship is congeniality of temperament. This means that a good man is attracted by other good men; he wants to annex them for themselves. This is almost like an ordinance of nature, as if the two of them were bound together by ties of blood. For nature has a greedy urge towards everything that is in conformity with itself. That, Fannius and Scaevola, is a cogent and evident reason, in my opinion, why good men feel for one another the kindly inclinations which nature has made the very wellspring of friendship. And these noble feelings are found in perfectly ordinary people. There is nothing inhuman or uncooperative or stand-offish about goodness. It protects whole nations and looks after them extremely well, which it could certainly never do if it disdained the affectionate feelings of the man in the street.

Anyone who wants to allege that a friendship is formed for the sake of advantage seems to me to be doing away with the most attractive things such an association can offer. What we enjoy in a friend is *not* the profit we derive from him, but the affection. Any practical benefit that goes with this affection only gives satisfaction when it is the product of a warm heart. It is quite untrue to say that people only form friendships because there is some deficiency in themselves. On the contrary, the most generous and liberal friends are those who have the very least need of anyone else, because they themselves already possess wealth and power and, above all, goodness, which is the strongest resource a man can command. And, in any case, perhaps it is rather frustrating if one's friends do not lack anything at all! If Scipio, for example, in his civil and military occupations, had never needed any advice or assistance from myself, it would have meant that I had no opportunity to show how fond of him I was. However, friendship does not develop out of advantage; the process works the other way round.

*

If people whose lives are just constant wallowings in self-indulgence want to discuss friendship, let us not pay them the slightest attention. They do not understand the subject, either in practice or theory. Because heaven knows – surely we all ought to know – that there is not a man upon the whole earth who would want to live surrounded by unlimited wealth and affluence if the price he had to pay was to renounce both loving and being loved. That is how a tyrant lives – without mutual trust, without affection, without any assurance of enduring goodwill. In such a life suspicion and anxiety reign everywhere, and friendship has no place. For no one can love the person he fears – or the person he believes himself to be feared by. Tyrants are courted, naturally: but the courting is insincere, and it only lasts for a time. When these despots fall, as they normally do, it becomes very evident how short of friends they have been. Tradition reports that Tarquinius Superbus made this point as he went into exile. 'At last,' he said, 'it is clear to me which of my friends are true and which are false – now that I am no longer in a position to pay them back!'

Tarquinius, however, was an arrogant bully, and I doubt if he was able to have any friends at all. His character must surely have made this impossible; and in any case friendships are generally ruled out when there is an excess of resources and power. Fortune is not only blind herself, but blinds the people she has embraced. They become puffed up with disagreeable insolence, and there is nothing more insufferable than a fool whom fortune has blessed. You can see how military command and power and success transform people who had been decent enough before, and cause them to discard their old friendships in favour of new ones.

When a man is overflowing with wealth and goods and all kinds of abundance, and has got hold of everything that money can buy – horses, slaves, splendid clothes, expensive plate – he will be very foolish if he fails to add friends to that list, since *they* are the finest equipment that life can offer. Besides, when it is material property that people are acquiring, they have no idea who is really going to benefit from these goods in the end; they cannot guess on whose behalf, ultimately, they have gone to all this bother. For possessions of this kind get passed on – they go to the next man whose turn it is to rise to the top. Friendship, on the other hand, remains a firm and durable asset. Indeed, even if a man does manage to keep his hands on fortune's transitory gifts, his life will still remain unhappy if it is empty and devoid of friends.

*

So much, then, for this side of the matter. It remains to make up our minds what limits and restrictions ought to be set to our affection for a friend. I know of three separate answers to this question; and I do not approve of any of them. The first opinion is that our feeling for our friends should be identical with our feeling for our own selves. The second is that our goodwill towards friends should correspond in every respect to their own attitude towards us. The third point of view is that the value we attach to our friends should be exactly the same as the value they attach to themselves. Now, as I said, I disagree with every one of these pronouncements. The first of them, suggesting that a man should have the same feelings for his friends as he has for himself, is entirely wrong. We do a great many things for our friends that we should never dream of doing for ourselves. We are prepared, on their behalf, to ask and even beg favours from the most inferior individuals. We are also ready to attack other people in savage, relentless terms which would be odious if we were launching these onslaughts in our own interests but are entirely respectable if their motive is to help a friend. And decent men are often willing to throw away or let themselves be deprived of substantial gain with the deliberate intention that the profit should go to their friends instead of to themselves.

The second attitude, which restricts friendship to an equal interchange of services and feelings, reduces it to a too mean and narrow calculation of payments and receipts meticulously balanced. Friendship, to me, is something altogether richer and more abundant; it is not going to keep a close watch on whether it pays out more than it receives. Fears that something may slip over the side, or fall on to the ground, or overflow the proper measure of friendship, are completely out of place.

But the third limitation is the worst of all. This is the theory that a man's friends ought to estimate him at his own valuation of himself. A lot of people happen to be too humble about themselves, or too pessimistic about the possibility of self-betterment. In such cases it is by no means the duty of a friend to accept the other man's estimate of himself. What he ought to do, on the contrary, is to exert every effort to increase his friend's self-confidence and lead him towards a more hopeful and optimistic opinion of his own capabilities.

Evidently, then, these are all unacceptable definitions of friendship; and we must think of something else. But first I must mention one other standpoint which Scipio used to regard with particular distaste. This was the belief that 'we ought to love as if we are one day going to hate'. Scipio said he regarded this idea as totally incompatible with true friendship. He refused to credit the generally accepted belief that the maxim was attributable to Bias, who was considered to be one of the Seven Wise Men.[1] Scipio preferred instead to suppose that the utterance had emanated from some degraded character, perhaps an unscrupulous politician who was looking at everything in terms of his own career. For how could you possibly form a friendship with a man whom you foresaw all the time as a future enemy? If that were really your approach, you would inevitably find yourself hoping and praying that your friend would do wrong on every possible occasion. And if, on the contrary, he acted creditably and fared well, you would be obliged to feel pain, distress and envy. So whoever it may be who originally made this statement, its effect is assuredly to consign friendship to destruction. The right view, in fact, is the exact opposite. We ought to have it instilled in us that we must *never* make a friend whom we might some day come to hate. And if, Scipio maintained, we prove mistaken in our choice of a friend, we have just got to put up with it. Under no circumstances must we look for an occasion to convert the relationship into a hostile one.

So we still have not found the right way to define friendship. My suggestion is this. When two men of sound character are friends they should unreservedly share all their concerns and aims with one another. Indeed, even if by some chance a friend of ours possessed ambitions which, while not entirely laudable, nevertheless needed our assistance since

1. See p. 178 above. Bias of Priene was renowned for the justice of his verdicts.

either his life or his reputation were at stake, then we should have some justification in turning aside from the path of strict moral rectitude – short, that is to say, of doing something absolutely disgraceful, since there are limits beyond which friendship could not excusably go. I mentioned a danger to the man's reputation as well as his life, because one is entitled to consider this side of things – and recollect that, in a public career, the goodwill of one's fellow-countrymen is an exceedingly powerful weapon. Certainly, to acquire such goodwill by obsequious flattery would be wrong. But it is also entirely possible to gain popularity without the slightest departure from decent moral standards.

*

But let me get back to Scipio, since he had a lot to say on the subject. He used to complain, for example, that people are prepared to take more trouble about everything else in the world than about friendship. Everyone has an idea how many goats and sheep he owns, but nobody can say how many friends he possesses. And an immense amount of care is devoted to acquiring the cattle, but none, Scipio believed, to choosing friends; and no one has at his disposal any definite signs or criteria for determining which candidate satisfies the necessary conditions for friendship and which does not. The friends we select ought to be sound and stable and reliable. But such people are distinctly scarce, and, besides, it is extremely difficult to pick them except by practical experience: and the problem is that this experience can only be acquired *after* the friendship has actually begun. That is to say, the friendship comes first and the material for estimating its desirability only becomes accessible later on; it is impossible to try one's friend out in advance.

Any sensible person, then, will behave like a charioteer applying the reins to his team, and will check the vigorous impulses of his affections. In this way he will be able, to some extent at least, to subject his friends to the same sort of preliminary testing operation that men apply to their horses. For example, one fault which may turn up in one's friends is unreliability in small money matters; whereas another sort of person would never succumb to corruption by a trivial sum, but shows himself a bad friend as soon as more imposing amounts are involved. There are some people, it is true, who would agree that it is always sordid to rate financial considerations above friendship. But we should be hard put to it to find anyone at all who would not be prepared to sacrifice a friend to his political or military career. Place the lucrative attractions of office on one side, and the claims of friendship on the other, and far too often the former will easily come first. For human nature is too weak to refrain from coveting power. And, indeed, even when a person has sunk so low as to abandon his friends in the effort to become powerful, he will still somehow manage to convince himself that a veil will be drawn over the defection, because it was prompted by such an irresistible motive.

Consequently, men engaged in politics and the business of the State discover that true friendships are extremely hard to come by. For where on earth are you going to find anybody who will be keener to advance his friend's career than his own? Besides, if someone in public life gets into difficulties, people find it deeply disagreeable and painful to remain friends with him; those who are prepared to step down and join him in his trouble are very few indeed. As Ennius rightly said, a friend in need is a friend indeed. There are two opposite charges on which most men stand convicted of fickleness and unreliability. When they are doing well, they forget their friends; and when a friend is in difficulties they desert him. Anyone who proves himself a serious, reliable and steadfast friend in both these sets of circumstances clearly belongs to an extremely rare and indeed almost superhuman class of person.

The foundation of this reliable steadfastness which we look for in friendship is trust – trust and friendship go together. We require our chosen friend to be straightforward and companionable and congenial – in other words we hope he will have the same interests as ourselves. And that is what makes for trust. No one with a devious or tortuous disposition inspires confidence, and no one who fails to share one's own concerns, who lacks sympathy with them, can really be trustworthy or reliable as a friend. I must add one further requirement too. A true friend will not enjoy criticizing you: and, what is more, when other people criticize you, he will refuse to listen. Both these points are extremely relevant to this question of reliability. All of which is to repeat what I asserted at the beginning: only good men have the capacity to be good friends.

And so when good men, which means the same as wise men, enter into a friendship, they conduct it according to two rules. First, there must not be the slightest element of pretence or hypocrisy. Any decent person would rather hate openly than conceal his true thoughts behind an insincere expression. And not only, if there is criticism of his friend, will he take no notice, but he himself will never believe or entertain the slightest suspicion that the other person has done wrong. Secondly, a friend should be pleasant in conversation and manner, since these are things which add spice to any relationship. To be solemn and austere on all occasions may be impressive, but friendship ought to be something freer and more relaxed and more agreeable, paying greater attention to pleasant and amiable behaviour.

*

At this point there arises a bit of a problem. Should new friends, assuming they deserve the designation, sometimes be ranked above old ones – in the same way as we prefer young horses to old? However, this is not a question which any human being really ought to ask. There are some things we can easily have too much of: but friendship is not one of them. The older it is, the better it ought to have become, like a wine that has improved with age. There is truth in the saying that men must eat many a peck of salt together before they can know what friendship really means.

I am not saying that new friendships are to be despised – on the assumption that they really offer a prospect of bearing fruit, like blades of corn that fulfil their promise at the harvest. Yet the old friendships must still keep their place, for length of time and familiarity are by no means negligible factors. To go back to horses for a moment: other things being equal, everyone would prefer to use the mount he knows rather than an untrained and unfamiliar one. Indeed, habit applies equally strongly to our attitudes even towards inanimate objects. A place in which we have spent a long time, for example, arouses our affection, however rocky and wild it may be.

*

A particularly important point between one friend and another is this. The superior must place himself on an equality with his inferior. It often happens that one man stands out among the others, as Scipio stood out in what you might call our group. All the same, he never had the slightest desire to place himself above Philus or Rupilius or Mummius, or even his other friends of lower rank. And his brother Quintus Maximus, a distinguished man but by no means Scipio's equal, actually received deference from him, because Quintus was the older of the two.[1] Indeed, Scipio's greatest wish was that all his friends should gain, not lose, in stature because of their association with himself.

1. Publius Rupilius was said to have secured his consulship of 132 BC through the influence of Scipio. For Lucius Mummius Achaicus see p. 164. Quintus Fabius Maximus Aemilianus was consul in 145 and died in 130.

And that is the lead which everyone should follow. If an individual happens to be superior in character or intellectual qualities or worldly wealth, it is his duty to pass on this advantage to his kinsmen and friends, thus making sure that the people who are closest to him have their share. If, for instance, his parents were of humble birth, it is up to him to improve their status and social position; and if his relatives are his inferiors in ability or wealth, he should provide them with material assistance. It is something like the situation in the myths when someone has been obliged for a time to live a menial existence because his origin and lineage were unknown. Finally he is discovered and recognized to be the son of a god or a king, but still he retains affection for the shepherds whom he believed for many years to be his parents. And when there is an important personage in real life, when his humble parents are authentic parents, his feeling for them ought to be a great deal stronger still. For whatever gifts of mind and character we may possess, we only reap their finest fruits when we are able to share them with our nearest and dearest.

So much, then, for the necessity that in any relationship with friends or kinsmen the stronger partner must place himself on an equal footing with the weaker. And the latter, on their side, ought not to be distressed because the other man surpasses them in talents or possessions or rank. In reality, when such a situation arises, the weaker parties frequently indulge in complaints and reproaches. This is particularly apt to happen when they believe they can claim to have performed some friendly service to the other person, involving a certain amount of exertion. But this sort of individual who makes a grievance out of what he has done to help someone is thoroughly tedious. Certainly, the man for whose sake the services have been performed ought to remember them; but the individual who performed them would do better to keep his mouth shut. To sum up, then, not only should the superior partner in a friendship reduce himself to the level of his friend, but he is also under an obligation to do everything he can to lift the friend to his own level.

Some people make friendships very unpleasant because they are so ready to believe they have been slighted. However, the characters who adopt this attitude are usually those who have a strong suspicion that they deserved the slight. It is as well to disabuse them – and not merely by disclaimers, either, but by practical demonstrations. That is to say, you ought to give each of your friends just as much assistance as you have the capacity to provide – and as the object of your affection and assistance is capable of receiving. For however distinguished you may be, it would be beyond your powers to promote every one of your friends to the highest posts in the State. Scipio, for example, was able to get Publius Rupilius made consul,[1] but then for his brother Lucius he could not manage it. And indeed, even if you did possess the power to give your friend everything you wanted him to have it would still be incumbent on you to consider how far his capabilities extended.

*

Generally speaking, decisions about friendships should be taken after we have reached full physical and intellectual maturity. Suppose that a person was keen on hunting and ball-games as a boy; it is not to be expected that when he grows up he will continue to associate with the individuals who in those early days had shared his interests. If that was the principle we adopted, our nurses and the slaves who took us to school would have a claim on the major part of our goodwill because they were the first human beings we ever knew. We must not drop them of course; but our relationships with them will now have to be looked at in a different light. Friendships formed before one grows up cannot possibly be

1. Publius Rupilius was consul in 132 BC. See also p. 211 above.

stable or permanent. For young people's personalities change, and their tastes change with them – and altered tastes are what bring friendships to an end. The reason why bad men cannot be friends with good, and good men with bad, is because of the enormous gulf of character and tastes that yawns between them.

And there is another useful rule. Do not let your good intentions towards a friend become so exaggerated that by mistake you actually damage his major interests instead of helping them. This happens all too often. For example – to borrow another illustration from mythology – if Neoptolemus had listened to Lycomedes who had brought him up, he would never have taken Troy: since the old man had tearfully endeavoured to prevent him from leaving home.[1] Important business often makes it necessary for friends to part, and anyone who tries to prevent this because the separation will cause him unhappiness is displaying a weak, soft character, and behaving unreasonably as a friend. All the time you have got to consider how much you are going to demand of your friend; and how much you yourself are going to give him.

*

And now I must leave the relationships between men to whom some degree of wisdom may be attributed, because I want to descend to associations of a more everyday character.

Breaking off a friendship can amount to a disaster; though the step may well be unavoidable all the same. It is possible for a person's faults, on occasion, to erupt unpleasantly on top of his friends, either directly or with a third party as the cause. When this occurs, the friendship needs to be brought to an end, not suddenly, but by a gradual process of elimination.

1. The mythical Neoptolemus (Pyrrhus) was the son of Achilles and Deidamia, the daughter of Lycomedes, king of Scyros.

Or, as I once heard Cato put the point, it is better to unstitch the union than to tear it apart; unless, that is to say, there has been some outburst of intolerable wrongdoing, in which case the only proper and honourable course, indeed the only practicable course, will be immediate withdrawal and dissociation.

If, on the other hand, as more frequently happens, there has merely been a shift in attitude and interests, or a divergence of political views (for, as I said, I am now talking about ordinary relationships, not those between exceptional men), then something must be done to make it clear that what has happened is just a termination of friendship and not a declaration of war. For if a man has been your friend, it is the most discreditable thing in the world to let him become your enemy. As you both know, Scipio stopped being a friend of Quintus Pompeius on my own account. Scipio was also compelled, again by a political difference, to become estranged from my colleague Quintus Metellus.[1] In each instance he acted with dignity and restraint, and refused to allow his displeasure to deteriorate into bitterness.

Our first duty, then, is to ensure that if possible our friendships shall contain no rifts. But if these nevertheless occur, it is our duty to make it look as though the associations have just burnt themselves out and not been forcibly smothered. Under no circumstances must friendships be allowed to deteriorate into serious hostility, which would inevitably mean that one becomes the target for insulting, abusive criticism. And yet even this hostile comment, provided it does not become absolutely intolerable, may have to be endured. For the friendship that once used to exist is still entitled to this degree

1. The younger Scipio quarrelled with Quintus Pompeius because the latter defeated Laelius in the consular election for 141 BC by a trick, and was also on bad terms with Quintus Caecilius Metellus Macedonicus who resented Scipio's part in getting him passed over for the command against the Achaean League (146).

of respect – you ought to be readier to suffer offence than to cause it.

Against all these faults and troubles there is only one possible precaution and safeguard. That is, do not be too quick to form an attachment; make quite sure first that you are not attaching yourself to someone who does not deserve the association. The people who merit your friendship are those who genuinely possess some characteristic capable of inspiring devotion. Such men are rare – for of course it is the hardest thing in the world to find anything, in any field, that is altogether perfect of its kind.

*

Most people are not prepared, in their daily lives, to accept that anything can be good unless it is a source of profit. They choose their best friends as they choose their cattle, lavishing the greatest affection where they hope for the most lucrative results. But if this is what they are going to do, they will miss the finest and most natural sort of friendship; I mean the sort which is desirable for its own sake and for itself. Such people deprive themselves of the opportunity to experience for themselves how powerful, how wonderful, and how all-embracing this kind of relationship can be.

Think of the love any person feels for his own self. Why does he engage in all this self love? Not from any hope of profit, but simply because it is in the nature of things that he should do so. Now, this is just the sort of feeling that has to be transferred to friendship. There is no other way to find a real friend.

Birds and fishes and the beasts of the field, tame and wild – every living being loves itself! The feeling is inborn in every creature. And inborn, too, is the need to find other creatures of the same species on to which they can fasten themselves. The urge that impels them to do so bears some resemblance to human love. And indeed human nature engenders the same pair of feelings – with a special degree of intensity. For they, too, love themselves; and they, too, search for a partner whose personality they can unite so utterly with their own that the two are almost transformed into one.

*

Perversely, not to say shamelessly, most people want to have the sort of friend they cannot be themselves. They expect their friends to provide what they themselves are incapable of supplying. However, the ideal requirement for such a relationship (next to being a good man yourself) is quite the opposite: it is to find someone not different from oneself, but the same. That is the best guarantee of the permanence I have been discussing. And those, too, are the circumstances in which men united by mutual sympathy can learn to master the passions to which other men are slaves. They will take pleasure in fairness and justice; there is nothing they will not do for one another. They will be incapable of asking their partner for anything that is not right and good. And besides loving and cherishing each other, they will also feel mutual respect. Remove respect from friendship, and you have taken away the most splendid ornament it possesses.

People who believe friendship gives a good opportunity for all sorts of laxity and crime are making a dangerous mistake. That is not why nature gave us this blessing; she did not give it in order to pander to our vices, but to help us behave decently. For the highest standards of behaviour are impossible to realize on one's own; union with someone else, companionship, are the only things that can ensure them. Such an association, whether you are speaking of today, or of the past, or of any epoch in the future, ranks as the finest and most glorious of all possible connexions, embodying the highest good that nature has to offer. For friendships of such a kind embrace everything worth pursuing by mankind – goodness, and fame, and peace of mind, and satisfaction: the things which make life happy when we have them, whereas without them there can be no question of happiness at all.

This happiness is the summit of our best ambitions. But if we are to get it, we shall have to concentrate on raising our behaviour to the very highest standard that morality can achieve. If we fail to do this, we can achieve neither friendship nor, for that matter, any other worthwhile objective. Anyone who ignores these standards, but imagines that he has friends all the same, will discover his mistake as soon as some serious emergency obliges him to put their friendship to the test. Consequently, my warning needs to be repeated again and again. Become devoted to your friend only after you have tried him out. Do not first become devoted, and *then* try him out.

There is nothing which causes people to display worse carelessness, and pay graver penalties, than their selection and acquisition of friends. We are apt to plan, too late, for something that is already in the past; we start doing what has already been done – just the thing that the old proverb tells us to avoid. And then very often, after we have become involved with someone by meeting them every day or doing each other good turns, all at once, right in the middle of our friendship, some cause of offence arises and we break the whole thing off.

Negligence of this magnitude, in so utterly vital a matter, is singularly deplorable. For after all, the only thing in the whole of human life which everyone, without exception, agrees to be worthwhile is friendship. Even moral goodness is disparaged by a lot of people, who call it self-advertisement and display. And quite a number of people look down on riches, because they themselves happen to need very little, and are content with meagre food and a modest way of life. Or then again, if you consider the attractions of an important political career, although some men, it is true, are consumed with such ambitions, a lot of others contemptuously regard it as something utterly empty and futile. The same applies to anything else you like to mention. Whatever it may be, its admirers will be matched by many others who think nothing of it at all. Yet friendship is something which inspires the same opinion in everybody – politicians, scholars who devote themselves to study and learning, businessmen who stick to their own affairs and keep out of public life. Even those individuals who devote themselves entirely to the pleasures of the flesh feel the same. All these categories of person, if they feel the slightest aspirations towards a decent human existence, believe that, without friendship, life does not deserve the name. Somehow or other friendship inserts itself into all our existences. However we choose to live, there is no escaping it.

Picture someone who is by nature so savage and forbidding that he shuns and detests the company of his fellow-men. Tradition tells us that there once lived just such an individual at Athens, called Timon.[1] And yet even that sort of character would not be able to resist making contact with some other person – for at least he could not help wanting to find a target for his venomous bitterness. You can appreciate what I mean if you imagine the following situation. Suppose that some divine being lifted us out of the crowded human society in which we live, and planted us in some spot where nobody lived at all. Suppose, furthermore, that he supplied us with an abundance of every material provision which we could conceivably require – but made it utterly impossible for us to look upon any other human being. To put up with life on those terms would be beyond anyone's powers even if he were made of iron. If you are lonely, every pleasure loses its savour.

There was a famous saying which some sage always had on his lips – Archytas of Tarentum, I think it was.[2] I have

1. This semi-legendary misanthrope seems to have lived in the mid fifth century BC.

2. See p. 86 above.

heard it repeated by old men at Rome; and they in turn had heard it from their seniors. The saying went like this. If a man ascended into heaven and gazed upon the whole workings of the universe and the beauty of the stars, the marvellous sight would give him no joy if he had to keep it to himself. And yet, if only there had been someone to describe the spectacle to, it would have filled him with delight. Nature abhors solitude, and always demands that everything should have some support to rely upon. For any human being, the best support of all is a good friend.

Nature provides many a sign to let us know what she wants and seeks and demands. And yet somehow or other we turn a deaf ear, and fail to listen to her warnings.

*

The maintenance of a friendship is a varied and complex process, offering many perilous opportunities for suspicion and offence. If a man is wise, he will sometimes contrive to avoid these unpleasant occurrences, and will sometimes manage to make light of them; at other times he just has to put up with them.

Indeed, if we are going to preserve the value and sincerity of a friendship, there is one such cause of offence that has simply got to be endured. That is to say, you are under an obligation not only to advise your friend frequently but to rebuke him if necessary; and when this is done to yourself, and done in a spirit of goodwill, you must take it in good part. Unfortunately, however, there is also a good deal of truth in what my friend Terence said in his *Woman of Andros*: 'Flattery gets us friends, but truth earns ill-will'.[1] Certainly, truth of that kind can be very disagreeable, since it does indeed produce ill-will, and ill-will is what poisons friendships. But flattery is, in fact, much the more tiresome disadvantage of the two, because while it indulges a friend's misdeeds it is

1. Terence, *Andria*, 41.

also contributing to his ruin. And most culpable of all is the friend who spurns the truth and allows flattery to seduce him into doing wrong.

This whole matter requires rational and discreet handling. Advice must not be harsh, or criticism offensive. If we are going to flatter, to use Terence's word, let it be just a form of courtesy, entirely free of any servile elements: since servility is what aids and abets every sort of viciousness and is unworthy not only of a friend but of any free man at all. Life with a friend is not like life with a tyrant. A man whose ears are so completely closed to the truth that he cannot even hear it from a friend is a hopeless case. Cato spoke shrewdly, as so often, when he remarked, 'In some ways our worst enemies do us greater services than our friends who seem so agreeable: since enemies often tell us the truth, whereas friends never do.' Certainly, it is irrational, if you are criticized, not to feel annoyed when you hear something that warrants annoyance, but to feel furious about a remark which ought not to upset you at all. You are annoyed not because you have done wrong, but because you are blamed for it: whereas what you ought to be feeling sorry about is the wrong you have done and when it is corrected you ought to be glad.

So it is an essential feature of genuine friendship both to offer advice and to receive it. The advice should be given frankly but not harshly, and received with patience and no trace of resentment. There can be no worse blot on a friendship than fawning sycophancy and adulation. Call this by whatever name you like, it can only be branded as a vice, characteristic of unreliable, insincere men who like to speak in a fashion calculated to give pleasure, without the slightest regard for the truth. Hypocrisy is bound to be vicious, because it saps and contaminates our standards of truthfulness. And this makes it wholly incompatible with friendship, which must be truthful if it is to have any meaning at all.

The significance of friendship is that it unites human hearts.

But this cannot happen if one of the personalities involved fails to remain consistently the same, and instead takes on a variety of shifting and changeable forms. For it is impossible to imagine anything more devious and tortuous than an individual who is prepared to transform his own personality in obedience not only to someone else's feelings and opinions but even to the very expression on the other person's face.

> He says 'no' and I say 'no'. He says 'yes', and I say 'yes'. In other words I have made it my duty to agree with him in everything.[1]

That is Terence again, but now he is speaking in the character of Gnatho – the sort of friend whom nobody but a fool would want. There are a great many people about who, even if they are Gnatho's superiors in position and wealth and reputation, behave exactly like him all the same!

And when you have a man who is not only insincere but influential, this sycophancy becomes really dangerous. However, if you are careful, it is possible to tell a hypocritical friend from a real one. You can keep the two sorts apart, in the same way as you can distinguish any other sham or fake from the authentic original.

*

A public meeting consists of wholly inexperienced people; and yet, when gathered together, they can usually tell the difference between a demagogue, that is to say a politician of the smooth-tongued unreliable sort, and a statesman who is reliable and truthful and honest. A short time ago Gaius Papirius Carbo insinuated himself into the favour of the Assembly by proposing a law to make tribunes of the people eligible for re-election to a second term of office. I spoke against him. But never mind about me; it is Scipio I want to talk about. Heavens, what an impressive, imposing speech he made! You might have thought he was head of the whole

1. Terence, *Eunuchus*, 250.

Roman State, not just one private citizen among many. However, you were both there listening to him – and in any case his speech is available for all to read. As a result of his words, the bill in question, which was meant to please the people, was turned down – the people themselves turned it down.

To return to myself, you must remember, when Scipio's brother Quintus Fabius Maximus and Lucius Hostilius Mancinus were consuls, how popular Gaius Crassus's bill about priestly appointments seemed likely to be. Such appointments had previously been arranged by co-optation,[1] and it was now proposed to transfer them, together with all the immense patronage they carried, to the popular vote. (Crassus also made another democratic gesture; he was the first man who ever turned to face the Forum while addressing the Assembly.)[2] I was called upon to speak in reply, and it turned out that his specious arguments could be defeated quite easily: what I did was to appeal to the reverence we all ought to feel towards the immortal gods. These events took place while I was only praetor – I did not become consul for another five years. In others words, what won the debate was not influence derived from rank, but the merits of the case itself.

On the stage, then – for that is what those public meetings amount to – the ample opportunities that exist for lies and misrepresentations still cannot prevent truth from winning the day, once it is revealed and brought out into the light. How much more, then, must this apply to friendship, of which

1. i.e. the existing members of the boards voted for the new ones.

2. i.e. when speaking from the Old Rostra this tribune (145 BC) addressed much larger crowds (on the Forum side) than could gather on the other (Comitium) side. This had already been the practice for informal meetings (*contiones*), and Gaius Crassus extended it to formal Assemblies (*Comitia*). The biographer Plutarch says it was not Crassus but Gaius Gracchus who turned towards the Forum. According to Varro (1st century BC), what Crassus did was to lead the voters from the Comitium out into the centre of the Forum.

truth is the indispensable condition? Between friends, unless the other person bares his soul to you, and you bare yours to him, there can be no question of loyalty and certainty, or, for that matter, of loving and being loved, since concealment would make it quite impossible to estimate whether there is any genuine feeling at all. Just now I was speaking of those who flatter their friends. Disastrous though this practice is, it can only do real harm to someone who enjoys receiving the flattery: for anyone who listens readily to sycophants makes himself a victim of self-love and complacency.

Now here is an apparent analogy with genuine goodness or virtue, because that quality, too, shares this capacity for loving itself. For it knows itself best; and in consequence it apprehends that it is worthy of love. But people who enjoy being flattered are not really after virtue at all, but merely the outward semblance of virtue. For a lot of people are less concerned to be virtuous than to look it. Such are the individuals who enjoy listening to flattery, and when they hear talk calculated to please them they regard the empty phrases as clear demonstrations of what models of perfection they must be. But a friendship in which one partner does not want to hear the truth, and the other is prepared to tell lies, can only be utterly meaningless. When we are watching a comedy on the stage, it is true we find the servility of the parasites amusing instead of disgusting, but that is because the dramatist relieves it with the contrasting humour of that other stock type, the swaggering soldier. 'Did Thais really seem grateful for my present?' asks one of these warriors. It would have been enough to answer, 'Yes, very grateful.' But the parasite prefers to reply, '*Gigantically* grateful.'[1] If the person who is being flattered wants something to be large, a sycophant always makes it larger still. Now when people welcome and encourage this kind of obsequiousness, it has its effect on them. And even tougher, better balanced characters need to be

1. Terence, *Eunuchus*, 391; cf. also the *Miles Gloriosus* of Plautus.

warned that they must defend themselves vigilantly against the craftier forms of servile behaviour.

If someone goes in for servility of the most open kind, nobody but a downright fool will fall for it. But what we must be on our guard against is letting the subtle, secret operator worm his way behind our defences. He is hard to recognize, because he often conceals his flattery beneath the appearance of offering opposition. That is to say he pretends to disagree, but finally pays the other person the compliment of giving in and allowing himself to be defeated, thus creating the impression that his companion had been more far-sighted than himself. To allow oneself to be made a fool of in such a way is shameful. We must take precaution against such a thing happening to ourselves! 'Today you have tricked me,' said the character in a comedy, 'and made a worse fool of me than all the old fools of the comic stage.'[1] For in plays, too, the silliest characters are always the old men who have so little sense that they always believe everything they are told.

*

But somehow or other I have drifted away from my theme. What I had proposed to talk about was friendship between good men, that is to say, wise men – wise, I mean, according to practical human standards. But instead I have started discussing friendships of a more trivial nature. So let me now return to my original subject, and finally bring the matter to a conclusion.

What unites friends in the first place, Fannius and Scaevola, and what keeps them friends, is goodness of character. All harmony, and permanence, and fidelity, come from that. When this moral quality appears, and reveals its brilliant light, and perceives and recognizes the same illumination in another person, it is impelled in his direction and receives his radiant

1. From the *Epiclerus* of Caecilius Statius of Mediolanum (c. 219–166 BC).

beams. And that is how love or friendship comes into existence. Both words, *amor* and *amicitia*, come from *amare*, to love. And love is precisely the nature of the affection you feel for your friend. Certainly it does not require the prompting of any advantage. (Advantage does, it is true, grow out of friendship, whether you have intentionally pursued such a benefit or not; but that is another matter.)

This was the sort of affection which I myself, when I was young, felt towards certain men who were already quite old – Lucius Paullus, Marcus Cato, Gaius Sulpicius Galus, Publius Nasica and the elder Tiberius Gracchus, the father-in-law of my friend Scipio.[1] But the feeling shines brightest when it is shared by persons of the same age, like Scipio, Lucius Furius Philus, Publius Rupilius, Spurius Mummius and myself. However, now that I myself am old, I enjoy my friendships with young people such as yourselves and Quintus Aelius Tubero. I also greatly appreciate my friendly relations with very young men like Publius Rutilius Rufus and Aulus Verginius.[2] And yet, all the same – life and human nature being what they are – with a new generation always coming up, the most satisfying thing of all really is to reach the end of the race with the same companions who were with you at the starting post.

Since everything that is mortal is precarious and transient, we ought always to go on and on searching for people who can receive our love and be loved by us in return. Without affection and kindly feeling life can hold no joys. Scipio was suddenly snatched away, but for me he is still living and always will be. What I loved him for was his goodness; and this is

1. The younger Scipio Africanus married Sempronia, daughter of the elder Tiberius Gracchus and sister of the tribunes Tiberius and Gaius Gracchus. For these personages and Quintus Aelius Tubero see Genealogical Table (II), p. 361. Publius Cornelius Scipio Nasica Corculum was consul in 162.

2. Spurius Mummius was brother of the famous Lucius Mummius Achaicus (p. 164). Aulus Verginius was a well-known lawyer.

something that has not died. When he was alive it was always with me; and the vision remains with me still. Indeed every generation to come, for all eternity, will continue to be illuminated by the glory and renown of his noble character. All men, for evermore, who have the courage and hope to embark on great enterprises, will be certain to cherish in their hearts the memory and example of that man.

As for myself, not one of the good things that fortune or nature has bestowed on me could begin to compare with my friendship with Scipio. One of its features was the total harmony between us on matters of state. Another aspect was the advice he was always prepared to give me about all my private affairs. And our leisure hours together were a source of unfailing pleasure. To the best of my knowledge, I never caused him irritation; and he never once addressed to me a single word I would have preferred unsaid. We shared the same house, we ate the same meals, and we ate them side by side. Together we were soldiers, together we travelled, together we went for our country holidays. Every minute of our spare time, as you know, we devoted to study and research, withdrawn from the eyes of the world but enjoying the company of one another. If my recollection of all these doings had perished with Scipio when he died, the loss of my friend, who was so utterly close and dear to me, would be unendurable. But the picture of them in my mind has not passed away. My memory keeps the vision alive – and it becomes even more wonderful as time goes on. And besides, in any case, even if I *had* lost the power to recall these things, my age would be some comfort. For it means that I shall not have to endure my bereavement for very long. Even the severest of burdens can be borne provided their duration is short.

That, then, is what I have to say about friendship. No one can be a friend unless he is a good man. But next to goodness itself, I entreat you to regard friendship as the finest thing in all the world.

# ON THE ORATOR

*On the Orator* is a far more generally significant work than its title might suggest, in relation to our own preoccupations as well as those of the ancient world. For 'orator' means the same as 'statesman', and what the book deals with is a very urgent question: how must we train the men who govern us so that they will be efficient but will refrain from abusing their power?

Oratory was immensely important in the Roman Republic. It was the pre-eminent civil occupation. The whole of public life depended on it; and so did the whole of education. A public speaker swayed issues of breathtaking magnitude.[1] It was therefore infinitely worth while to stand back and consider how he should proceed. And when Cicero was the man conducting such an inquiry this was peculiarly valuable, since his political experience was great, he possessed extraordinary culture and humanity, and above all he was the most persuasive and successful orator who has ever lived. Moreover, his excellence as a practitioner was equalled by his attention to theory, which resulted in a number of highly important treatises.[2]

It may seem strange to us to find oratory elevated to the full status of an art or science. We do not share this view; but the Romans had learnt from the Greeks, who had thought of rhetoric in this light for nearly four hundred years.

The Greeks had always been great talkers, as was already clear enough from the Homeric poems. But the founders of speech as an art were said to have been Corax and Tisias of Syracuse in the fifth century BC (p. 268). Another Sicilian, Gorgias of Leontini, who came to Athens in 427, advocated

1. See *Cicero: Selected Political Speeches*, op. cit., pp. 15ff.

2. See List of Rhetorical Works, p. 357.

various devices, and stressed the value of emotional appeal; his arrival symbolized the passage of oratorical theory from Sicily to Greece, where, during the years that followed, he became the most famous practitioner of rhetoric. Then the Athenian Isocrates (436–338 BC) developed the teaching of the subject into a far-reaching moral and political training system which considerably influenced Cicero's later concept of the orator as the Whole Man. Like Isocrates (though he deplored Isocrates's description of the study as 'philosophy'), Plato faced the problem of the amorality of rhetoric, indicating that what must be done is to make it into an art that would be useful for advancing the truth – and for this purpose the orator himself has to *know* the truth first.[1] Plato stressed the need for native endowment and knowledge and practice, and emphasized the importance of psychological considerations, condemning spurious arguments and mechanical classifications and stylistic tricks. Aristotle, in his *Rhetoric*, accepted Plato's suggestion that this pursuit could be an art – endeavouring to meet his criticisms – and included the subject in his philosophical courses. Rhetoric seemed to Aristotle a genuine branch of reasoning, 'the observing of all the available means of persuasion', and his analysis displayed shrewd attention to commonsense and human foibles. It also laid the foundations of style; and then his pupil Theophrastus (p. 24), in works that are now lost, gave fresh impetus to this subject and to the study of delivery. Theophrastus also insisted on the union of rhetoric and philosophy. He and his master are hailed for this achievement by Cicero,[2] who deliberately by-passed the technicalities of the preceding centuries to reach the broader and more philosophical concepts of Aristotle and Theophrastus.[3]

1. Plato, *Phaedrus*, 260 D, 3ff. The Greek and Latin words for an 'art' (*techne, ars*) can also sometimes be translated 'science'.

2. *On Divination*, II, 1, 4.

3. The Stoics believed that the thought behind speech *is* speech:

An early example of the subsequent handbooks concentrating on technical points was the anonymous *Rhetorica ad Alexandrum* of the fourth century BC. By the middle of the following century – when the main political units were no longer city-states but great kingdoms – important oratory was no more, and rhetoric had become a scholastic discipline. The most eminent teacher of the subject in Hellenistic times was Hermagoras of Temnos (c. 150 BC), who developed methods of advanced instruction and encouraged a good deal of the hair-splitting that followed. Disturbed by this aridity, his contemporaries Carneades the Academic and Critolaus the Peripatetic, who visited Rome in 155, attacked the educational claims of the rhetoricians. Carneades insisted that, although some people might possess an inborn gift for flattery, there is no *art* of rhetoric: his implication was that there is no useful base for humane studies except philosophy.

The quarrel between philosophy and rhetoric was now in full swing: and Romans went to listen to Carneades's pupil Charmadas arguing the point against Menedemus the rhetorician (p. 252). The first great Roman orators, whom Cicero introduces as disputants in his work *On the Orator*, are thought of as carrying on and continuing the dispute. They are Lucius Licinius Crassus and Marcus Antonius Orator. Crassus, consul in 95 BC, was the most distinguished of all Roman orators before Cicero himself, who had been his pupil as a boy. In the dialogue, Crassus takes the broad view, and is thus the mouthpiece for Cicero's own opinions on oratory – as he was also in politics, where he stood for moderation and constitutionalism. Cicero called him 'the best lawyer among the orators'. Moreover, the pure, artistic style of Crassus, and his employment of choice and careful but unpedantic language, helped to mould Latin prose.

---

look after the subject-matter and the words will look after themselves (Cato the elder): the philosopher is the only orator.

So did the different methods of the other principal spokesman here. He was Marcus Antonius Orator (consul 99), the triumvir's grandfather (famous for a campaign against the pirates of the eastern Mediterranean). He alone could compete with Crassus as an orator, though Cicero did not altogether approve of his unstudied, almost casual method of speaking (behind which, in fact, lay considerable though unacknowledged theoretical training). Marcus Antonius wrote down some of his views on the subject, but he did not publish the treatise (p. 309), and like other early Roman essays on rhetoric, it is lost.

Cicero, always an admirer of the great men of the past, imagines that their conversation took place in the highly dramatic year 91 BC when he himself was in his sixteenth year. It had been a time of ominous crises, shortly before the outbreak of the terrible Marsian War in which the Italians rebelled against Rome. But Cicero supposes that a group of leading figures in the State took advantage of the holiday of the Roman Games (4–12 September) to retire to a pleasant country house at Tusculum (p. 51). There, after talking of the political emergency, they spoke about oratory.

Their host was Crassus. A few days after the date at which this discussion was supposed to have taken place, he died of a chill caught while delivering an impassioned speech in the Senate. Marcus Antonius survived until 87, when he was murdered in the civil strife which followed the Marsian War, while Gaius Marius and his 'democratic' followers were undertaking measures of revenge against the supporters of Sulla, who had just left for the east in order to conduct the war against King Mithridates VI of Pontus.

The other speakers are Publius Sulpicius Rufus, Gaius Aurelius Cotta and Quintus Mucius Scaevola. Soon after the imagined date of the discussion, in 88, Sulpicius became a highly controversial tribune, raising the hopes of the Italians and backing Marius against Sulla, who had him killed when he marched on Rome before leaving for the east. Though ignorant of general culture, Sulpicius was next only to Antonius as an orator. The other participant in the whole discussion, Gaius Aurelius Cotta, was another good speaker. He remained a moderate conservative reformer and survived the Civil War between the Marians and Sulla, and again survived Sulla's subsequent dictatorship (81–79), to become consul in 75 BC. Cotta was a cousin of Julius Caesar's mother.

One volume of the work – the first, which is translated here – also introduces Quintus Mucius Scaevola (consul 117 BC), known as 'the Augur' to distinguish him from his cousin's son of the same name who served as consul with Crassus in 95 and was known as 'the Priest'.[1] Scaevola the Augur, like other members of his family, was an eminent jurist. He was also a supporter of the Stoic school of philosophy, and had been one of the cultured associates of the younger Scipio. Cicero himself, as a boy of sixteen, had received instruction in Roman law from 'the Augur', as he later did from 'the Priest' as well.

In a letter to Atticus Cicero remarked that in view of the Augur's age he thought it appropriate to spare him the more technical arguments of the second and third books, in which Antonius and Crassus in turn enlarge upon the respective points of oratory at which each of them excelled. But first Book I, which is presented here, had provided a remarkable general discussion of the equipment needed by an orator, in which Antonius denies that such a man needs a higher education and Crassus argues that he does.

Cicero himself sat at the feet of other Romans as well as Crassus and the Scaevolas. But he did not attend the first school of Latin rhetoric, which was opened at Rome by Lucius Plotius Gallus in the middle or later 90s, since he thought it better, as far as professionals were concerned, to go

1. See Genealogical Table (I), p. 360.

to the Greeks.[1] Cicero worked on the practical side of oratory, especially style and delivery, with the eminent rhetorician Molon both at Rome and Rhodes, and studied rhetoric with a Syrian named Demetrius at Athens. He also learnt from the Stoic Posidonius the view that the philosopher is the only orator (pp. 27, 235n.). But what appealed to Cicero particularly was the practice of the Academic Philo of Larissa (p. 29), who taught both rhetoric and philosophy,[2] thus symbolizing the final resolution of the dispute between these two equally essential pursuits.[3] One of the reasons why Cicero liked the Academy was because it was the most adaptable of all schools to oratory.[4]

Cicero himself wrote a textbook on rhetoric, *On Invention*, early in his life. Later he became the author of a number of much more important works on the same subject.[5] These included the *Brutus* and the *Orator*, but first of all came *On the Orator*. It was written in a period of political disillusionment: not the epoch of Caesar's dictatorship and its aftermath which produced the philosophical treatises (p. 12), but an ominous time a decade earlier, when the suppression of the Republic was already clearly under way. In September 57 BC the worst period of Cicero's life came to an end when he returned from exile. But any hopes that he may have formed of making an effective re-entry into politics were quickly dashed when Pompeius, M. Crassus and Caesar, the members of the First Triumvirate whose alliance had seemed, to his hopeful eye, to be weakening, came together at the Conference of Luca (Lucca) in 56 BC, patched up their disagreements and planned

1. Suetonius, *Rhetoricians*, 2. cf. Crassus in *On the Orator*, III, 24. Cicero opposed Gallus because the latter's school was intended as a 'democratic' political reaction against the cult of Hellenism.

2. *Tusculans*, II, 3, 9.

3. *On Duties*, I, 1. For the Stoics and Academy see above pp. 26, 28.

4. *Paradoxes of the Stoics*, preface, 2.

5. See List of Rhetorical Works, p. 357.

a fresh period of shared dictatorial control. In this year Cicero still delivered important speeches, but during 55 he largely withdrew from the lawcourts and the Senate. A letter he wrote to his friend Atticus in November indicates that he was devoting this period of retirement to the three books (volumes) *On the Orator*, which he now brought to a conclusion after much time and trouble had been expended upon its composition.[1] The work was dedicated to Cicero's brother Quintus.

Written at a time when the political achievement of which he was so proud, the suppression of Catilina's conspiracy during his consulship of 63, was still fresh in his own mind, if not in the minds of others, the treatise has a strong practical bias: in determining what sort of man an orator, that is to say a statesman helping to rule the Roman world, ought to be, it is performing an urgent task. This urgency is accentuated because Cicero is at pains to point out that this is not just another rhetorical textbook, or treatise on the theory of speaking, like *On Invention* (p. 233).[2] It is much more. Yet Greek technicalities cannot, he agrees, be altogether forgotten, since he believed that discourse, being a human product, is susceptible to the refinements of an art. Indeed he regarded the art of oratory as one of the highest expressions of human dignity[3] – even superior to philosophy, because, although the orator has to know his philosophy first, he is the man who then adds perfection of form.

The work *On the Orator* is itself an artistic masterpiece, as fine as anything in the language. But where Cicero parted company with the textbooks was in his insistence that, in view of the exceptional importance of oratory, this powerful

1. *Letters to Atticus*, IV, 13, 2.

2. *On the Orator*, I, 6, 23.

3. Soon after this work was written Cicero's concept of this art was strongly contested by the Atticist school, which found him too ornamental and verbose.

weapon must be put into responsible hands. The orator, that is to say the statesman, needs both moral excellence and a wide and liberal culture: the combination of philosophy and oratory ensured right conduct *and* expression.

The blend seemed to him peculiarly appropriate to Rome.[1] Admittedly these are doctrines which could be found in classical Athenian thought – before the centuries of technicalities began – but no one had ever given them the vitality and impassioned relevance that Cicero put into them. It is true that the fundamental theoretical problems (such as the connexions between craft and art) are not subjected to the acute and profound analyses of Plato or Aristotle; but there is ample compensation in the sense we are given of intimate, unique contact with practical realities. Here we have the supreme practitioner of Rome's supreme civilian occupation, one of the greatest speakers of all time, imparting to future Roman statesmen and ourselves the fruit of the experience which had brought him – without any of the advantages of ancestry – to the summit of the Roman State. Book I of *On the Orator* ranks at the very top of those works which give us an insight into how Rome and Romans functioned at their best.

1. *On the Orator*, III, 15, 57. On the value of the liberal arts to national affairs see *On the State*, 3, 5.

## ON THE ORATOR (1)

I THINK about the old days very often, my brother; and whenever I do so I am constantly struck by the extraordinarily happy fortune of the men who lived in an age when the Republic was at its best. Noble careers came their way, and great fame, and yet all their political activities did not involve them in the smallest personal danger. And if they retired from politics, they were able to retire honourably.

There was once a time when I, too, imagined that I might well become entitled, with more or less universal approval, to retire from public life and devote my thoughts to the wonderful studies we both love so much. The endless toil of speech-making would be over, and so would all the business of getting oneself elected to state offices, since the progression from one post to another would have been completed, and I should have reached just the right age for the change to a new way of life. That is what I was thinking of and planning for! But my hopes have been dashed. The catastrophic experiences from which we are all suffering have frustrated such expectations completely; and so have my own various personal crises. The time which ought to have been the most serene and tranquil of my life proved exactly the opposite, producing a more pressing horde of vexations and tempestuous storms than I had ever experienced in all my days. What I wanted and longed for, I entirely failed to get. This was leisure: to enable me to pursue once again, in association with yourself, the studies you and I have been so devoted to ever since we were boys.

Instead, just when I was growing up the old order started to collapse. Then came my consulship, which plunged me right into the middle of a conflict of the most critical character and of universal proportions. And ever since that moment I have been trying to stem that flood. I succeeded in saving all our fellow-countrymen from its onslaught – only to find the waves engulfing myself instead.

Events are deeply worrying, and time is short. But all the same, when those studies of ours beckon, how can I fail to respond? When the intrigues of my enemies, the calls of friendship, the demands of public service, allow me an instant of spare time, I intend to devote every moment I can get to writing. Besides, when it is *you*, my brother, who urge me to do precisely this, in no uncertain fashion, I cannot possibly refuse to obey – because no man's wish or influence carries greater weight with me than yours.

The way in which I propose to meet your request is by evoking the memory of something that happened long ago. Though the precise details of what took place are not available, I believe the story fits in very well with what you want. It will also give you an opportunity to see what the most famous orators thought about the whole business of public speaking. You have often expressed to me the view that the essays which came out of my notebooks while I was still a boy, or a very young man, are hardly worthy of my present time of life, and the experience I gained from all the important cases I have handled.[1] And you have therefore urged me to compose some more careful and comprehensive study of the theme.

All the same, when we discuss the subject, I have noticed that we do not quite see eye to eye! For what I like to argue is that effective speaking requires extremely wide theoretical knowledge; whereas you prefer to maintain that oratory is entirely independent of systematic learning, and merely depends on a special kind of natural gift, supplemented by practice.

*

1. Cicero is referring to his study *On Invention* (c. 86 BC).

I have often thought it worth trying to find out why oratory has produced a smaller number of outstandingly distinguished and talented representatives than any other occupation. Examine and inquire anywhere you like, and you will find a whole host of people excelling in every sort of activity, and I do not mean merely trivial accomplishments but pursuits which approach any in the world in importance. Take, for example, the army. Anyone who had the idea of drawing up a priority list of professional careers, based on usefulness and importance, would obviously rank generals above orators. Yet it is an unmistakable fact that our own country alone has been able to offer almost innumerable examples of exceedingly able war leaders; but it has scarcely supplied even a minimum number of really good public speakers.

A comparison with statesmen shows the same result. Individuals possessing the shrewdness and wisdom necessary to conduct the government of the State have been forthcoming in considerable quantities even in our own day, and were even more abundant in our fathers' time, and proliferated still more in the age of our ancestors. Whole epochs, on the other hand, have failed to yield one single really good orator, and whole generations have scarcely even provided a tolerable one. Or take other pursuits, involving abstruse branches of learning; take the whole wide range of cultural studies. The result will be the same as when we were considering generals or competent senators. That is to say, you will find that all these subjects have produced a considerable multitude of first-class authorities. So this, again, makes one appreciate how scarce orators are – and how scarce they have always been.

And then consider the activity which we call by the Greek name of philosophy. You will recall that the most learned opinion identifies this as the creator and mother of every other noble art. Yet here, too, the distinguished practitioners have been very numerous indeed, and the diversity and scope of their studies have been correspondingly vast. I am not merely speaking about men who have devoted themselves to some single part of the field, but I am thinking of scholars whose scientific researches and logical investigations have embraced the greatest possible range they could command. Mathematics, again, are well known for dealing with exceedingly obscure questions, based on an art that is recondite, complex and rigorous. Yet this, too, is a branch of learning which has produced remarkable exponents in such numbers that one is sometimes tempted to think that almost everyone who has ever gone in for the subject with any seriousness at all has managed to hit whatever target he had happened to set himself. And the same is true of other subjects such as music and literature. These studies are almost boundless in scope, and yet it has been quite common for people who have really gone in for such topics thoroughly to achieve complete mastery of them.

I believe I should be right in saying that, if you compare all these noble arts and disciplines and the people who have gone in for them, the fields which have produced the smallest number of distinguished exponents are poetry and oratory. Anyone really good at either of these two pursuits is indeed hard to find; and when you consider who they have been a careful review of our own record here at Rome compels one to conclude that orators are far rarer even than poets; and the same applies to the Greeks. This must be regarded as all the more remarkable because unlike other subjects, which derive most of their material from specialized and hidden sources, the whole art of speaking lies open to anyone and everyone and is concerned with the ordinary life and customs and speech of mankind. Indeed, when you think of other arts, their very choicest aspects are actually those remotest from the understanding and appreciation of the uninitiated, while for orators, on the other hand, it is a major fault to depart from everyday language and the accepted usage of the community in general.

And yet it would be impossible to maintain either that the devotees of other arts are more numerous or that they have deeper satisfactions, higher hopes or more ample prizes to spur them on. I say nothing of Greece, which has always claimed to take the lead in eloquence. And I will not even refer to Athens, the birthplace of every single branch of learning, the centre where oratory of the very highest kind was both invented and perfected. But in our own city, too, no pursuit has ever flourished with greater vigour than public speaking.

For once our world empire was established, and enduring peace gave us some time to spare, almost every ambitious young man felt he ought to bestir himself to the best of his ability to become eloquent. At first, it is true, they were wholly ignorant of method, and had no inkling that there could be such a thing as rules; their attainments were no more than what natural ability and hard thinking were able to achieve. But then later on, when they had heard the Greek orators and learnt about Greek literature and procured Greek instructors,[1] our people became quite unbelievably keen speakers.

Lawsuits abounded; and they dealt with extremely important and varied issues. And this state of affairs gave the orators such incentives that whatever degree of learning any of them may have been able to acquire through his own efforts was now supplemented by extensive practice. This proved to be of greater value than all the precepts of the teachers put together. And even in those days the rewards, in the form of popularity and wealth and position, were already as outstanding as they are now. And besides – as a great many things go to show – our countrymen have far excelled other people in the world in natural ability. In view of all these considerations, we may well feel surprised that the

1. The reforming tribunes Tiberius and Gaius Sempronius Gracchus (d. 133, 122 BC) were taught by Diophanes of Mytilene and Menelaus of Marathon respectively.

entire histories of prolonged epochs and profoundly varying conditions and multitudinous cities have thrown up such an extraordinary small number of able speakers.

*

But the fact of the matter is that oratory is a much more considerable activity, and depends on a far wider range of different arts and branches of study, than people imagine. The trouble cannot be lack of incentive. A great number of persons want to learn how to speak; there are teachers in abundance; outstanding talent is available; the legal issues that come up display an infinite diversity; and the rewards, as I said, are truly splendid. In view of all these circumstances, there can only be one possible reason for the scarcity of speakers of any competence: the incredible vastness and difficulty of the subject.

For, first, one has to acquire knowledge about a formidable quantity of different matters. To hold forth without this information will just mean a silly flow of windy verbiage. And then one has to be able to choose one's words well, and arrange them cleverly. It is also essential to have an intimate understanding of every emotion which nature has given to mankind: it is in the processes of calming or exciting the feelings of an audience that both the theory and practice of oratory find their fullest expression. Other requirements include a certain sparkle and wit, and the culture appropriate to an educated man, and a terse promptitude both in repartee and in attack. A sensitive, civilized lightness of touch is also desirable. One's memory, too, must be capable of retaining a host of precedents, indeed the complete history of past times. Nor is it by any means advisable to be ignorant of the law and existing statutes.

As regards delivery, I am sure I need not go into a great deal of detail. The principal relevant factors include physical deportment, gestures of the arms, facial expression, voice production, and the avoidance of monotony. How important that last consideration is, we can see from a less serious art – I refer to the stage. For although all actors go to great pains to regulate their expressions and their voices and the movements of their body, all the same it is undeniable that there are extremely few whom it is tolerable to go on watching and hearing at any length; and there has never been a time when it was otherwise.

To go back to the memory, this serves as a universal treasure house, and it has to be given the safe keeping of every single aspect of the speech one is going to make, all its substance and all its words. Without this precaution, however remarkable all these items were when the orator originally conceived them, they will one and all be totally wasted.

So there is no longer any need to wonder why orators are rare. They have to display a whole host of different qualifications: and to possess even a single one of them is a considerable achievement. So let us urge our sons, and everyone else whose glory and reputation are dear to us, to appreciate the gigantic scope and range of this activity. They must not suppose they can achieve their object by just relying on rules or on teachers or on ordinary exercises. It is not beyond their power to get where they want to; but they must use different methods altogether.

I hold the view that no one can be the complete and perfect speaker unless he has learnt about *all* the important subjects and arts that exist. For he needs such a background in order to enrich what he says, and give it depth. Unless he has all this material at his disposal, thoroughly comprehended and absorbed, every word he utters will be vapid and childish. Certainly I will not burden orators with the demand that they should be omniscient; and least of all would I insist on such a thing from our own speakers here at Rome, who have to operate amid all the bustle of city life. All the same, the term 'orator', as I understand it, and the art of good speaking which he professes, does seem to me to imply an undertaking and a promise that, whatever subject he is called upon to deal with, both the form and substance of his performance will attain an impressively high quality.

I know most people will regard this as an immense and indeed endless undertaking. I also recall that the Greeks, who not only possessed great talents and learning but had at their disposal ample spare time for study, have divided up the field of knowledge into separate branches. With regard to oratory, this has meant that no one individual was expected to work over the entire field by himself. For what these Greeks did was to pick out, and isolate from other types of speaking, the sort of speeches which are concerned with legal cases and public debates: and this was the only branch of the activity which, according to their definition, remained the orator's concern.

In the present book I shall follow their definition and deal with this judicial and deliberate kind of oratory. That is to say, I shall restrict myself to those elements which the experts, after prolonged investigations and arguments, have almost unanimously agreed to ascribe to this category of speaking. However, I do not propose to go right back to the cradle and bring out all over again that string of precepts I used to go in for when I was a boy. What I propose to do instead is to set down a discussion which took place, so I was told, a number of years ago. The participants were certain compatriots of ours who were unrivalled for their eminent position in our national affairs; and, above all, they possessed a unique reputation for eloquence.

Not that I underestimate the guidance which Greek rhetoricians and professors have handed down to us. But their maxims have been published and made generally available, and no new version that I might be able to offer would add to the elegance and clarity with which they themselves have already set these matters out. So you will forgive me, brother, I expect, if instead of speaking about the Greeks I devote my attention to these authoritative countrymen of our own, whom our fellow-Romans have judged the greatest of our speakers.

*

I remember being told how, when Philippus was consul, he furiously attacked the policy of our leading statesmen at the time; and the position of the tribune Drusus, who was speaking up for the Senate, seemed seriously shaken and undermined.[1] Lucius Licinius Crassus, I was informed, took the opportunity of the Roman Games to retire to his country house at Tusculum, on the pretext of restoring his energies. Quintus Mucius Scaevola the Augur, the man who had formerly been his father-in-law,[2] went there too, it is said, and so did Marcus Antonius who was Crassus's close political ally and personal friend. Crassus was accompanied on his journey from Rome by two great friends of Drusus, young men whom the older generation hoped would become notable defenders of the senatorial cause. One of these youths was Gaius Aurelius Cotta, who at the time was a candidate for the tribuneship; the other was Publius Sulpicius Rufus, thought likely to stand for the same office in the following year.

*

On the first day this group conferred together at great length until very late in the evening. They were discussing the current crisis, and the political situation in general; indeed, that was why they had come. Later on, Cotta reported that the three ex-consuls who were present spoke in truly prophetic fashion about the lamentable signs of the times. Not one of the evils that subsequently befell Rome, he declared, had they failed

1. Lucius Marcius Philippus (consul 91 BC) opposed the attempts of Marcus Livius Drusus (tribune) to heal the split between Senate and knights and to appease Italian unrest.

2. See Genealogical Table (I), p. 360.

to foresee, right on to times far ahead in the future. However, when they had completed their discussion, Crassus behaved with such charming tact that after they had finished their baths and taken their places at table, the melancholy atmosphere of the earlier conversation was completely dispelled. He made himself most agreeable and amusing: after a day which had rivalled the Senate-house for solemnity, the dinner-party was truly worthy of his Tusculan retreat.

On the following day, Cotta continued, the older men took things quietly to begin with, and then came out into the garden-walk. Whereupon Scaevola, after walking round once or twice, remarked, 'Crassus, why don't we imitate Socrates in Plato's *Phaedrus*? What reminded me of it was this plane-tree of yours, with its spreading branches which cast a deep shadow over this spot, like the plane whose shade Socrates once enjoyed (a tree, incidentally, which surely owed its dimensions more to Plato's eloquent pen than to any "little rivulet" which in sober fact may have watered its roots!).[1] Moreover Socrates, before delivering himself of those utterances which the philosophers have exalted as divine, had proceeded to throw himself on the grass: and since the feet *he* relieved by so doing were very hard ones, would it not be even more justifiable for these feet of mine to obtain similar relief?'

'Yes, certainly,' replied Crassus; 'and let us make things more comfortable still.' And so he called for cushions, and they all sat down on the seats beneath the plane-tree. When they were settled, according to Cotta's account, Crassus thought it would be a good thing to provide some relaxation after the serious discussions of the day before. And so he launched a debate about the profession of oratory. He began by saying that Sulpicius and Cotta needed no exhortations from himself but, on the contrary, deserved his congratulations, because they had already acquired a degree of skill

1. Plato, *Phaedrus*, 229 A, 230 B.

which ranked them above all their contemporaries and which, indeed, invited comparison with men much older than themselves. 'It seems to me the most marvellous gift upon earth,' he commented, 'to be able to employ one's powers of speech to rivet men's attention, so that their wills are subjected to one's own and they are persuaded and dissuaded in whatever direction one wishes. In all free countries, and particularly in those enjoying peace and tranquillity, oratory has always flourished exceedingly and reigned supreme. It is one of the most striking things that can happen when all the infinite multitudes of human beings (not one of whom, by natural endowment, is potentially lacking in the faculty) on very rare occasions indeed produces an individual quite in a class by himself or at most with only a very few others like him: a person who has the capacity to give truly effective expression to the gift.

'Besides, I can think of nothing more agreeable to the brain and ear than a speech adorned and embellished with wise thoughts and fine language. And it is indeed a uniquely impressive and imposing experience to see the tumult of an enormous crowd, the convictions of a conscientious bench of judges, the solemn judgements of the Senate, all completely transfigured by the eloquence of one single man. Think, moreover, of the *power* an orator possesses: power to rescue the suppliant, to raise up the afflicted, to bestow salvation, to dispel danger, to preserve citizens' rights; what in the whole world could be more noble, more generous, more princely? Once you possess the perpetual access to weapons which will give you the means to defend yourself, furnish you with the opportunity to stand up for good men, enable you to challenge the enemies of your country, grant you the ability to strike back when you are attacked, then, surely, you are armed to perform the most necessary tasks in the world.

'But now, for a change, turn your gaze right away from the Forum, and all its lawcourts and public meetings and senatorial sessions. Consider your leisure hours instead. While you are enjoying these, what more agreeable and civilized occupation could you have than witty, well-informed talk? The one special advantage we enjoy over animals is our power to speak with one another, to express our thoughts in words. For this reason it is a peculiarly satisfactory experience for a man to take pleasure in conversation and seek to excel at it. He will then be excelling other human beings in the very respect in which human beings surpass animals.

'However, I must pass on to the highest achievements of human eloquence. For there is no other force in the whole world which could have been strong enough to gather scattered mankind together in one place, to transplant human beings from a barbarous life in the wilderness to a civilized social system, to establish organized communities, to equip them with laws and judicial safeguards and civic rights.[1] I could give almost numberless illustrations, but instead I will sum the whole matter up in one brief sentence. When a consummate orator offers his listeners wise guidance, he is not merely furthering his own personal ambitions: he is also protecting the safety of a host of other people as well. Indeed, he is protecting the entire Roman nation.

'So I urge you to continue as you have started, young men. You have set your hands to this occupation: get on with it. For by so doing you will have the power to gain glory for yourselves, to do good to your friends, and to perform splendid service to the State.'

*

Then, in his usual pleasant way, Scaevola started to speak. 'With most of what you have asserted, Crassus,' he said, 'I am in complete agreement; and I certainly have not the slightest

1. The idea that speech was the basis of civilization had been developed by the Athenian rhetorician and educationalist Isocrates (p. 229), *Nicocles*, 5ff., *Antidosis*, 253ff.

desire to disparage the oratorical talents or reputation either of my father-in-law Laelius[1] or of yourself, who married my daughter.

'All the same, you made two points which I do not feel able to accept. First, your pronouncement that it was orators who first founded human communities and, after their foundation, often maintained them as well; and secondly, your assertion that the orator cannot restrict himself to the Forum and public meetings and courts of justice and the Senate, but is also obliged to achieve excellence over all the entire range of speech and culture. Human beings, we know, ceased to be scattered in mountains and woodlands and began to shut themselves up within walled cities. But no one is going to agree with you that they did all this because eloquent speakers talked them into it. Obviously the reason why they collected together was because clever men decided that this was the best thing to do. The same applies to all the advantageous consequences that followed from establishing states and keeping them in being. These results cannot have been due just to fluent and elegant speakers. Surely the particular qualities that distinguished the people who made these decisions were wisdom and courage, not eloquence. Wise judgement, not talent as a speaker, was what enabled the great Romulus to gather together his shepherds and refugees, and arrange marriages with the Sabines, and suppress the hostile neighbours. Can you honestly claim that Numa Pompilius, or Servius Tullius, or all the other kings who made so many wonderful contributions to the development of our State, possessed even so much as one single trace of eloquence? And afterwards, too, when the kings were expelled, it is clear enough that their ejection was the work of Lucius Brutus's brain, not his tongue; and all the other events which then followed, one after another, were triumphs of wise planning,

1. See *On Friendship*.

without oratorical gifts making any contribution whatsoever.[1]

'As a matter of fact, I could easily quote illustrations both from Roman and foreign history to demonstrate that men of outstandingly skilful speech have damaged communities more often than they have helped them. But let me just offer two examples. With the exception of yourself, Crassus, and of Antonius here, I believe the best speakers I have ever heard were the tribunes Tiberius and Gaius Gracchus. Their father, on the other hand, possessed no talent in this direction whatsoever. Yet he had been a man of sound sense and integrity, and on a number of occasions, especially when he was censor, he had performed great services for the Republic when he had the freedmen transferred to the city tribes.[2] But it was not by any elaborate flow of oratory that he attained these results. On the contrary, he did whatever was needed by a nod, and a mere word. And yet had it not been for what he achieved, our government, which we are finding it hard enough to keep going today, would have completely collapsed long ago.

'The sons of Gracchus, on the other hand, were fine speakers, equipped with every oratorical qualification that nature or training could provide. Because of their father's wisdom and their grandfather's military victories, Rome, as they found it, was prospering exceedingly. Yet they managed to bring our flourishing nation to ruin: and this they did by their eloquence, which according to you guides states so splendidly!

1. The traditional dates of the reigns of Romulus's legendary successor Numa Pompilius and of the semi-legendary Servius Tullus were 715–672 and 578–534 BC. Lucius Junius Brutus was believed to have expelled Tarquinius Superbus and to have become consul in 509.

2. Tiberius Sempronius Gracchus, father of the tribunes Tiberius and Gaius (p. 142), was one of the censors of 169 BC who restricted the rights and voting power of freedmen by limiting them (unless they possessed a property qualification of 30,000 sesterces) to a single one of the thirty-five tribes (the urban *tribus Esquilina*). Freedmen had earlier been restricted to the four urban tribes, but in 189 and 179 BC this rule had been to some extent relaxed.

'And then think of our ancient legislation and the customs of our ancestors. Consider, for example, the institution of augury, over which you and I, Crassus, preside, greatly to the national advantage.[1] Reflect also upon all our other religious rituals and ceremonies. And what about the law, the occupation in which members of our family have so long been engaged? They certainly did not need eloquence to help them! Indeed, the whole profession of the orators has contributed nothing whatever towards the creation or comprehension or practice of legal affairs. I retain the clear impression that Servius Galba, who spoke like a god, and Marcus Aemilius Porcina and Gaius Carbo, whom you yourself spoke successfully against in court when you were still a very young man, all remained utterly unaware of our statutes, completely at a loss in dealing with our ancestral institutions, and, in a word, thoroughly ignorant of the law.[2] And when you yourself, Crassus, learnt law from my family, you did not pursue these studies because it was something that a speaker ought to do; you pursued them because you found the subject interesting. (Apart from you, our contemporaries have so little legal knowledge that one sometimes feels ashamed.)

'Then, at the end of your statement, you put forward the claim that an orator ought to be able to speak with full understanding on any subject whatsoever; and you spoke as though such a claim were perfectly legitimate! Had we not been here on your own personal territory I should certainly not have felt prepared to put up with this. On the contrary, you would have found me taking the lead in a mass move either to oppose you by injunction, or to challenge you to prove your title for having wantonly seized other people's

1. Cicero, *On Divination* (44 BC), sets out the arguments on both sides of this question.

2. On Servius Sulpicius Galba and Gaius Papirius Carbo, see pp. 318, 144. Marcus Aemilius Lepidus Porcina (consul 137 BC) was described by Cicero as the first man to speak artistically.

possessions. People would have come flocking to bring law-suits against you – first and foremost all the disciples of Pythagoras and Democritus,[1] and then every other natural philosopher, too, would put in his own individual claim: a whole host of accomplished and authoritative speakers, who would assuredly lose you your deposit! Great troops of other philosophers, too, would assail you, going right back to their originator and fountain-head, Socrates himself. They would complain that you had learnt nothing about what is good and evil in life, or about human emotions and conduct, or the theories about how people ought to live. It would seem to them that you had carried out no investigations on any of these subjects, and indeed that your knowledge in all these fields is non-existent.

'Then, after this combined attack, one individual school after another would launch action after action against you. The Academy would be after you, compelling you to deny anything and everything you had said. Our friends the Stoics would make sure you were firmly entangled in all the snares their arguments and questionings could contrive. The Peripatetics, too, would demonstrate that the people one ought to ask for the aids and ornaments of eloquence, which you regard as the orator's special property, are themselves! And they would remind you that Aristotle and Theophrastus wrote more sensibly, as well as more copiously, on these subjects than all the professors of oratory put together. About the mathematicians and literary experts and musicians I need say nothing; because it is obvious that their subjects have nothing whatever to do with oratory.

'So in my view, Crassus, you have got to avoid making such sweeping and abundant claims. Surely what you are able to guarantee is valuable enough: that when you present a case in the courts you can make it sound better and more

1. See pp. 22, 106.

plausible than your adversary's argument; that your speech in a public meeting or senatorial debate will carry more weight than anyone else's; and, finally, that you can convince intelligent listeners that you are speaking eloquently, and make ignorant people believe you are speaking the truth! If you can achieve anything more than this, I am sure it will not be the orator who is doing it, but Crassus – because he happens to have some particular gift of his own, which other speakers lack.'

'Yes, Scaevola,' replied Crassus. 'I know the Greeks make a habit of putting forward and debating this sort of view. I had the opportunity of listening to their principal experts when I visited Athens as quaestor from Macedonia.[1] The Academy was said to be at its best at that time, with Charmadas and Clitomachus and Aeschines as its directors. And Metrodorus was in Athens, too. Like the others, he had been a particularly keen pupil of the famous Carneades himself, who was reputed to be the most vigorous and fluent orator of them all. Mnesarchus, too, a pupil of your friend Panaetius, was in his prime, and so was Diodorus, who studied with Critolaus the Peripatetic.[2] And many other famous and distinguished philosophers were there as well. But they were quite unanimous, I noticed, in declaring that the orator should be

1. Crassus was quaestor in Asia (western Asia Minor) in 110 BC. He may have returned via Macedonia; or Cicero has made a slip.

2. Carneades of Cyrene visited Rome in 155 BC and was head of the Academy until 137. He died in 129. Charmadas was a pupil of Carneades. Clitomachus of Carthage, originally named Hasdrubal, succeeded Carneades and recorded his teaching; Cicero used Clitomachus's work in his treatise *On the Nature of the Gods*. Then came Aeschines of Neapolis (Naples). Metrodorus of Stratonicea, though at first an Epicurean (like Metrodorus of Lampsacus), later joined the Academy. Mnesarchus succeeded the famous Panaetius of Rhodes (p. 27) as director of the Stoic school at the beginning of the first century BC. Diodorus succeeded Critolaus of Phaselis (who was with Carneades at Rome) as leader of the Peripatetics.

excluded from governmental affairs altogether. They were determined not to let him have anything to do with any of the more important branches of knowledge and learning, relegating him to lawcourts and trivial public meetings, and penning him down there, like a slave put to the mill.

'Personally, however, I thought this was going too far. Nor did I agree with the man who actually invented this whole type of discussion that we are having now, and was himself far and away the most authoritative and eloquent speaker of all. I refer to Plato: whose *Gorgias* I read pretty carefully with Charmadas during those days at Athens.[1] I must say I was very intrigued by the way in which Plato kept on making fun of orators, although he himself, it seemed to me, was the most accomplished orator of all.

'But controversy about what the word actually means has long been a bother to the poor Greeks, who find argument more absorbing than truth. You have suggested that we ought to restrict an orator to speaking as best he can before the praetor or judges or the Assembly or the Senate. All the same, even under that definition, he has got to be allowed to possess a certain number of qualifications. For even if he limits himself to this restricted range of activities he is not going to command the necessary skill and expertise unless he first acquires extensive experience in public affairs, and a mastery of our ordinances and customs and law, and a knowledge of human nature and character. Without this information, no orator can even begin to conduct his cases properly; but once he is equipped with it, it would be difficult to name an important branch of study that is outside his range. What you say seems to be that all an orator has to do is to arrange his speech properly, and make it attractive and fluent. But how is he going to achieve even that much if he is not allowed the

1. Cicero's work *On the Orator* may to some extent be a deliberate attempt to reply to Plato's estimate of oratory in the *Gorgias*.

knowledge which you are refusing him? How can anyone be a good speaker unless he understands what he is talking about?

*

'If, then, the great natural philosopher Democritus was an attractive speaker – as he is reliably said to have been – his subject matter belonged to him as a physicist, but I maintain that the attractiveness of his language must be ascribed to him in the capacity of an orator. And if Plato, as I admit, spoke like a god about matters far removed from political debate, if Aristotle and Theophrastus and Carneades, each on their own themes, held forth with eloquence and charm and grace, then, granted that the substance of what they were saying relates to other branches of study, yet their actual style is the peculiar product of this art of oratory, which is what we are considering today.

'And indeed it is clear enough that some of the philosophers who wrote about these topics possessed dreary, feeble styles. One of them was Chrysippus. Yet he is regarded as having been exceedingly clever;[1] and his renown as a philosopher has not been damaged in the slightest by his failure to express himself well. For the gift of eloquence, which he lacked, has nothing to do with philosophy at all: it belongs to another activity altogether.

'But how, in fact, is it possible to distinguish between a good speaker and a bad one – what rules should we employ to define the differences between a fluent, eloquent orator and the performer who is weak, monotonous and unattractive? The distinction, evidently, is a stylistic one; the particular characteristic of a good speaker is a harmonious, attractive manner, marked by a certain artistry and polish.

'All the same, unless the speaker grasps and understands what he is talking about, his speech will be worthless – and may well

1. Chrysippus of Soli succeeded Cleanthes as head of the Stoic school in 232 BC.

be received with ridicule. However beautiful and alluring his words may be, if he just pours them out in a meaningless flow, without sense or knowledge behind them, he will be behaving like a fool. Yet whatever the topic may be, whatever the branch of knowledge involved, the orator, if he has taken the same amount of trouble to master what he is trying to talk about as he would have taken if he were getting up a case for a client, will be able to express it better and more attractively than the specialist from whom the actual material originated.

'And now to answer the argument that there are certain themes and ways of thinking to which the orator ought to restrict himself: namely, those which you can find behind the railings of the lawcourts and nowhere else. Well, I am quite prepared to concede that we speakers spend a large part of our time in such work. Nevertheless, even this sort of occupation includes a good many aspects which those who profess to give instruction in rhetoric neither teach nor understand.

'For example, it is widely appreciated that an orator's special strength lies in his capacity to rouse men's hearts to anger, hatred, and indignation, or to soothe these violent emotions and transform them into gentleness and compassion. But he will never be able to produce the right words to achieve these results unless he has a thorough understanding of human nature and psychology, and knows all the ways in which people's minds are susceptible to persuasion and dissuasion. All this, surely, must be regarded as the special province of philosophy; and the orator, if he takes my advice, will never attempt to dispute its claim. For these are precisely the subjects on which the philosophers have concentrated their attention, and he must concede their special knowledge. But the fact remains that all this learning continues to be of no value whatever until he, the orator, has put it into words. That is what he claims to be able to do, and, as I said before, it is the proper achievement of his métier: the creation of a style that is dignified and attractive, and well adapted to the feelings and intelligences of his audience.

'I admit that Aristotle and Theophrastus have written on these matters, although they were not orators at all, but philosophers. But I would ask you to note, Scaevola, that this is really an argument in my favour. I, for my part, do not ask the philosophers to lend me the features they share with the orator. But when they discuss any of these oratorical subjects, see how ready they are to admit that it falls within the orator's sphere: accustomed as they are to naming their writings after the theme they deal with, the name they choose to define these treatises on how to speak is *Rhetoric*. The converse process also sometimes occurs: an orator, that is to say, will have occasion to make some general reflection about the immortal gods, piety, concord, friendship; about the rights shared in common among citizens or all human beings or nations; about equity, moderation, generosity, or other virtues. When this happens, however, I am perfectly sure that any and every philosophical school and sect will at once raise the cry that these matters belong to themselves, and are not the orator's business in any way whatsoever.

'By all means, if they wish, let the philosophers get on with discussing these matters in their own secluded corners, to pass an idle hour. All the same, the man who will have to set forth, with all the power and attractiveness he can muster, the themes which these philosophers have been discoursing about (in their tame and bloodless way) is the orator. I used to debate these questions at Athens face to face with the philosophers themselves. This was under the impulsion of our friend Marcus Marcellus who is now curule aedile and would surely be taking part in our conversation today if he were not at this moment organizing the Games. For even as a very young man, he already showed great enthusiasm for the subject.

*

'And now let us consider institutions such as legislation, war and peace, the position of our allies, the levying of taxes, and the legal rights assigned to the various categories of citizen according to rank and age. We may accept the Greek tradition that Lycurgus and Solon knew more about such things than those superlative orators Hyperides and Demosthenes – though Lycurgus and Solon were eloquent speakers too.[1] And let us accept, also, our own fellow-countrymen's contention that the Board of Ten, who compiled the Twelve Tables[2] and must surely have been very able men, should be ranked, as regards this sort of knowledge, above Servius Galba and your father-in-law Gaius Laelius, although both of these are well known to have been orators of the highest rank.[3] For I am always prepared to agree that certain activities must be regarded as the speciality of anyone who has devoted his whole attention to their understanding and practice. But the complete and perfect orator I define as the man who is capable of speaking on *all* subjects with versatile thoroughness.

'Even in dealing with themes which by universal consent belong to the orator's sphere, it is often necessary to make use of some fact derived not just from the daily experience of the courts (which is all you will permit the orator to know about) but from some more abstruse branch of knowledge. I do not see, for example, how someone can make a speech attacking or defending a general if he understands nothing whatever about military affairs, and does not even know, perhaps, the

1. Lycurgus was the legendary founder of the Spartan code (p. 55), and Solon the statesman and poet of early sixth-century Athens (p. 305). Hyperides and Demosthenes died in 332 and 322 BC respectively. On Demosthenes see also above, p. 106. Marcellus is otherwise unknown.

2. The Twelve Tables, the earliest Roman code of law, were believed to have been drawn up by a special board of ten commissioners in 451–450 BC.

3. On them see p. 318, 173.

geographical location of the relevant lands and seas.[1] How can he address the Assembly for or against a bill, or speak in the Senate on some political issue, unless he has a thorough theoretical and practical knowledge of affairs of state? And then take that business of inflaming and calming his audience's emotions and passions which is so extremely important for a speaker. How can his words achieve this until he has first made the most careful researches into every theory the philosophers have ever put forward about human psychology and ethics?

'On my next point I am not at all sure I am going to convince you. However, I am going to speak my mind. I grant you that physics, and mathematics, and the other specialized sciences which you spoke of just now, do belong peculiarly to the professors of the individual studies in question. Yet it still remains true that anyone who wants to display the fullest significance of these sciences cannot possibly do so without calling upon the resources of the orator.

'I admit that Philon, the architect who built an arsenal for the Athenians, is also understood to have supplied them with an eloquent description of his project. But if he did so, his eloquence came to him not as an architect but as an orator.[2] In the same way, if Marcus Antonius here had been called upon to speak for Hermodorus about dockyard construction, first he would have got up his case from his client and then he would certainly have made a very attractive and thorough speech – but the skill he put into it would not have come from the science of dock-building at all.[3] Asclepiades, too, whom we

1. Cicero himself wrote a work on geography, the *Chorographia*, of which only fragments survive.

2. Philon of Eleusis (4th century BC) designed the arsenal at the Piraeus. His books on the subject and on the proportions of sacred buildings are now lost.

3. He may be the same man as a Hermodorus of Salamis who built the temple of Mars in the Flaminian Circus of Rome, and was for a long time the only Greek architect employed in that city.

know as a doctor and a friend, was the most eloquent member of his profession.[1] But his excellent speeches were the product not of his medical learning, but of his oratorical gifts.

'Socrates used to say that every man who is called upon to speak about a subject he understands is capable of achieving eloquence. That sounds plausible enough; but it happens not to be true. It would be nearer the truth to say, first, that no one can be eloquent on a matter he knows nothing about, and, secondly, that even if he does know the subject to perfection, he can still only speak eloquently about it if he knows how to dress his remarks in an attractive style.

*

'Now for an attempt at a general, comprehensive definition of what an orator ought to be. In my opinion, he will merit this splendid designation provided that, whatever the topic of discussion, he is able to display sound knowledge, and proper arrangement of his material, and a good style, and a retentive memory, and an impressive delivery. Some people may think that when I said 'whatever the topic' I was aiming too high. In that case, they can trim and prune the phrase according to their taste. But I shall propose to stick to my point. I am prepared to grant that a speaker will sometimes be ignorant of the other arts and branches of knowledge, and that his knowledge will be restricted to deliberative and judicial oratory. But if he is called upon to take on some theme he knows nothing about, once he has picked up its technicalities from the experts he will speak about the subject far better than they themselves ever could.

'Imagine, for instance, that Sulpicius here is required to make a speech about military affairs. Well, first he will make

1. Asclepiades of Prusa, physician and atomic philosopher, lived on until c. 40 BC.

the necessary inquiries from my relative Gaius Marius.[1] Then, once he has got the information, he will make even Marius feel that he himself knows less about the subject than the orator does! Or if Sulpicius has to talk about the law, you are the person he will consult; and although you are the supreme authority in this field he will express what he learnt from you even better than you could ever express it yourself.

'Or perhaps he might be confronted with a case in which he had to offer pronouncements about human nature, people's failings and passions, moderation and self-control and other moral qualities, or the acceptance of pain and death. These, admittedly, are things an orator ought to know something about. However, the man faced with making such a speech can always, if he thinks fit, seek the advice of Sextus Pompeius, who is a learned philosopher.[2] And in any case, whoever he consults, and whatever the subject may be, the orator will unquestionably give it a very great deal more attractive expression than his informant ever could.

*

'Philosophy, as we know, has three branches, relating to the mysteries of nature, the subtleties of logic, and the life and behaviour of human beings. All right then, if Sulpicius will listen to me, this is what I suggest: let us agree to give up the first of these branches as a concession to human laziness. But the third has always been the orator's special sphere, and unless, on his behalf, we keep a firm hold of this, we shall be depriving him of the one province in which he has a real chance of distinguishing himself. For the fact is that this entire field of human life and conduct is something which he ought to study very thoroughly indeed. The other subjects are dif-

1. The adoptive(?) son of Marius (Gaius Marius, consul 82 BC), he had married Crassus's daughter Licinia. See Genealogical Table (I), p. 360.

2. Sextus Pompeius, Stoic and mathematician, the uncle of Cnaeus Pompeius Magnus (Pompey the Great).

ferent. Even if he has not learnt about them himself he only has to get the necessary information collected and handed over to him, and then he will be able to transfigure them by the eloquence which is his personal contribution.

'Learned men accept the fact that a man who knew nothing about astronomy composed fine and beautiful poetry about the sky and stars: I refer to Aratus. It is also agreed that Nicander of Colophon, although he had not the slightest acquaintance with country life, wrote brilliantly about rural affairs. His skill, of course, was that of a poet not a farmer.[1] And so, by the same token, what is to stop an orator, once he has got up a subject for some special purpose and occasion, from handling it with consummate eloquence? Poets, after all, have a lot in common with an orator. They are slightly more tied down in respect of form, and possess more freedom in matters of vocabulary; but in many other points of style they are his allies, and resemble him a good deal. Indeed, in one feature, the two sorts of writer are practically identical. That is to say, poets set no limits or boundaries to their sphere of action, but reserve for themselves the full right to range wherever they please with complete ease and freedom – and the orator does just the same.

'I claimed, you will remember, that he ought to be well qualified not only in every type of speaking but in every single branch of culture as well. And your comment was, Scaevola, that you would never have felt able to tolerate such an assertion unless you had been on my own territory.

'However, I should naturally never have made a claim of such a kind if I had seen myself as the perfect orator I was thinking of! But I remember something Gaius Lucilius used to say – an individual, incidentally, who did not care for you

1. Aratus of Soli (d.c. 240 BC) wrote the *Phaenomena*, which Cicero translated when he was a young man, and Nicander of Colophon (mid second century) was the author of the *Georgica*, of which fragments survive.

very much, and was for that reason less intimate with myself than he would have liked to be.[1] Well, Lucilius, who was a learned and very civilized person, used to express the opinion that no one should be counted as an orator unless he has a thorough acquaintance with the subjects an educated man ought to know. It is not so much that one actually needs to draw upon these themes while one is making a speech. The trouble is that if we are ignorant of such topics it very soon becomes painfully evident!

'One could draw an analogy with the technique of playing ball. During the course of any particular game, it is very likely that the players will not have to give any display of the actual movements they learnt in their training school. Nevertheless, the way they move their bodies shows very clearly whether they have ever performed the exercises in question. It is the same with sculptors, too. Even if, at a given moment, they are not making any use of the instruction they once received in draughtsmanship, it is always very easy to see whether they have been taught the subject. And the same applies to speeches in lawcourts and public meetings and the Senate. Even if, outwardly, the other arts are not brought into play, it is the simplest thing in the world to detect whether the speaker is just ignorantly floundering about, or whether, before he embarked on speech-making, he has really been trained in the full range of liberal studies.'

*

Scaevola smiled. 'Crassus,' he said, 'I'm going to stop trying to argue against you. For although what you have just been saying was ostensibly directed *against* the view I had put forward, in some ingenious fashion you have managed to agree with me about the things I took away from the orator;

1. Gaius Lucilius the poet and satirist. It is not known why he disapproved of Scaevola the Augur, of whose father-in-law Laelius he was a close friend.

and yet at the same time you have somehow or other contrived to get hold of them again and hand them back to him to keep!

'What you say about these wider studies reminds me of the occasion when I visited Rhodes as praetor. There I was able to discuss with Apollonius, that great professor of rhetoric, the things I had been learning from Panaetius.[1] Apollonius, as was his manner, made fun of philosophy and poured scorn on the whole thing, talking, on the whole, more wittily than seriously. But you, on the other hand, have been careful not to belittle any art or branch of learning whatever. What you have done instead is merely to demote every single one of them into being the attendants and maid-servants of the orator!

'My own view is this. If there was ever a man who had mastered every single one of these subjects, and if that same person simultaneously possessed the power of attractive self-expression, there is no doubt whatever that he would be a remarkable and outstanding individual. But if such a person exists, or has ever existed, or ever could exist, then unmistakably you yourself would be the man! For everyone would agree with me – with due respect to our other friends who are here today – that the truly outstanding nature of your reputation really means that no one else has been left the possibility of acquiring any fame at all. And if even you yourself, in spite of your thorough knowledge of practical law and politics, have fallen short of mastering all that additional erudition which you regard as obligatory for the orator, ought we not to conclude that you are expecting from him more than the realities of the situation could ever allow?'

But Crassus had a reply to this. 'I again ask you to remember,' he said, 'that I have not been speaking of my own

1. Apollonius of Alabanda, founder of a school of rhetoric at Rhodes, was visited there by Scaevola the Augur in 121. Apollonius was probably succeeded by Molon, who was one of Cicero's teachers.

qualifications. What we are discussing is the perfect orator. As for myself, I have never acquired any learning, or had a chance to. Before I had any opportunity to tackle the theory of the subject at all, I was plunged straight into practice. Speeches in the courts, candidatures for office, the multifarious obligations of a public figure, the help one has to give one's friends – all these activities took up every bit of my energies before I could even begin to get the slightest idea of the wider implications. And so I have certainly lacked both knowledge and spare time – and indeed I must also admit that I have not really felt that keen desire to get on with studying! In spite of this, you are still kind enough to detect some merits in me, and to suggest that the ability is there. But if so, just imagine if there should emerge some individual who possessed my degree of ability, or more, combined with all the knowledge that I have never had the occasion to acquire. Think of the quality and stature of the orator you would have then!'

'In my opinion, Crassus,' answered Antonius, 'you prove your case. I entirely agree that if anyone managed to absorb every subject and every branch of knowledge, his speaking would benefit enormously. But, in the first place, this is hard to achieve, especially as we lead such extremely busy lives. There is also the danger that we might get drawn away from our traditional use of a style adjusted to the requirements of the lawcourts – in other words to the needs of the general public. For the eloquence of the people you were just talking about seems to me to belong to quite a different category. Certainly, they spoke attractively and convincingly, whether their subject was natural philosophy or human behaviour. But their methods of delivery are polished and florid, suggesting the oil of the training school masseurs rather than the rough and tumble of politics and the courts.

*

'My own introduction to Greek literature came late in life,

and was not very extensive at that. The occasion was my journey to take up the governorship of Cilicia.[1] On the way I stopped for some days at Athens, because weather prevented my ship from sailing. I spent all my time there in the company of Greek scholars, more or less the people you were just talking about. Somehow or other the report had spread among them that I, like yourself, have to do with important legal cases. And so all these learned individuals came to exchange views, to the best of their ability, about the functions and methods of the orator.

'Some of these Greeks, including Mnesarchus whom you quoted, expressed the opinion that the man we describe as an orator is just an artisan who happens to have a quick and practised tongue. They went on to argue that no one can be a real orator unless he is a wise man, that eloquence, being the art of speaking well, must be classified as one of the virtues, that a person who possesses one of the virtues possesses them all, and that every virtue is equal and equivalent to every other. It follows, therefore, that an eloquent speaker possesses all the virtues and is a wise man. However this seemed a thorny, arid sort of logic, which bore no relation to the way in which we Romans think. Charmadas, on the other hand, was a good deal more forthcoming on the subject. Certainly, he avoided defining what he himself believed, because of the inherited tradition of the Academy which requires its members to speak for the opposition in any and every debate. Yet on this occasion he set out to demonstrate that the people who are called rhetoricians and teach rules of speaking have no real grasp of the subject at all, and that no one can become a good orator unless he has mastered the doctrines discovered by the philosophers.

'Other Athenians, talented speakers with political and legal

1. In 102 BC Marcus Antonius the Orator commanded an expedition against the pirates and contributed to the establishment of the province of Cilicia (southeastern Asia Minor).

backgrounds, refused to accept this point of view. One of them was Menedemus, who recently came to Rome as my guest.[1] During the discussion at Athens he insisted that matters such as the establishment and government of states require knowledge of a special kind. But, on hearing this, Charmadas was up in arms at once. This nimble-minded polymath, who was almost incredibly well equipped with erudition of all conceivable kinds, maintained that any and every aspect of this sort of learning has to be acquired from the philosophers and no one else. A nation, he went on to say, does not exist at all, or at the very least finds itself in an extremely poor moral situation, unless it is furnished with a lot of things like religious and educational institutions, and qualities such as justice and endurance and moderation. However, he added, nothing whatever about any of these subjects can be found in the slim volumes of the rhetoricians. And yet these same professors of rhetoric interpret their art as embracing an enormous multitude of the most important things in the world. Why, then, asked Charmadas, are their writings crammed with so much talk about forewords and perorations and other such trifles, as he called them, while there is not even the faintest mention of the science of government, the formulation of laws, the virtues of equity and justice and loyalty, the conquest of the human passions, the improvement of human conduct? He also argued that the rules which rhetoricians lay down are enough in themselves to demonstrate that these professors are not only devoid of the wisdom they claim for themselves, but even ignorant of the true principles and proper methods of the rhetoric which is supposed to be their own subject.

'The proposition Charmadas himself put forward was that the orator's main purpose is to make his audiences regard him in the same way as he regards himself. And the way to achieve that, according to him, was by living a good life – a matter that these teachers of oratory do not even begin to cover at

1. Not otherwise known.

any point throughout all their regulations. And another thing, he maintained, which is a particularly important part of the speaker's job is to ensure that the feelings of his audiences are affected in just the ways he wants them to be. This, too, can only be achieved by investigating all the methods and approaches and varieties of language which incline people's minds in one direction or another. However, according to Charmadas, these problems lie buried, hidden in the profundities of philosophy. And that is a subject which these rhetoricians had not so much as touched with the tips of their tongues.

'Menedemus attempted to refute these assertions. His method was not so much to offer arguments as to quote concrete examples. Repeating from memory one noble passage after another from the speeches of Demosthenes, he demonstrated how the great orator was able to sway the minds of judges and audiences alike in any direction he desired; and how, in addition, he was perfectly well aware of the means by which these aims must be attained. This was an endeavour to refute Charmadas's claim that no one is capable of possessing such knowledge without philosophy.

'Charmadas, in his reply, agreed fully that Demosthenes was not only a supremely powerful speaker, but possessed outstanding wisdom as well; though it was worth considering, he added, whether the Athenian owed these qualities entirely to his natural gifts, or whether the acknowledged fact that he had been a pupil of Plato did not also have something to do with it. The present question, however, Charmadas pointed out, was not the particular case of Demosthenes and his talents, but the general claims rhetoricians are accustomed to make for their own profession.

'Often, as he held forth, Charmadas got so carried away that he even began to deny altogether that any such thing as an art of speaking exists at all. And he offered arguments in support of this denial. We are born, he said, with an aptitude for coaxing the people we want something from, and insinuating ourselves like suppliants into their favour. We are also born with a capacity to intimidate our opponents, to tell stories about how things have happened, to bring accusations and endeavour to substantiate our charges, to refute what other people say against us, and then to wind up our speeches with some sort of entreaty or lamentation. And these procedures, after all, are precisely what the orator says his art consists of. But the whole business is really just a question of habit and practice, Charmadas said; habit and practice are the things that sharpen our understanding and enhance our fluency.

'Then he produced an extensive array of examples in support of the case he was trying to make. In the first place, he argued, not one single writer on rhetoric had ever been even moderately eloquent himself, all the way back to certain individuals called Corax and Tisias, who were known, he said, to have been the discoverers and founders of the art.[1] Conversely, Charmadas claimed to be able to cite an infinite number of extremely eloquent speakers who had never learnt the rules of rhetoric at all, or shown the slightest desire to do so. Among these, as a joke – or perhaps he really believed it, unless he was just going by hearsay – he named myself, suggesting that I was precisely the sort of man he had in mind, since I too had never learnt the rhetorical art and yet he regarded me as an orator of some ability. One of these points, that I had never learnt anything, I accepted very readily. But as regards the other, I felt he was either making fun of me or had just got it wrong.

'What Charmadas maintained was that every authentic art consists of the thorough knowledge and comprehension of a certain assemblage of incontrovertible facts, all of which are

1. Corax and Tisias of Syracuse (5th century BC) were traditionally regarded as the founders of judicial rhetoric: possibly Corax was a political speaker and Tisias a writer of judicial speeches.

related to the same general purpose. Whereas everything, on the other hand, that oratory has to deal with is quite uncertain and ambiguous, since the speakers have no real understanding of what they are talking about, and their listeners do not acquire any genuine knowledge, but only some fleeting opinion that is either untrue or, to say the very least, unclear. In short, he seemed determined to convince me that there is no such thing as an oratorical art, and that no one can speak with the smallest skill or ability unless he has absorbed the doctrines of the most erudite philosophers. However, your own gifts, Crassus, received very favourable comment from Charmadas throughout his discourse. As for myself, he called me an excellent listener; but he described you as a very formidable man to argue against.

'Personally I found his views convincing. And I indicated as much in a little essay I composed, which without my knowledge or consent got around and came into people's hands. I stated in this treatise that, although I had known a number of good speakers, I had never come across a single one who was really eloquent. By a 'good' speaker, I meant somebody who could express himself with reasonable intelligence and clarity, standing before an average audience, and adjusting the level of his discourse to an average mental outlook. The term 'eloquent', however, I reserved for those who can command a style capable of elevating and enhancing anything they want to say, and whose intellect and memory enable them to obtain a complete grasp of all the sources relating to oratorical matters.

'For people like myself this is difficult to achieve, because before we have got down to studying at all we find ourselves heavily involved in the pursuit of office and the business of the courts. All the same, we must accept this ideal as not being beyond the natural bounds of possibility. And indeed – if I may offer a personal guess based on the abundance of talent which I can see in our fellow-citizens – I do not despair that one day there may emerge a man who is going to study harder than I myself do (or ever did), and will have more time to spare, and a greater capacity for hard work. That is the man who, once he has carried out a concentrated programme of listening, reading and writing, will be the orator we are looking for; not merely an adequate speaker but truly eloquent.

'But, after all, we already have such a man. For we have Crassus. Even if epochs still to come should manage to produce someone who has all the ability of Crassus but can also claim to have heard, read and written more than he has, this product of the future will only be able to improve on Crassus to a very small extent.'

*

At this point Sulpicius intervened. 'We didn't dare to expect it, Crassus,' he said, 'but this was exactly what Cotta and I were hoping for – that you and Antonius would get on to this subject. As we were on our way here we remarked to one another how satisfactory it would be if your conversation, even if it was on other subjects, gave us an opportunity to pick up something that might come in useful for ourselves. But the prospect of your embarking on a thorough and comprehensive discussion of this whole art or craft or mental function of orators, call it what you like, seemed to us almost more than we could expect.

'Ever since I was a very young man I have admired both of you enormously; and my devotion to Crassus has been so assiduous that I could hardly bring myself to leave his side. Yet as regards the theory and practice of speaking I was never able to get a word out of him, although I used to appeal to him to break his silence, as well as constantly asking Marcus Livius Drusus to intervene on my behalf.[1] Whereas you, on the other hand, Antonius – I must admit without hesitation –

1. On Marcus Livius Drusus see also p. 244.

have never failed to answer any request or inquiry I put to you, whatever it might be. And many is the time that you have explained to me the principles you yourself are guided by as an orator.

'But now the two of you have actually combined forces to produce exactly what we are after! Indeed, it was Crassus himself who began the discussion. So please do us the favour, both of you, of conveying to us, in the most exact detail you can manage, every one of your thoughts about the entire subject of oratory. If you and Antonius agree to do as we ask, Crassus, you will have made this villa of yours at Tusculum into a training ground which I shall look back on with immense gratitude. I shall not have the slightest doubt that your educational facilities here, on the fringes of the country, surpass even the illustrious Academy and Lyceum themselves!'[1]

'Well, Sulpicius,' replied Crassus, 'we had better ask Antonius, who has the power to grant your requests, and indeed, according to what you say, has already been in the habit of doing so. I personally, as you have just indicated, have always shunned such discussions, and that, quite often, has compelled me to decline even your most pressing appeals. But the motive behind my evasions was neither arrogance nor unkindness, and certainly no feeling of reluctance to fall in with your enthusiasm, which seemed to me, on the contrary, entirely legitimate and most admirable. Moreover, I had already appreciated your remarkable, indeed quite exceptional, natural qualifications to become an orator. The fact of the matter was that I was quite unfamiliar with this sort of

1. The Academy (p. 23) was founded by Plato in c. 385 BC in a park and gymnasium sacred to the hero Academus (or Hecademus) in the north western outskirts of Athens. The Lyceum, east of the city in a grove sacred to Apollo Lyceius, is where Aristotle taught. Cicero had an 'Academy' and a 'Lyceum' in the grounds of his own villa at Tusculum.

discussion, and all too conscious that I lacked the skills needed to deal with the principles of this so-called art.'

'Well then, Crassus,' said Cotta, 'we have at least got over the most difficult of our problems – which was how to get you to open your mouth at all about these questions. After that, we shall only have ourselves to blame if we let you go before you have given a complete explanation of everything we want to ask you about.'

'All right,' replied Crassus, 'but limiting your interrogations, I assume, to the subjects which fall within the range of that formula they use in inheritance cases, *as far as lies within my knowledge and capacity*.'

'Certainly,' answered Cotta. 'Because if there should happen to be anything which lies outside your knowledge and capacity, certainly none of us here would have the presumption to claim it lies within our own range!'

*

'So can we ask you this first of all?' said Sulpicius. 'What is your opinion about the point Antonius raised just now – do you believe there exists such a thing as an "art" of oratory?'

'Well, really!' exclaimed Crassus. 'Do you imagine I am just one of those idle and talkative Greeks, the sort of little man, no doubt scholarly and erudite enough, whom you can ask trivial questions to give him a chance of coming out with any kind of answer that may occur to him? You must be very well aware that I have never devoted the slightest attention or thought to this kind of point. On the contrary, I have always laughed at the impudent characters who sit on their chairs in the schools and call out to the assembled crowds that anybody can interrogate them on any subject he likes. They will tell you that Gorgias of Leontini invented this practice.[1] When he advertised himself as ready to talk on any question anyone

1. Gorgias headed a delegation to Athens (427) and was believed to have introduced rhetoric there (p. 228).

wanted to ask him, he was thought to be professing and promising something very impressive. Later on, however, people began to do the same thing all over the place. And they are still doing it today, with the result that, however vast and unexpected and unfamiliar a topic may be, they still claim to be perfectly ready to cover every possible aspect of it in their replies!

'If that was the sort of thing I thought you wanted to hear about, Cotta and Sulpicius, I would have brought some Greek along with me to amuse you with a discussion on those lines. Indeed, even now that would present no problem. For Marcus Piso, who although young is extremely clever and particularly keen on this subject – and is also a devoted friend of mine – has the Peripatetic Staseas staying with him at this moment. I know Staseas pretty well, and I believe the experts agree that he is quite supreme in that particular field.'[1]

'Staseas!' said Scaevola, 'what Staseas? What is all this talk about Peripatetics? No, Crassus, you must do what the young men want. They are not after the commonplace chatter of some inexperienced Greek, or slogans chanted in the philosophical schools. What they want to hear is the views of a man who is pre-eminent both for wisdom and eloquence, a man, moreover, who gives these qualities peerless expression not in academic treatises, but in mighty practical issues. Yours, Crassus, are the footsteps they desire to follow, yours the opinion they are eager to discover! As a speaker I have always ranked you as superhuman; but I have also, invariably, had occasion to praise your kindness quite as highly as your eloquence. And now it is up to you to show how kind you really are – by agreeing not to withhold the explanation which these two extremely talented young men are so anxious to have from you.'

1. Marcus Pupius Piso had given the young Cicero instruction, but in Piso's consulship (61 BC) the two men became estranged. Staseas of Neapolis may have been the first Peripatetic to reside in Rome.

'Very well then, I shall obediently do as they wish,' replied Crassus. 'And they will not find me in any way reluctant to indicate, in my own brief fashion, what I think about the various points. And besides, Scaevola, I am very well aware how improper it would be if I tried to disregard your own authority!

*

'So let me take the first question first, about whether such a thing as an art of speaking exists.

'My reply is that it does not. Or, if it does, it is negligible. All the argumentation in learned circles is merely founded on a dispute about what the word 'art' means. Antonius indicated just now that an art, in the sense in which we want to use the term, is something founded on things which are thoroughly examined, clearly understood, segregated from the arbitrary caprice of mere opinion, and comprised within the limits of exact knowledge. If he was right, then I do not believe that there is any such thing as an art of oratory at all. However, provided that the procedures that people actually follow in the practical business of making a speech have all been noted and recorded and put into words by a man of experience and skill, each one of them with its appropriate classification according to divisions and subdivisions – and I note that every stage of this analysis has, in fact, been undertaken – then there is no reason, as far as I can see, why the result should not be regarded as an art, perhaps not according to the precise definition of Antonuis, but at any rate in the popular sense of the term. But in any case whether oratory really is an art, or only looks rather as if it may be one, it would certainly be a mistake for us to underestimate its significance. Nevertheless, it does remain important to understand that a good orator does not need all these rhetoricians' rules anything like as much as he needs a number of entirely different things.'

At this point Antonius put in a word of agreement with

Crassus: for his keenness on describing oratory as an art was not so great, he said, that he went along with the people who declare it is *only* an art and nothing else. However, said Antonius, he was equally unprepared to reject its description as an art altogether, as most of the philosophers do. 'But I am quite sure, Crassus,' he added, 'that these young men would appreciate it very much indeed if you would now go on and indicate what you mean when you suggest that there are certain qualifications which are more useful to an orator than the actual regulations of the rhetoricians are.'

'Certainly I will do my best to oblige,' replied Crassus, 'now that I have started – though I beg you not to let my trifling remarks get around! All the same, I propose to observe a measure of self-restraint. For I do not at all want to give the impression of being an instructor and a professional. Please think of me merely as one Roman citizen out of many, with some experience of the courts and a modest degree of capacity; not an absolute novice, but equally not someone who has spontaneously offered to put his own views forward; just a man who has accidentally come in upon your discussion.

'I have to confess that in the days when I was standing for offices of state I used, while canvassing, to tell Scaevola to go away and leave me alone. For I was proposing, I explained to him, to do something quite fatuous – that is to say I must make myself pleasant to people in order to get their votes. This was a thing that could only be done well if it was done fatuously; and Scaevola was the last man in the world whom I wanted to see me displaying fatuous behaviour. And yet here he is now appointed by Fortune to be the witness and spectator of my imbecility. For since any sort of talking, except when absolutely necessary, is a silly activity, talking about talking must surely be the most imbecile procedure in the world.'

'Yes, but do go on all the same, Crassus,' said Scaevola; 'and as for the blame you seem to be so worried about, I am quite prepared to accept it all myself.'

'All right then,' resumed Crassus, 'this is what I think.

'To take first things first, what a good speaker needs most of all is natural ability. Antonius was talking just now about the men who have written about rhetoric. They did not lack knowledge of the theory and method of oratory. What they lacked was the innate capacity for its performance. For certain active intellectual gifts and talents are absolutely essential: swiftness of invention, fluency of exposition and elaboration, and a strong and retentive memory. People who think these are assets that can be picked up by theoretical study are quite mistaken. It would, indeed, be most agreeable if qualities of this kind could be awakened and brought to life in such a fashion, but there is no art in the world which can possibly graft or implant them on to anyone. They all have to be implanted by nature: nature has to do it, and nature alone.

'If anyone feels disposed to deny this, I do not see how he can explain away other characteristics which are quite obviously inborn, such as a ready tongue, a loud voice, powerful lungs, physical strength, and the shape and build of a man's face and body. I am not for a moment trying to deny that the art can add polish; I am perfectly well aware that teaching can make good things better – imperfections can be rectified and corrected. All the same, some people are so tongue-tied or harsh-voiced or boorishly uncouth in facial appearance and bodily gesture that even if they possess all the talent and learning in the world they will still never be capable of becoming an orator. Others, however, are so well qualified in these respects, so admirably equipped with nature's gifts, that they seem to exceed human limitations altogether; they must surely have been formed by some divinity.

'Whenever a man puts himself forward as the one and only speaker worth hearing on some issue of major importance, in front of an enormous crowd waiting in silence to hear what he has to say, he is accepting a truly enormous burden and responsibility. When someone is making a speech it is almost universal practice for a sharper and more penetrating eye to be cast on his faults than on his merits. Consequently, any and every mistake he makes will completely efface whatever good points he may happen to possess.

'However, my intention in reminding you of this is certainly not to discourage young men from attempting to become orators altogether – even if their innate talents are by no means substantial. Consider, for example, the case of my contemporary Gaius Coelius. Although his origins had not been noble, he acquired a great reputation: and he did so by means of oratorical powers that can only be described as modest. And think of Quintus Varius, who is the same age as you are. He is a clumsy and barbarous fellow. Yet he has made himself very popular – by using such gifts as he has.[1]

'But what we are looking for is "the Orator". This means that we have to envisage a speaker who is wholly flawless and endowed with every conceivable merit. It is true that the mass of lawsuits that crop up, and the illiterate rabble who crowd into the Forum, give even the most deplorable speaker a chance. But that is no reason why we should lose sight of our ideal. On the contrary, we must adopt the same standards as we apply to those arts which aim not at indispensable utility, as oratory does, but at intellectual pleasure pure and simple.

'When that is what we are after, we judge very critically, indeed fastidiously. The theatre, for example, does not have to stage the lawsuits and disputes which force listeners to put up with mediocre oratory in the courts; and so there is no need to tolerate bad actors. But the orator, too, ought to aim equally high, not merely seeking to satisfy the audiences he has got to satisfy, but also trying to win admiration from people who are at liberty to offer entirely disinterested judgements.

1. Gaius Coelius Caldus was consul in 94 BC, the first man of his family to attain that office. Quintus Varius Hybrida, as tribune in 90, prosecuted Antonius, Cotta and others for rousing the Italians against Rome.

'And now, if you really want to know my opinion, I will tell you – since we are all close friends here – just what I think about one matter on which I have always hitherto kept silent because this seemed the wisest policy. In my view it is proper for even the best of orators, the men who speak really fluently and eloquently, to display some diffidence at the beginning of a speech, and some discomposure when they bring their discourse to a close. Otherwise they will tend to be regarded as shameless. However, for good speakers the problem does not, in fact, arise. For the better he is at his job, the more frightened he feels about the difficulty of making a speech, and about its uncertain fate, and about what the audience expects of him.

'But the most shameless person of all, in my opinion, is the speech-maker who shows in the clearest possible way that he falls completely short of his subject, and the title of orator, and the expectations of his audience. For the way to avoid being shameless is not by being ashamed of something one has done wrong but by not making the mistake in the first place! Most speakers, I notice, have no feelings of shame at all. In which case, I maintain that they deserve to be not merely rebuked but heavily penalized.

'Personally, I react to making a speech in the same way as I know you both do. That is to say, when I start, I find myself turning deadly pale and trembling in every limb and to the very depths of my soul. In fact once in my earliest days, when I was just beginning a prosecution, I got into such a complete panic that I felt deeply grateful to Quintus Maximus when he adjourned the case promptly because he saw I was overwhelmed and incapacitated by nerves.'[1]

At this point Crassus's listeners all showed by their nods and murmurs of approval how they agreed with what he had been saying. For he really was an exceptionally modest man. And

1. Quintus Fabius Maximus Eburnus was praetor (he became consul in 116 BC).

far from being a hindrance to his oratory this quality actually helped him, because it showed his complete integrity.

Antonius took the point up. 'Yes, Crassus,' he said, 'I too have noticed what you have been reporting to us; that you yourself, like other first-class orators (not that anyone has ever been as good as you are!), get agitated when you are starting to make a speech. I once tried to find out the reasons for this phenomenon: why is it that the better the speaker, the worse the state of nerves he gets into? And I discovered two reasons. First, able and experienced orators are only too well aware, when they are delivering a speech, that its reception may not come up to their hopes. Consequently every time they perform they fear, with good reason, that the sort of disappointment which they have found to be such a familiar occurrence is going to come their way yet again.

'The second reason for this nervousness is something I have often had occasion to complain about. In other activities, when some recognized, approved figure falls below expectations this is explained by his not having been in the mood, or not having done as well as he could because he had felt ill. People say about an actor, for example, "Roscius wasn't in good form today", or "he was suffering from indigestion".[1] But if, on the other hand, it is an orator whose faults are being criticized, defects of this kind are just set down to stupidity. And nobody regards that as a good enough excuse! – because stupidity is something which cannot be just explained away on grounds of indigestion or because one was not in the mood. In other words, orators are subjected to severer standards of judgement. Every time we open our mouths, we are judged. If an actor gets one of his gestures wrong, people do not immediately jump to the conclusion that he is totally ignorant of acting. But as soon as the slightest fault is detected in a

1. The famous actor Quintus Roscius Gallus of Solonium (Lanuvium), who gave Cicero lessons in elocution and his first important brief, and died in the late 60s BC.

speaker, he is dismissed as thickheaded for ever afterwards, or at least for a very long time indeed.

*

'One thing you said was that a great many qualifications have to be inborn in an orator as a natural endowment, since no teacher on earth is going to be able to help him acquire them. Here I agree with you completely. I have always thought Apollonius of Alabanda was on the right lines here.[1] Although he taught to earn money, he would never allow students whom he believed incapable of becoming orators to waste their time with him. He used to send them away, urging them to transfer to whatever job he considered them best suited for.

'In other subjects, a pupil only has to be an average human being, capable of grasping and memorizing what is taught him or, if he happens to be more than usually slow-witted, what has been hammered into his head. He does not need quickness of tongue or readiness of speech or, for that matter, any of the other things which we have no control over, such as those relating to our physical shape and facial appearance and vocal powers. But in an orator, on the other hand, we demand the acuteness of a logician, the profundity of a philosopher, the diction virtually of a poet, the memory of a lawyer, the voice of a performer in tragic drama, the gestures, you might almost say, of an actor at the very top of his profession. Here, then, are some of the reasons why a first-class orator is one of the rarest things in the world. For qualifications which the member of another profession gets praised for, even if he merely possesses a single one of them and only a modest ration of that, fail to win the slightest approval for the orator unless he commands the whole lot of them, and commands them to a superlative degree.'

'Quite true,' said Crassus, 'and note how people dedicate a

1. See p. 263.

far greater amount of care to quite trivial and unimportant pursuits than they are prepared to devote to oratory, although everyone agrees what an exceptionally important job the orator has. Again and again one hears Roscius declaring: "I have never yet found a single pupil I really thought well of – I do not deny that some of them were worth praising, but the trouble is that, if they had so much as one single defect, I found it quite intolerable!" The slightest mistake stands out and is remembered for ever. And the analogy between actor and orator can be carried one stage further. You will observe that everything Roscius does is the very height of excellence, utterly appropriate to the occasion, ideally adapted to move and delight his entire audience. Because of this, he has long since gained a unique distinction: if a man excels at any activity at all, whatever it may be, he is described as a Roscius in his own line. Now I demand the very same absolute flawlessness of the orator as well. In demanding this perfection, of which I fall so very far short myself, I know I am behaving outrageously: I want indulgence for myself, but I am not prepared to grant it to others. No, the man who can never become a speaker, who gets it all wrong, who ought not to be making the attempt at all, should in my opinion, just as Apollonius said, be demoted, and made to do something he can manage.'

'So what about Cotta and myself?' interposed Sulpicius. 'Are you going to tell us we must abandon oratory and study the law instead, or soldiering perhaps? For who on earth is ever going to attain the sublime total perfection you are insisting upon?'

'On the contrary,' replied Crassus. 'It was precisely because I recognized a really remarkable and exceptional talent for oratory in both of you that I wanted to make the point. What I said was intended not only to warn off the people who lack the capacity but to stimulate you and Cotta, who are its fortunate possessors. You are both very gifted; and you show no lack of industry either. And as for you, Sulpicius, you also enjoy, to an almost supernatural degree, the advantages of personal appearance, about which I have perhaps said more than Greeks usually do. I do not believe I have ever known a speaker who had the better of you in bodily movement and deportment and appearance generally or in strength and beauty of voice.

'All the same, even a person whom nature has endowed less generously still has the chance to make judicious and sensible use of such advantages as he can mobilize. He must exploit these assets up to the limit of good taste. For that is a very important point. However, it is particularly difficult to apply rules to such a matter. It is hard enough for myself, who am talking just like a father laying down the law! But it is also hard even for Roscius, whom I often hear declaring that the essence of art is taste – though he goes on to point out that it is the one thing an instructor in the art cannot possibly teach.

'But please! Do let us change the subject. Why can't we just chat to one another as we usually do, and stop debating as though we were rhetoricians?'

'Sorry: but I'm afraid not,' replied Cotta. 'For since you are kind enough to let us remain orators, reprieved from expulsion to another profession, the time has now come for us to get from you the secret of your own powers of oratory – which you rate so inordinately low. Don't imagine we are going to be grasping! We are perfectly content with your own "ordinary" amount of eloquence, as you call it; your humble oratorical success is good enough for us. You are kind enough to assure us that our own natural endowments for oratory are not totally deficient. Well, then, we should like to know what we need to supplement them.'

Crassus smiled at this, and said: 'You need just one thing: enthusiasm – a passion little short of love! Without such a passion, no one is going to achieve anything outstanding in life, least of all what you are looking for. However, this, I can see for myself, is an exhortation I do not need to give you. Your importunity towards myself shows clearly enough that you are by no means short of keenness – indeed you have too much of it!

'Nevertheless, nobody can reach any objective at all, however hard he tries, without first mapping out the path which will lead him to his goal, Since, then, the burden you now impose on me is not as heavy as it might be – what I mean is that you are not asking me about the entire oratorical art but only about my own moderate ration of ability – I shall try to explain the procedure I used to adopt at an earlier time of my life, when I was young and free to devote myself to this sort of study. It is nothing very abstruse or difficult; there is nothing grand or imposing about it.'

'Excellent!' declared Sulpicius. 'At last the day we were waiting for! Hitherto no amount of appeals or stratagems or even attempts to spy, either at first hand or based on hints from his secretary and reader Diphilus, ever succeeded in procuring me the slightest information about Crassus's methods of practising or rehearsing his speeches. But now I am full of hopes that we have really got what we wanted and are going to learn from his own lips everything we have been eager to hear for so long.'

'All the same, Sulpicius,' continued Crassus, 'when you have heard what I shall be saying, I'm afraid you won't be particularly impressed – you're more likely to conclude that your eagerness has been misguided! For I shall not be explaining anything at all mysterious or worthy of your high expectations.

'Indeed, I am sure that you and everyone else will have heard it all before.

'However, let us start at the beginning. Well, first I have to record that, in the course of my normal liberal education as a Roman citizen, I learnt all those trite and commonplace maxims that everyone goes in for. First of all, that it is the duty of an orator to speak in a manner calculated to persuade. Secondly, that speeches can be divided into two categories, those dealing with general questions, without any particular reference to this or that person or occasion, and those concerned with specific individuals and times. Addresses of both these types, whatever the question at issue may be, are generally concerned with investigating whether something has been done, or, if it has been done, how it was done, or maybe how it should be classified, or perhaps – for some include this as well – whether it ought to be regarded as right or wrong. Disputes also sometimes arise concerning the interpretation of a document in which there is some ambiguity or contradiction or discrepancy between written word and intention. Each one of these themes requires its own special type of treatment.

'Other definitions I learnt were specially concerned with the disputes which relate to particular rather than general issues. One subdivision in this category comprises judicial proceedings, and another covers deliberative oratory. There is also a third kind, which deals with praising or censuring particular individuals. One can draw upon a whole series of stock comments and arguments adapted to different types of occasion. Some of these observations are for employment in the lawcourts, where justice is the object. Others are reserved for deliberative speeches and calculated to serve the people for whose advice orations of this kind are intended. Other stock themes again are designed for panegyrics, in which the sole consideration is to glorify the particular person concerned.

'One was also told that an orator's theoretical and practical task is divided into five parts. First, he must think of what to say. Secondly, once this has been decided, he has to organize his material. Then he has to arrange it in the right order, and attach due weight to its various elements according to his estimation of their relative importance. His next task is to devise suitably embellished language to clothe the results of all this thinking. Subsequently, he must commit this form of words to memory. And then at last comes the time when he has to deliver the end product verbally.

'With reference to this final part of the process they taught me that before passing to the actual substance of the speech one ought to pronounce a preamble aimed at winning the audience's goodwill. Thereafter, the character of the case should be stated. After that one has to prove that one's own contentions are right and those of one's adversary wrong. And finally, there should be a peroration, to amplify and reinforce all the points which support one's own arguments, while invalidating and demolishing those that favour the other side.

'I also listened to instructions about making one's oration attractive. The first rule is to speak pure and correct Latin. The second is to express oneself clearly and lucidly. Then comes the time to add some ornaments. And what one says must be appropriate, and in keeping with the dignity of the theme. On each of these matters I learnt the relevant precepts. I also heard the rhetoricians urging people to study the entire subject carefully, with a view to enhancing whatever qualifications nature has already provided them with. As regards matters such as delivery and memory, I got a taste of certain rules which could be stated concisely enough but required a great deal of practice.

'This is the sort of thing to which the theoreticians devote their learning, almost every bit they possess. If I rejected all these efforts as a waste of time, I should not be telling the truth. For the rules certainly supply a speaker with useful reminders. They never let him forget the standards which he always ought to apply and must keep in mind if he is not going to stray away from his objectives. But, in my view, the principal significance of these regulations is somewhat different. The reputation this or that speaker may have gained by following them is not really the point. What the compilers of the maxims have really done is to note carefully, and collect together, a set of procedures which good speakers had hitherto employed anyway, following their instinct. That is to say, eloquence is not derived from the rules: it is the other way round.

*

'Nevertheless, I repeat that I have no intention of rejecting the validity of these precepts. The art which has been built up out of them may not be really necessary for good speaking; but its study is by no means out of place for an educated man. And clearly orators have got to have some sort of preliminary training. I don't mean your two selves, because both of you are already embarked on your careers. But I'm referring to the men who are just starting the race. They still have the opportunity to prepare themselves by trying out their powers in a mimic arena before they have to launch out into the actual battlefield of the courts.'

'Exactly!' said Sulpicius. 'That is just the sort of training we hope to hear about from you. Certainly, we should also like to learn more about what you think of the rules of the art, since your treatment of that topic was so brief. But we know something about the rules ourselves; we can always return to them later on. At the moment we want to hear your views about the educational process.'

'The method I like best is the one you yourselves follow,' continued Crassus. 'I refer to the way you set yourselves a theoretical case very much on the lines of the actions that come into court, and then argue the issue, as far as possible, as though it were a real lawsuit. But all that most people manage to do, when they attempt this sort of thing, is to exercise their voices (and in a thoroughly unscientific way at that) and test out the strength of their lungs, and acquire the habit of speaking at a greater speed; in fact they just revel in their own flow of verbiage. The reason they cannot fail to go wrong is because people have told them that the way to become speakers is to speak. But it is equally true that speaking badly is a remarkably easy way for them to become bad speakers!

'That is why, when you are doing those exercises of yours, although practice in impromptu speaking is certainly useful, it is even more valuable to take time to consider what you are going to say, so that when you do finally express yourself you have put a lot of careful preparation into it. But the most important education of all is something which, to tell the truth, we go in for much too rarely; because it requires a great deal of labour, which most of us shirk. What I mean is writing. Far and away the best creator and professor of eloquence is the pen; and it is not very hard to see why. For just as a casual, improvised piece of speaking is easily outdone by an oration that has been well prepared and thought out, so the latter again, in its turn, will obviously be eclipsed by an effort which is the product of care and industry not only in its background thinking but in the actual composition as well. For when we really put a great deal of work and concentration into a speech, then, after that, all the arguments we could possibly need for what we want to say, arguments derived either from our studies or from the natural workings of our intelligence, will automatically surge forward and present themselves all ready for our use. That is how to make all the most brilliant thoughts and expressions crowd on to the point of our pen. And that, too, is the way to ensure that every single word is located and arranged in its proper place, according to the particular rhythmical scheme which is appropriate to oratory as opposed to poetry.

'These are the things that earn a good speaker shouts of applause and admiration. But, however strenuously one may have practised extempore speech-making, the only way to achieve this acclamation is by writing and by continuing to write. Anyone who comes to oratory from long experience as an author brings with him a great advantage: even when he is improvising, what he says will be as good as if he had written it down first. Furthermore if, in the course of a speech, he has to introduce written evidence, he will be able, after he has finished reading the document out, to continue speaking without any abrupt change of style.

'If the oarsmen of a fast-moving ship suddenly cease to row, the suspension of the driving force of the oars doesn't prevent the vessel from continuing to move on its course. And with a speech it is much the same. After he has finished reciting the document, the speaker will still be able to maintain the same tone without a break, borrowing its momentum and impulse from the passage he has just read out.

'I myself, when I used to do my daily exercises as a very young man, liked to adopt the method which I knew that our political enemy Gaius Papirius Carbo had been accustomed to employ. That is to say, I would read a piece of poetry, the best I could find, or I would work through as much of a speech as I could memorize, and then I went on to deliver a recitation on the subject I had just been reading about – in *other* words, as far as possible. But later I detected a flaw in this procedure. The trouble was that Ennius, if his was the poetry I had chosen for my exercise, or Gaius Gracchus, if I had set myself one of his speeches, had already appropriated the best, finest and fittest words on whatever the subject might be. If, therefore, I used the same words as they did, I was doing myself no good; and if the words I used were different I was actually doing harm, since this inculcated the habit of using words that were less suitable than those of the original authors. Afterwards, when I was grown up, I adopted a different practice; I used to declaim free translations of speeches by leading Greek orators. The advantage of this method was that by rendering in Latin what I had read in Greek I not only found myself using the best words, familiar though they might be, but also, by imitating Greek terms, I invented new Latin forms of my own, which, provided they were accurate, constituted additions to our language.

'As to voice and breath control, and physical exercises, and training of the tongue, the question is here not so much one of art as of sheer hard work. The important thing is to be very careful whom we choose as our models. To make sure that bad habits do not land us in undesirable and faulty practices, it is a good thing to study actors as well as orators. The memory, too, must be trained, by learning by heart as many Latin and other writings as we can. And in the course of this training programme, I have no objection, if the practice attracts you, to the mnemonic system prescribed by the textbooks – the method which defines the various types of argument by different symbols.

'And then, at long last, comes the time when our speech-making has to be brought out of this secluded domestic training-ground into the front line: into the dust and uproar, the fighting men's camp, the battlefield of the Forum itself! Now is the moment when our oratory has to brave the gaze of the whole world, and summon up all the powers it can muster. Now we must endure the exposure of all that sheltered preparation to glaring reality!

'But, to return to the question of training, a speaker also ought to read the poets and historians. Indeed he must peruse and scrutinize the writers and experts on every liberal art. He will find it good practice to explain their merits and meanings, to criticize and attack and refute what they say. He must be ready to argue on both sides of any issue, and to bring out the persuasive elements in a theme and put them into words. He must know all about our law and our statutes, he must have a thorough understanding of ancient history; he must master the usages of the Senate, the nature of the constitution, the rights of the subject allies, our national treaties and agreements, the interests of our empire. And finally he must be able to sprinkle a little salt on his speech, in the form of a civilized, well-varied supply of humorous and entertaining touches.

'That is everything I can offer you – out it has all come for your benefit. And very likely any father figure you happened to get hold of at a party would have answered your inquiries in exactly the same way!'

*

When Crassus had finished his statement, there was a silence. His listeners appreciated that he had done what they asked him to. But all the same they felt he had wound up his exposition with disappointing speed. 'Well, Cotta?' said Scaevola finally. 'Why are you both so silent? Can't you think of anything more you want to question Crassus about?'

'Most certainly I can,' answered Cotta. 'And that is precisely what I am pondering at this moment. But his speech flew along at such speed that while one was just getting a general impression of hustling briskness it was almost impossible to keep pace. Or, to put it in another way, I felt as if I had entered some richly furnished mansion where there were no tapestries unrolled, no silver plate displayed, no pictures and statues placed on view, but quantities of all these magnificent objects were huddled away together somewhere in heaps so that you could not really see them. That was my reaction to Crassus's speech. I got a glimpse of the opulence and splendour of his talent through a mass of coverings and wrappings; but when I wanted to obtain a closer view I could not get near enough to get a clear view of anything. If I were to say, therefore, that I know nothing at all about the goods he possesses, I should not be telling the truth; but equally I cannot claim that I really know what those possessions are, or have got a proper sight of them.'

'Well, then,' said Scaevola, 'you ought to behave just as you would if you came to the treasure-filled mansion or country house you were speaking of. If the treasures were hidden away, as you describe, and you very much wanted to see them, you would not hesitate to ask their owner to have them brought out, particularly if the two of you were close friends. And the same applies to Crassus here and now; you can appeal to him about his abundant treasures which we just managed to catch a passing glimpse of through a lattice, all piled up together on top of one another. You can ask him to bring them out and arrange them as they ought to be arranged.'

'No, Scaevola, you do it for me, please,' Cotta replied. 'Both Sulpicius and I would feel embarrassed to ask the great man himself. After all, he has always looked down on this sort of thing as mere schoolboy stuff. Do us this favour, Scaevola. Make Crassus go back to the points which he crowded and crammed into such a very brief survey just now; get him to amplify and expand all the various themes one after another.'

'I must say I agree with you,' declared Scaevola. 'At first, I admit, I was insisting more for your sakes than my own; since my desire to hear him discussing the subject was not so keen as the pleasure I invariably feel when I listen to him pleading a case in court. But here we are, with more spare time on our hands than we have had for ages, and so on my account as well as theirs, Crassus, I do want to take the opportunity to support their appeal. Complete the edifice you have started to build, and let us hear no objections. For the whole enterprise, I now see clearly, has taken on a finer and more significant shape than I ever thought it would; and this is something really splendid.'

'So you too, Scaevola, are associating yourself with what these young men ask,' said Crassus. 'That really surprises me! After all, my understanding of these matters cannot be compared with that of a professional instructor on the subject. And even if I understood the various points very well indeed, they are really not the sort of thing, are they, that a man of your talents would find any use to listen to.'

'What do you mean?' Scaevola replied. 'Even if we agree that the commonplace, hackneyed maxims of the rhetoricians are hardly worth hearing for a man of my years, one obviously ought not to disregard all the other subjects you declared an orator ought to know: the different sorts of human nature and behaviour, the ways of exciting and calming people's emotions, the study of history and antiquity, the government of the State, the law of the land. I was well aware that you yourself possessed all this abundance of knowledge, because you are a man of extraordinary intellectual gifts. But no orator I had ever seen before could boast of anything like so magnificent an equipment.'

*

'Well,' said Crassus, 'can we perhaps pass over all the other aspects, vast and countless though they are, and come to your own speciality, the law. Think back to the day when Scaevola's uncle Publius, though impatient to be off and play ball in the Field of Mars, was kept waiting for hour after hour, undecided whether to be more angry or amused.[1] This was the occasion when Hypsaeus, pouring forth a torrent of words at the top of his voice, was doing his very best, without realizing it in the least, to make the judge (the praetor Marcus Crassus) pronounce against him.[2] The speaker on the other side was Cnaeus Octavius, who as a former consul ought to have known better: because he delivered an oration which was not only of equally inordinate length, but, if successful, would have won the case not for himself but for the other side! Because his argument, had it been accepted, would have made it impossible for his own client to escape a degrading and

1. This Publius Mucius Scaevola (consul 133 BC) was cousin of Quintus 'the Augur' who is taking part in this discussion (consul 117) and father of Quintus 'the Priest' who was Crassus's fellow-consul in 95. The Field of Mars (Campus Martius), outside the Republican walls in the angle of the Tiber, was used for parades and for exercise.

2. Marcus Plautius Hypsaeus was consul in 125 BC and Cnaeus Octavius in 128.

damaging verdict of dishonest guardianship. If, on the other hand, Hypsaeus's stupidity had been left to itself, Octavius's client would undoubtedly have been acquitted.' 'Yes, I remember hearing the story from Publius', said Scaevola. 'Surely, if speakers cannot do any better than that, they are not fit to appear in court at all, much less to be accorded the title of orators!'

'All the same,' Crassus went on, 'the advocates in question were not short of eloquence, or knowledge of oratorical theory, or fluency of utterance. What they lacked was knowledge of the law. For Hypsaeus was claiming more than the maximum allowed by the Twelve Tables for a statutable action – so that if he had gained his point his own case would have been defeated. Whereas Octavius thought it unjust that his opponent's claim exceeded what was permissible, failing to understand that if the claim had gone forward Hypsaeus would lose the action, and he himself would win it.

'A similar thing happened a few days ago when we were sitting as assessors in the court of our friend Quintus Pompeius Rufus, the city praetor.[1] On this occasion a barrister who has a reputation for eloquence was defending someone in a debt case, and requested the insertion of the ancient and well-known special plea, *in exclusive respect of payments already due*. He quite failed to realize that the only person this saving clause would protect was the plaintiff; since the intention of the clause was to provide that, if a defendant tried to get out of repaying a debt by persuading the judge that the claim for its payment had been made prematurely, the plaintiff and creditor should not be stopped from bringing a new action by the fact *that the matter had been in court before*. Surely that is as stupid a mistake as you could imagine! The speaker was a man who had taken it upon himself to defend the interests of a friend involved in litigation. He was supposed, in other

1. Quintus Pompeius Rufus was praetor in 91 and consul with his father-in-law Sulla in 88.

words, to be helping a man in trouble, healing his suffering, cheering him in his affliction. And here was this supposed helper instead making himself an object either of pity or ridicule – people could take their choice – by allowing some quite negligible and simple point to trap him into the grossest of blunders.

'Our relative Publius Crassus, surnamed Dives, "the Rich", was a man of versatile culture and accomplishments.[1] But what I consider the most praiseworthy and commendable incident in his life was an assertion he often made to his brother Publius Scaevola about his own career. First, he said, he would never have become a good lawyer unless he had also made himself a fluent speaker – advice conspicuously followed by Publius Scaevola's son, with whom I served as consul. And conversely, Crassus added, he had not started to defend his friends in the courts until he had first done everything possible to master the law. And what about the great Marcus Cato?[2] No one at that period of the Republic's history could possibly have been more eloquent than he was. But in addition his knowledge of law was altogether exceptional.

'However, while I have been enlarging upon this theme I have begun to feel an increasingly strong sensation of embarrassment. For as an orator Antonius, who is with us here, seems to me more admirable than anyone else in the whole world. And yet he has always despised this study of the law. However, you have said you wanted to share my opinions and views, and so I have no intention of concealing anything from you; on the contrary I shall exert myself to let you know what I think about any and every aspect of oratory. About Antonius,

1. Publius Licinius Crassus Dives Mucianus was Chief Priest, and held the consulship in 131 BC. His family relationship with Lucius Crassus, who is speaking here, is uncertain (but see p. 360).

2. Cato the elder (censor 184 BC) published his own speeches; Cicero knew more than 150 of them, and fragments of 80 have survived.

then. He is a man of unbelievable gifts: they are virtually unparalleled, almost superhuman. Even without the protection of legal learning, therefore, he has all the other weapons of his genius to guard and defend himself with. So let us agree to regard him as an isolated exception. But as for all the other people who know no law, I shall not have the slightest hesitation in pronouncing my personal verdict of "Guilty", Guilty of laziness, not to speak of impudence!

'For to flit around the Forum, to hang about the courts and the praetors' tribunals, to undertake weighty private suits depending, often enough, not on questions of fact, but on points of equity and law; to show off before the Board of One Hundred about such matters as long user's rights, guardianship, kinship by clan or paternal descent, changes in shore-lines, formation of islands by rivers, disputes about pledges, transfers of property, rights relating to partition-walls and lights and rain-drips, the validity and invalidity of wills – to tackle all this infinite array of subjects without equipping oneself with the slightest knowledge of what legally belongs to oneself or the next man, or even of the distinction between a citizen and a foreigner, or the difference between a free man and a slave: that really is the last word in effrontery.

'If you heard someone confessing that he is not much of a hand at managing small boats but that all the same he knows how to navigate great ships with five men to the oar, or even larger vessels still, his pretentiousness would make you laugh. And so when I see a man who even in the relaxed atmosphere of a mere private conference, without any of the hazards of a lawcourt around him, still manages to get himself trapped by some quibble perpetrated by his opponent; a man perfectly prepared to set his seal on a deed containing words that will completely ruin his own client's case; how can I possibly suppose that an individual like that could ever be capable of handling any lawsuit even of the very slightest importance?

I would sooner let a man who has overturned a two-oar dinghy in harbour steer the ship of the Argonauts in the open Black Sea!

'Just suppose that this creature had to deal with the sort of really important case which has major legal implications. Imagine the nerve of a barrister who could venture to tackle a problem of those dimensions without knowing anything about the law at all! For example there was that significant dispute about the soldier who was wrongly reported dead. When the army sent home news of his death, his father believed the report and changed his will, choosing a fresh heir; then the father died himself. The soldier, however, eventually returned home, and thereupon he brought an action for the recovery of his paternal inheritance, and the matter came before the Board of One Hundred. Clearly the issue was a legal one – whether or not, that is to say, a son could be disinherited of his father's property after the will left by the father had neither named him as heir nor disinherited him explicitly by name.

'And then there was that other controversy that came up before the same Board, between the family of the Marcelli and the patrician branch of the Claudian clan.[1] The Marcelli claimed that the estate of a freedman's son should revert to them by lineal descent, whereas the patrician Claudii maintained the property was theirs by title of clan. In such a case, the arguments on both sides obviously involved the entire question of the law relating to family and clan entitlements.

'The Board of One Hundred also had to decide another issue recently. A certain foreigner was allowed to live in exile at Rome, provided that he attached himself to some citizen as client to patron. Subsequently this foreigner died intestate; and so here was a case in which the pleaders had to expand and clarify to the court the obscure and little-known

1. The Claudii included the patrician Pulchri, Nerones and Centones and various plebeian families including the Marcelli.

legal position relating to such cliental attachments. And when I myself recently defended Gaius Sergius Orata in a private suit against our friend Antonius here, my entire case likewise hung on a point of law. For Marcus Marius Gratidianus had sold a house to Orata without stating in the terms of sale that a portion of the building was subject to an easement.[1] My argument was that, if the vendor had known of the existence of such an encumbrance and had failed to disclose this defect, he was obliged to indemnify the purchaser.

'This was the kind of action in which our friend Marcus Bucculeius, who is no fool in my opinion and the greatest of sages in his own – and one does have to admit that he shows no disinclination for the study of the law – went badly astray on a recent occasion. For when he was selling a house to Lucius Fufius, his deed of transfer made a reservation of all lights existing at the time.[2] But Fufius, as soon as anyone anywhere in the city began to construct a building which he could so much as glimpse from his house, would instantly proceed to bring an action against Bucculeius, because Fufius took the view that his entitlement to light was infringed upon if even the most minute portion of his outlook was blocked, no matter how far away from his house.

'And then think of that famous dispute recently between Manius Curius and Marcus Coponius – another of the Board of One Hundred's cases.[3] The debate attracted great crowds, and aroused correspondingly high expectations. One of the

1. Gaius Sergius Orata was praetor in 97 BC and Marcus Marius Gratidianus in 86 and 82; he was the nephew of Cicero's grandmother Gratidia and was murdered by Catilina on Sulla's orders. Easement or servitude: the condition of a piece of land in which the owner had given his neighbour a right, e.g. a right of way.

2. i.e. he sold the house subject to all existing easements (see last note) with regard to the obstruction of its light.

3. This case took place in 93 BC, two years after the consulship of Crassus and Quintus Scaevola the Priest (who, like the Augur of the same name, taught Cicero, p. 232).

speakers was my contemporary and former fellow-consul Quintus Scaevola the Priest, a man of exceptional legal learning, extremely acute and wise, a most sensitive master of language. I always call him the best orator among lawyers and the best lawyer among orators. Now Scaevola was basing his contention on the literal interpretation of a will. His argument was that the person who had been appointed second heir – as substitute for a posthumous son, had such a child been born and then died – was not entitled to inherit unless such a posthumous son had in fact come into the world and then died, while still under age. I, on the other hand, maintained that the intention of the testator had been for the person in question, Manius Curius, to become his heir in the event of no son coming of age. Here, then, was another matter where the pleaders on both sides had to delve constantly into past decisions and precedents and the technicalities of wills. In fact they had to deal with fundamental questions of law.

'I shall forbear to mention further instances of highly important cases hinging on legal points; there have been any number of them. But I would just add that actions involving civil rights frequently turn on questions of such a kind. That, for example, was what Gaius Mancinus found. Here was a fine man of the highest rank, a former consul, who had become unpopular at Rome because of the treaty he had made with Numantia;[1] and so the Senate had decreed that the official herald should surrender him to the people of that city. They, however, refused to accept him; whereupon Mancinus returned home, and even put in an appearance at the Senate-house. But the tribune Publius Rutilius Rufus, son of Marcus, ordered that he should be ejected from that place, on the grounds that he was not a Roman citizen any longer. In

1. This was the result of his disastrous campaign against rebel Numantia (in Spain) during his consulship of 137 BC. Subsequently he got his civil rights back again.

making this demand Rutilius cited the accepted tradition that a man who had been sold by his own father or the people of Rome, or who had been disposed of by the chief herald, could never become entitled to rehabilitation. It would be hard indeed, over the entire range of public life, to think of a more far-reaching problem. Here was an issue which affected the rank, nationality, liberty and civil rights of a man of consular seniority: and once again the decision depended not on some specific charge, which the man involved might have been able to refute, but on a point of law.

'A similar case arose in an earlier generation, though the rank of the individual concerned was not so high. The member of a people which was one of Rome's subject allies, he had been reduced to slavery in our city, but later obtained his freedom. Subsequently he returned to his home; and the question which came up was whether the process of his liberation did, or did not, mean that he reverted to his original nationality, thus forfeiting Roman citizenship.

'Such questions on which the whole future of a person's freedom hangs are of course of paramount importance. To take another example, litigation can easily arise on the problem whether a slave, who has been entered upon the censors' roll with the agreement of his master, is entitled to regard himself as a free man from that moment, or only from the later time of the five-yearly ceremony which actually brought the new register of citizens into operation.

'There was also the occasion, a generation ago, when the head of a family came to Rome from Spain, and left his pregnant wife behind in the province. In Rome he married again without having sent the first wife notice of divorce. Then he died intestate, after a son had been born to the second woman as well as the first. The dispute which now arose had significant implications, since it involved the civil rights of two Roman citizens, the boy born of the second marriage and his mother. If the ruling was to be that the first wife could only be divorced by a specific form of words, and not just by her husband's remarriage to someone else, then the second woman would merely be regarded as a concubine.

'And so, when you see a man who has not got a clue about these and similar statutes of his own country roaming at large all over the Forum with a grand and lofty demeanour and a keen and complacent expression, attended by an impressive crowd; and when you see such a person promising and offering protection to his dependents and help to his friends and the exalted brilliance of his counsel to virtually every citizen of Rome, this can only be regarded as scandalous.

'So much, then, for impudent behaviour. Let us now go on to point out how lazy and idle some people can be. For even if this legal study were a large and arduous matter, nevertheless its extraordinary advantages ought to impel people to take the trouble to learn what the subject is all about.

'Heaven knows, I should never be venturing to say such a thing with Scaevola among my hearers, if it were not for the fact that he himself declares so repeatedly that he regards the law as the easiest of all the arts to master! However, most people think otherwise – and I can tell you why. In the first place, they are able to point out that the men who presided over this branch of knowledge in ancient times were never willing to disclose its contents to the general public. And even later on, when these secrets had finally been published and Cnaeus Flavius had set out the various forms of procedure for the first time,[1] there still proved to be nobody capable of arranging the subject methodically in categories. For nothing can be organized in scientific fashion until someone appears who thoroughly understands the subject and has the ability to

1. Cnaeus Flavius, the son of a freedman of Appius Claudius Caecus (the Blind), was a magistrate's clerk who was elected aedile in 304 BC. It was stated that Appius helped him with his handbook, or that he stole it from Appius.

systematize all these elements that have never been set in order before.

*

'But I see that my desire to be brief has caused me to express myself rather obscurely. Let me see if I can't make my meaning a bit plainer.

'Nearly all the things which have now coalesced as elements in arts and sciences were originally quite unconnected and uncoordinated with one another in people's minds. As regards music, for example, that was the position with rhythms, sounds and tunes. In geometry it was true of lines, figures, dimensions and magnitudes; in astronomy, of the rotations of the heavens, and the risings and settings and other movements of the stars; in literature, the same applied to the study of poetry, historical research, the interpretation and correct pronunciation of words.

'And just the same must be said of oratory. Invention, style, arrangement, memory, and delivery were all once thought of as obscure matters that have no particular relation one to the other. And so another art was called in from that further range of ideas over which the philosophers claim exclusive control. The intention was that these various factors, which had previously been separate and unconnected, should be welded together and given some sort of logical cohesion. That is to say, they were to be made the components of the law – which may be defined, in this context, as the application of equity, founded on statute and usage, to the concerns and disagreements of Roman citizens.

'Once the elements of an art have been brought together, the next thing is to classify them under general headings, reducing these to a definite number, which should be as small as possible. General headings, in their turn, fall into two or more secondary subdivisions, which have certain things in common but differ from one another in some special feature.

And when the subdivisions are all marshalled under their general headings, subdivisions and headings alike have to be given names which will define the scope and significance of each of the categories in question. (I interpret the term 'define' as indicating a concise and succinct description of the peculiar features of the item concerned.)

'I might add specific illustrations of what I mean; but I appreciate the calibre of my listeners too well to attempt any such thing. Instead let me briefly indicate to you a project which I have long been turning over in my mind. If I am ever permitted to carry this plan out, or if owing to my many other preoccupations someone else gets in first, or carries out the undertaking after I am dead, my idea is that the procedure I have been talking about should be applied to the legal field.[1] First, that is to say, the law has to be divided under main headings, which will not need to be numerous, and then the second step will be to establish the various subdivisions. Next, the peculiar features characterizing each general heading and subdivision will require to be identified and defined. And then, finally, you will have a complete legal system. It will be a splendid asset, containing a great deal of valuable material: but not particularly difficult or obscure. And even in the meantime, before the collection of all this scattered material is complete, by gathering up what he can from here and there and collecting information from every source a man can ensure that his knowledge of the law will meet his requirements. Have you considered the case of the knight Gaius Aculeo, who lives with me, and always has?[2] He is an extremely intelligent man, but very far from

1. Cicero himself compiled, or at least started, a work on jurisprudence (according to the writers Quintilian and Gellius). It was perhaps an attempt to codify.

2. Gaius (Visellius?) Aculeo is probably the Aculeo who is mentioned in the second book of *On the Orator* as being defended by Crassus against Marcus Marius Gratidianus. He had a connexion with Cicero's aunt Helvia.

learned in any other branch of knowledge except the law. Yet his mastery of that subject is so complete that, with the one exception of our friend Scaevola here, there is not a single expert, however distinguished, who can be ranked above him.

'For the fact is that all the constituents of this subject are fully accessible to our view, being part of our everyday experience both in the lawcourts and in the ordinary relationships between one man and another. In consequence, these matters have not been set down in written works of any quantity or volume. A number of authors, it is true, have dealt with the subject, but what they have published has all been very much the same; and indeed even the same writers have repeated themselves over and over again with only minor alterations.

'There is also another thing which makes it all the easier to learn and master the law: though most people find this hard to believe. For the fact is that legal study is so utterly fascinating and absorbing! For example, it would be very easy to become attracted by the sort of researches which Lucius Aelius Stilo has brought into fashion.[1] Once he has embarked on that line, the whole range of the law and our priestly chronicles and the Twelve Tables will give him a remarkable picture of what ancient times were like. For one thing, these records provide invaluable evidence about primitive linguistic usage; and, besides, some of the types of legal action they preserve are extremely informative about our ancestors' customs and ways of life. Or if you are studying the art of government – which Scaevola does not consider to be an orator's business, preferring to attribute the subject to some other branch of knowledge – you will find all the material in

1. Lucius Aelius Stilo Praeconinus, who was born at Lanuvium in c. 150 BC and died after 90, was a knight, a Stoic and the first important Roman scholar. The reference here is to his literary and linguistic work, which included the study of etymology and grammar. Cicero was one of his pupils.

the Twelve Tables, including descriptions of every aspect of public life and all the various interests that play a part in its conduct.

'Or suppose someone is keen on this philosophy of yours, with all its grand and assertive claims – for it really is necessary to describe them in this way. If so, he will find every kind of philosophical disputation has its sources in the law and the statutes. For it is from them that we learn to give preference to true merit above everything else – honours, rewards and distinctions are won by genuine, honest, and conscientious labour, whereas misdeeds and crimes, on the other hand, lead to fines, degradation, imprisonment, flogging, exile and death. And it is not the endless squabbling in debates, but the authoritative ruling of the statutes themselves, which teaches us to check our passions, hold our lusts under control, and protect our own property while keeping our thoughts and eyes and hands off what belongs to our neighbour.

'Let everyone grumble as much as they like, I am going to say what I think. If you want to study the sources and origin of the law, I insist that the single little book of the Twelve Tables, all by itself, is more authoritative and useful than all the libraries of the philosophers. It is our own, and nothing ought to delight us so much as our own country. So strong and so profound is this emotion that the epic hero, wise man that he was, placed even immortality itself second to that Ithaca of his, fixed among the roughest of rocks like a little nest.[1] And if this be so, ours is the patriotism which ought to be the most ardent in the world, since ours is the land that surpasses all others as the home of virtue and empire and excellence. The spirit and custom and government of this commonwealth of ours ought to come absolutely first and foremost among all the things we learn, not only because it is

1. In the *Odyssey* Odysseus (Ulysses) rejected Calypso's offer of immortality because of his desire to return to his island home of Ithaca.

the fatherland and parent of us all but because Rome's laws are manifestly the product of every bit as much wisdom as inspired the acquisition of its mighty territories.

'And legal learning provides another delight and satisfaction too. Compare our laws with those of other communities: with the laws of Lycurgus and Draco[1] and Solon. You will then find it extremely easy to understand why our ancestors surpassed every other nation in the world in wisdom. For the laws of all other countries are incredibly disorderly; one might almost call them ridiculous. This, however, is a subject that will be familiar to you from my daily conversation, since I am always repeating how much wiser we Romans are than the Greeks and everyone else.

'So these, Scaevola, were the reasons why I declared that a knowledge of the law is essential for anyone who wants to become an orator.

'Besides, everyone can see that leading Roman advocates become important, popular and famous. In Greece the custom is for men of insignificant status, described as attorneys, to offer themselves as assistants to pleaders, for a miserable fee. In our community, on the other hand, a great number of distinguished and famous personages have done this sort of legal work. Among them was Sextus Aelius Paetus, who knew the law so well that our greatest poet called him "a man of consummate wisdom and shrewdness".[2] And yet Paetus was only one of many lawyers who became so eminent by their talents that in their subsequent careers, in advisory capacities, they could almost have lived on their reputations and nothing else, even if they had been completely incompetent!

1. Draco drew up a code of laws for Athens in 621 BC. For Lycurgus and Solon see also pp. 257, 178.

2. The line is quoted from the *Annals* of Ennius. Sextus Aelius Paetus Catus (the Shrewd) was consul in 198 BC and the author of a famous legal work, the *Tripertita*, later described as the *ius Aelianum*.

'Furthermore, the interpretation of the law is a splendid haven for the old – something to ennoble and dignify a man's advanced years. Personally I have been storing up this resource ever since I grew up. Partly, of course, this is to help my practice in the courts, but another motive was to make sure of honour and respect in my old age. When my strength begins to fail me – a time which is now not far off – that is how I shall be able to make sure that my home does not become a lonely place. For it is a fine thing for an old man, after he has held the highest honours and offices of the State, to be justified in claiming for himself what Pythian Apollo said in Ennius, that if not "the peoples and the kings", at least all his fellow-citizens seek his advice: "Men doubtful how to act; I rescue them and let them go their way. Their doubts resolved; their plans brought to a head; fated to tread a troubled path no more."[1]

'For you can quite plausibly compare a lawyer's house to an oracle serving the entire population of the city. Look at the entrance and ante-room of our friend Scaevola's home. He is by no means strong in health or young in years, and yet every day there comes to him an enormous throng of citizens, including the most eminent in the land.

'It will not take long to explain why I think the orator also requires a knowledge of public law – the law concerning governmental and imperial affairs; and why he should also be familiar with ancient history and all its wealth of precedents. In private cases and suits, as I have mentioned, his language will often require to be derived from common law, which is why he cannot do without this branch of study; and in precisely the same fashion any speaker who takes part in public issues – whether in the lawcourts or public meetings of the Senate – has got to realize that he must learn about past times, and the precedents in public law and governmental

1. From an unidentifiable play of Ennius. The Pythian Games were held in connexion with the oracle of Apollo every four years at Delphi.

theory and practice that the study of these ancient periods furnishes.

*

'For what we are looking for, in all this discussion, is not just the sort of pleader who makes a loud noise and gets involved in a row. The person we have in mind is very different indeed, being nothing less than the high priest of an art which, although generously implanted by nature in mankind, was nevertheless deemed to be the gift of a god. Certainly, it is something peculiar to the human race. And yet we believe that we did not acquire the gift unaided, but were vouchsafed it from heaven.

'Even on the field of battle the practitioner of oratory is able to remain unharmed – his ability to speak is more effective than a herald's staff. His eloquence also gives him the power to throw culpable and guilty men to the wrath of their own fellow-countrymen: to suppress crime, by ensuring that it is punished. The protection his talent affords others can bring salvation to the innocent by rescuing them from condemnation in the courts. It is even within his capacity to transfigure a spiritless and misguided nation, to revive its sense of honour, to reclaim a whole people from its errors. He can stir up anger against evil men, or, when such anger has attacked innocent people, he can calm it down. Indeed his might as an orator will give him the power to instil or eradicate within the hearts of mankind any and every passion that circumstances and occasions may demand.

'Anyone who supposes that this oratorical power has been adequately explained by writers on the art is going to be seriously disappointed; and the same applies to people who may imagine that this phenomenon can be explained in so brief a space by myself. For, if so, they must have failed to comprehend the magnitude of the subject, not to speak of my own ignorance. All I have tried to do was to respond to your request by suggesting the fountains you can draw from, and the paths which lead towards them. I was not setting myself up as your guide, which would be an endless labour – and unnecessary, since you have no need of such a thing. What I have attempted to do was merely to show you the road, like a man pointing in the general direction where the springs are to be found.'

'All the same,' said Scaevola, 'I am sure you have done enough, and more than enough, to stimulate the efforts of these young men, if they really have the enthusiasm. The great Socrates, we are told, used to describe his work as completed as soon as his exhortations had stimulated someone to tackle the study of ethics: once people had become convinced that they really wanted to lead good lives, and wanted this more than they wanted anything else, everything else that had to be learned was easy. That is how I myself feel; I am convinced that if the two of you are really determined to embark on the pursuits which Crassus indicated, you must first manage to open the gateway and get through the door, and then you will find the rest of the journey quite easy.'

*

'Your advice is indeed acceptable,' declared Sulpicius, 'and it suits us extremely well. But we still want a little more. In particular, we should be glad to hear further details about the various aspects of the actual art of oratory. Far from despising these matters, Crassus, you declared that you had taken trouble to learn about them. However, you dealt with the different points all too briefly. If you would kindly go into them at greater length, then indeed you will really deserve our thanks for satisfying the ambition we have cherished for so long. So far, we have learnt what we ought to aim at, and that in itself is very important. But we are also extremely eager to be given a more detailed indication of what the theory and method of the subject really amount to.'

'Well,' said Crassus, 'I have already gone beyond my own custom and inclination to meet your wishes. I was afraid that if I didn't you would go away! But how would it be, at this juncture, if we asked Antonius instead to tell us about the things he has been keeping to himself unpublished, apart from the single little volume that slipped out, as we heard him complain just now? Would it not be a good thing to get him to divulge these mysteries of the oratorical profession?'

'Yes, why not?' said Sulpicius. 'And besides, even if it is he who is going to do the speaking and not yourself, we can be sure that his words will represent your views as well.'

'Very well, then, Antonius,' Crassus continued, 'since nothing will stop these determined young men from exploiting us seniors, I call upon you to take up the theme! You know what is required of you. Kindly let us have your views.'

'I see I am caught,' replied Antonius. 'That is perfectly clear. And the trouble is that the questions you are asking me about are right outside my knowledge and experience. Furthermore, our friends here are forcing me into a situation which I always take good care to avoid in the lawcourts – the situation of having to follow after a speech made by Crassus!

'But there is one reason why I shall not feel too utterly diffident in approaching the task. What I mean is this: I expect to be accorded the same favour which I customarily receive in court – that no one should expect me to display the graces. For I am not going to speak about the art of rhetoric; I never learnt such a thing. What I shall be talking about is my own experience. The stock arguments in *my* notebooks are not theoretical points I picked up in the course of any reading but actual problems that have arisen in lawsuits. And if you, being men of great learning, do not think much of what I shall be telling you, then you will have only yourselves to blame for having been so unreasonable as to ask me about matters I know nothing about. And you must also, please, admit that I am a good natured man, because I have allowed your enthusiasm to get the better of my own judgement, so that here I am humouring your request without making too much of a fuss about it.'

'Just go ahead then, Antonius,' said Crassus, 'and stop worrying; because it is quite safe to assume that what you are going to say will be so sensible that none of us will in the least regret having brought all this pressure to bear on you.'

'Then go ahead I shall,' Antonius answered. 'And I propose to begin by doing what I believe should come first in every discussion. For one ought to start by defining one's theme: since it is essential to prevent the inquiry from just rambling on and meandering about, which is what would surely happen if its participants all harboured contradictory definitions of the subject we were trying to discuss.

'If, for example, we were talking about the art of generalship, I should feel we ought to get it quite clear, at the very outset, just what a general is. He is a man, one could say, who has been put in charge of conducting a war; and then we could go on to speak of troops, encampments, marching orders, engagements, sieges of towns, questions of supply, the ways to set and avoid ambushes, and all other matters relating to warfare. Good generals, I should then say, are the men whose capacity and knowledge have made them masters of these subjects; and I should cite as examples the elder Africanus and Fabius Maximus and Epaminondas and Hannibal and commanders of that calibre.

'Or if we were seeking to discover the essential characteristics of the man who devotes his experience, knowledge and endeavours to the government of the State, I should offer some definition such as this: a successful statesman, the person who guides the nation and controls its policy, may be defined as the individual who knows and employs the means of securing and promoting the interests of his country. And then I could mention Publius Lentulus, that distinguished leader of the Senate, and Tiberius Gracchus senior, and Quintus Metellus Macedonicus,[1] and Scipio Africanus the younger, and Gaius Laelius, and countless other eminent figures in our own and other lands.

'And if, again, we were trying to find out what sort of person it would be right to define as a lawyer, I should describe him as the man who possesses an expert knowledge of the statutes, and has studied the customs followed by the citizens who belong to his community; the man who is qualified to offer legal opinions, give instructions regarding the conduct of an action, and safeguard his clients. And in this category I should cite Sextus Aelius Paetus, Manius Manilius and Publius Mucius Scaevola.[2]

'Next let us turn to less important arts. If we were examining the qualities of musicians, or literary experts, or poets, I could explain their various claims in similar terms, and indicate the limits of what can be required of each category. As for the philosopher he stands alone because of his own claims that his peculiar faculty and wisdom are virtually all embracing. Nevertheless, he too can be defined after a fashion, as the man who seeks to learn the meaning, nature and causes of every heavenly and human phenomenon, and claims to understand and put into practice the entire science of right living.

'Now, however, the person we are attempting to analyse is the orator: and I do not see him in the same light as Crassus does. What Crassus was doing, it seemed to me, was to group together within this one single profession the entire range of human knowledge on every subject that exists. I, on the other hand, just envisage the orator as a person who can employ

1. Publius Cornelius Lentulus was consul in 162 BC and leader of the Senate from 125. For the elder Tiberius Gracchus and Quintus Caecilius Metellus Macedonicus see pp. 142, 215.

2. For Sextus Aelius Paetus Catus, Manius Manilius and Publius Scaevola see pp. 305, 327, 292.

language agreeable to the ear, and who is capable of putting forward convincing arguments in lawsuits and public debates. That is the man I would describe as an orator. And I would also want him to be equipped with vocal powers, good delivery, and a certain amount of wit.

'Crassus's own much wider definition of oratory was surely based not so much upon any theoretical delimitations as upon his own personal abilities – which practically have no boundaries at all! For according to his verdict, the entire business of statesmanship was handed right over to the orator; and I was very surprised, Scaevola, to hear you conceding this point. After all, you yourself have succeeded in convincing the Senate on innumerable occasions, although the speeches by which you did so were only of the briefest and plainest character.

'And take that outstanding statesman Marcus Scaurus (who is staying at his country house not far from here, I believe).[1] If he ever heard that the great personal authority which he derives from his impressive character and intellect was being allocated by yourself, Crassus, to the sphere reserved for the orator, I really think he would at once come over here in person and frighten us into silence just by the expression on his face. For, although by no means contemptible as a speaker, he is another who depends much more on his knowledge of great affairs of state than on oratorical techniques.

'And besides, even if a man does happen to possess both capacities at the same time – if he is an influential political speaker as well as a good politician – that does not necessarily make him an orator. When an eloquent orator happens also to be a first-class administrator, the latter sort of expertise has not come to him from his oratory at all. The two sorts of talent are completely distinct; indeed they are separated by a wide

1. Marcus Aemilius Scaurus (consul 115 BC) wrote his memoirs. He had a villa at Tusculum, which in his son's time was burnt down by his slaves.

gulf. Marcus Cato, the younger Scipio, Quintus Metellus Macedonicus and Gaius Laelius were all eloquent men who possessed both sets of gifts at the same time. They became brilliant orators; and their statesmanship enhanced the glory of Rome. But to achieve these two ends they had employed entirely different approaches and methods.

'For the fact is that there is no earthly reason why a man should limit himself to the knowledge of one art and one only. Neither nature nor statute nor usage demand any such restriction. Pericles, for example, although he was the most eloquent man in Athens, also directed its national policy for very many years. But his combination of both these talents does not at all signify that they are one and the same thing. Nor does the fact that Publius Crassus combines gifts for oratory and law by any means warrant the conclusion that legal knowledge is a part of oratorical ability.[1]

'For just suppose that, whenever an expert in some branch of knowledge acquired some information in another field, we were then compelled to regard this second field as a subdivision of the branch in which he was an authority. If that were so, we should be obliged to assert that playing ball and shooting dice are an essential activity for a lawyer – since Publius Scaevola happens to be very good at both! And by the same line of reasoning the men the Greeks call physicists would have to be automatically regarded as poets as well, merely because the physicist Empedocles wrote a good poem.[2] As for the moral philosophers, they already claim universal possession and control of everything; their special province extends to all things that exist! And yet even they do not go so far as to assert that geometry or music form part of the equipment of a philosopher just because Plato is known to have been a master of both those arts.

1. For Publius Licinius Crassus Dives see above, p. 151.

2. Empedocles (p. 189) wrote poems *On Nature* and *Purifications*; 450 lines of them survive.

'However, if we really *must* subordinate every other subject in the world to oratory, at least let the matter be expressed in some unobjectionable way such as this. We do realize that eloquence cannot just be left bald and bare. Certainly it has to be adorned and embellished by a pleasing diversity of additions. So let us accept that the good speaker will find it necessary to have heard and seen a great deal, to have covered extensive ground in his thoughts and his reflections and his reading. But these are not things that have become his own personal property: they still belong to other people. What he has been doing is to get a good taste of these advantages. For I entirely agree that he has got to show himself a clever sort of man; in no subject can he just be an untrained novice. It is absolutely right for him to have made excursions into every topic. He must not be a stranger to any of them.

'At one point you started becoming very dramatic, Crassus, in the authentic philosophical style; but it didn't worry me. It was when you were talking about speakers whipping up or calming the feelings of their hearers. This, we agree, is precisely an orator's principal talent and job. But you maintained that he is incapable of achieving these aims until he has first obtained a profound insight into the nature of everything that exists, including human characters and motives. And this being so, you went on to say, the orator has to master philosophy: a pursuit in which, as we know, men of outstanding abilities, with ample spare time at their disposal, have actually spent their whole lives! I do not in the least underestimate the immense range of scientific learning they achieved. Indeed, such achievements have my warmest admiration. But as for ourselves who have to go down into the Forum and deal with the people of Rome, let us learn, and teach others, just as much about human nature as a human being can reasonably master; and we shall be entitled to feel content.

'Picture some powerful and impressive advocate who is doing everything in his power to work up a judge's feelings against his opponent. You cannot suppose that such a speaker has ever got stuck because he had failed to solve some philosophical problem – whether anger, shall we say, is a heated state of the emotions or an urge to avenge a smart. Or imagine, for that matter, an orator who is trying to stimulate judges or audiences to feel any other passion you like to mention. When will he ever feel the slightest need to repeat the commonplaces philosophers go in for? Indeed, some of them even refuse to concede that a person ought to have any feelings at all! They would regard it as criminal to try and arouse such emotions in a judge; while even those who pride themselves on being more tolerant and realistic are only prepared to allow them in the smallest and most modest doses.

'The orator, on the other hand, makes a point of overcolouring and exaggerating everything in daily life which is regarded as evil and disagreeable and undesirable, and he likewise does all he can to magnify and beautify whatever is commonly held to be pleasant and attractive. He takes the greatest care not to present himself as a sage among fools, for if he did that his listeners would just regard him as a tactless little Greek; or at all events, even if they admired his eloquence and wisdom, they would want to avoid looking like idiots themselves. Yet in any case the orator himself possesses such power to range through men's hearts, he is so good at penetrating their deepest feelings and thoughts, that he quite genuinely does not need all the definitions of the philosophers at all. It is not for him to worry whether the supreme good lies in the soul or the body or whether it consists of moral right or pleasure, or whether there is some way of uniting and blending morality and pleasure, or even whether, as some have maintained, nothing at all can be known or understood or apprehended with any certainty.

'These studies, I know very well, are imposing and complicated; and the theories based on them are numerous, lengthy and diverse. But this is not the sort of thing we are concerned with at all. What we are looking for, Crassus, is entirely different. What we want is an intelligent man, with a good brain sharpened still further by experience, who is able to form an incisive assessment of the thoughts and feelings and beliefs and hopes entertained by his fellow-countrymen, and indeed by any person whatsoever whom he may wish to convince on some subject or other by his eloquence. He must have his finger on the pulses of individuals of every sort, age and degree and must be able to sense the feelings of any audience he is pleading before, or likely to plead before.

'His philosophical books, on the other hand, he should keep for a leisurely holiday at a Tusculan villa, like the holiday we are enjoying now! Because if he ever has to talk about justice and loyalty, for example, he would be well advised not to let the idea of borrowing from Plato enter his head. For when Plato had to write down his views on such matters, the Republic he depicted was an unfamiliar bookish affair in which the concept of justice, as he interpreted it, was totally divorced from the actual everyday lives and customs of human societies.

'If Plato's ideas had actually been accepted by the nations and communities of the world, even your great reputation, Crassus, as one of Rome's most distinguished leaders, would not have allowed you to get away with an appeal you were once heard to utter in front of a huge crowd of your fellow-citizens.[1] "Deliver us from our miseries!" you cried. "Deliver us from the jaws of the men whose cruelty even a torrent of our blood will never sate! Suffer us not to be slaves to anyone but yourselves, the Roman nation: *your* slaves it is both practicable and right for us to be!" Well, I will say nothing about your use of the word "miseries" – though the philosophers declare that no man of moral strength can ever be involved in any such thing. And I had better not dwell on the

1. This was the speech made by Lucius Crassus in favour of the Servilian Law (106 BC), championing the Senate against the knights.

"jaws" from which you hope to be delivered. For you imply that, failing this rescue operation, your blood might be squandered by an unjust sentence. But surely, to quote the philosophers again, such a sentence is something which the Wise Man is incapable of experiencing.[1]

'However, did you not also venture to indicate that you yourself and indeed the entire Roman Senate, whose interests you were on that occasion upholding, were slaves? But can Virtue possibly be a slave, Crassus, according to these same philosophical authorities whose precepts you include within the orator's sphere? On the contrary she, and she alone, is free, and free forever. Even if our bodies are captured in war or bound in chains, it is axiomatic that virtue's rights and liberties remain inviolate and unrestricted. And when you went on to declare that the Senate not only can but must be slaves of our country, no philosopher in the world would be such an unmanly, soft and feeble fellow, so determined to subordinate everything to the standard of physical pleasure and pain, that he could agree to the idea that the Senate is the nation's slave! The opposite is surely the case: the nation has placed the reins of government in the Senate's hands and entrusted it with the power to act as controller and guide of the people as a whole.

'I admit that when you delivered that oration I regarded it as supernaturally eloquent at the time. But Publius Rutilius Rufus, who was a learned man and extremely devoted to these philosophical studies, took the opposite view, maintaining that what you said was injudicious – and indeed downright disgraceful and immoral. He also expressed very severe criticism of Servius Galba (whom he claimed to remember well) for working on the compassion of his audience in the same sort of way. Marcus Cato, who was Galba's bitter and implacable enemy, had attacked him with great ferocity in

1. A doctrine of the Stoics – who also, and alternatively, maintained that if a man did lose his life by an unjust verdict it would be no evil.

the Assembly (Cato has published the speech himself in his *Origins*), and next Lucius Scribonius brought forward a motion that there should be an inquiry into Galba's conduct. Galba then made the gesture which Rutilius, as I have said, viewed with such disfavour. Galba had a ward named Quintus, the orphan son of his kinsman Gaius Sulpicius Galus,[1] and what the little boy's guardian now did was to lift the little boy up high in the court, indeed he practically hoisted him on to his shoulders, so that the memory of the child's illustrious father should draw tears from the crowd. Then Galba appealed to the assembled multitude to look after his own two sons, behaving just as if he were a soldier making an emergency will on the eve of a battle; and he cried out that he was appointing the Roman people to take over the guardianship of the poor fatherless children. Although, at the time, Galba was the target of widespread unpopularity and hatred, this playing to the gallery, according to Rutilius, actually got him off the charge; and Cato, too, declared in his book that "if Galba had not exploited children and tears, he would have paid the penalty". Rutilius strongly condemned this sort of method, declaring that exile or even death was preferable to such humiliating behaviour.

'And that was not just empty talk on his part, since Rutilius meant what he said and practised what he preached. He was, as you know, a model of integrity; there was no more honourable and blameless man in all Rome. Consequently

1. Publius Rutilius Rufus (consul 105 BC) was a friend of the younger Scipio and of the Scaevolas (the Augur and the Priest). Servius Sulpicius Galba (consul 144 BC) had been prosecuted in 149 for massacring Lusitanians in Portugal and western Spain. Cato the Censor's *Origins* were a history of Rome up to the time of his death (149). Lucius Scribonius was a tribune, and Gaius Sulpicius Galus (consul 166 BC) an eminent astronomer. A verbal declaration of the testator's last wishes, given in the field 'without scales or tablets' (this is the phrase Cicero uses), was valid if made in the presence of three or four comrades.

when he himself on a later occasion came up for trial,[1] he flatly refused to utter any appeal to his judges, and would not even allow his counsel to add the slightest embellishments or embroideries to the bare facts of the case. Cotta here, who was a most able young barrister and was also the son of Rutilius's sister, was only allowed by his uncle to handle a minor part of the action. Quintus Scaevola the Priest also shared in the defence, speaking in his own unadorned fashion, and delivering a straightforward, terse oration.

'You were saying just now, Crassus, that a speaker ought to improve his fluency by drawing upon the material the philosophers use in their debates. Well, if on that day you yourself had defended Publius Rutilius, and I do not mean after the fashion of the philosophers but in precisely your own style, then, however crooked and villainous and guilty the judges may have been – and that is just what they were – the force of your eloquence would have been able to purge all trace of cruelty from their hearts. But what, in fact, happened was that Rutilius lost his case – and so we, for our part, lost a very fine man. And the reason why this happened was because his defence was conducted just as if the whole affair was taking place in Plato's ideal Republic. None of Rutilius's counsel produced any moans or shouts, none displayed the slightest sign of grief, there was not a sign of any protests, or calls upon the name of Rome, or pleas for mercy. In short, nobody so much as stamped a foot during the entire course of the trial. They behaved as if they were afraid they were going to be reported to the Stoics!

'Well, that is how a Roman of consular rank imitated the example of the great Socrates of old. For Socrates, though the wisest and most upright of men, had to stand trial for his life. He defended himself in person. But one would certainly not

1. Publius Rutilius was convicted in 92 BC for having engaged in corrupt practices while serving under Quintus Scaevola the Priest in Asia (western Asia Minor) two years earlier.

have thought he was a defendant or suppliant at all, for he behaved towards the men who were judging him more as if he was their tutor or slave-master. Lysias, who was an extremely eloquent orator, brought him the draft of a speech to learn by heart, if he wanted to, and then deliver at his trial.[1] Socrates read through the speech willingly enough, and remarked that it was agreeably phrased. But then he added; "If you had brought me a pair of shoes from Sicyon, I should not wear them, however well-fitting and comfortable they might be, because it would not be manly to do so. And the same applies to this speech of yours; it seems to me eloquent oratory, but deficient in the courage a man ought to show."

'And so Socrates was convicted, not only on the first count, when all the judges had to do was to decide whether they should condemn or acquit, but also on the second, which was a feature of Athenian law. For whenever a man was found guilty of any crime (other than murder, for which the punishment was fixed), there followed a sort of assessment of his penalty: when the judges were preparing to reach their decision, the convicted man was himself asked to name the maximum penalty he would acknowledge that he deserved. When Socrates was asked this question, he replied that what he deserved was to be granted the highest honours and rewards, and to be maintained at the public expense at the Prytaneum[2] – an honour which the Greeks rated above all others. This answer so infuriated the judges that in spite of Socrates's complete innocence they condemned him to death. If only he had been acquitted! It is no business of ours, of course – but he was such a genius.

1. The orator Lysias (c. 459–380 BC) was the son of a Syracusan who had settled in Athens.

2. A sort of town hall (also known as the Tholos) where the Prytaneis (executive committee of the Council) had their meals, and entertained foreign ambassadors at the public cost. Citizens of exceptional merit, and the children of those who fell in battle, were given seats at the table.

'Even if he *had* got off, the contempt which philosophers display for any eloquence not derived from their own field would still have been intolerably irritating. But as it is, seeing that the verdict was guilty – seeing that *he*, their own master, was condemned purely and simply because he had no idea how to defend himself, how can they still have the nerve to tell us that the whole art of oratory has to be learnt from themselves? The question whether their occupation is better or truer than ours I will leave on one side. All I am asserting now is that the two arts are entirely different. Eloquence, the finest possible kind of eloquence, can perfectly well exist without any assistance from philosophy at all.

*

'And now, Crassus, to turn to what you said about law. I can see why you embraced its cause with such warmth. Indeed, I already detected the reason before you had finished speaking. In the first place you wanted to pay a compliment to Scaevola, whom we are all very fond of because he is such an extremely charming man. You noted that his legal art was bare, unendowed and unadorned, and you enriched and adorned it with a dowry of fine words. And it is an art to which you yourself had dedicated a great deal of labour and effort, since you had living with you in your house a man who encouraged and stimulated your devotion. In consequence, you were afraid that unless you amplified the importance of the law by claiming that eloquence was merely one of its subdivisions you would have wasted your endeavours.

'Not that I have any quarrel with these legal studies of yours. By all means let us accept that the law is every bit as important as you say. Certainly no one can question that it is great and far-reaching, that it affects multitudes of people, that it has always been held in the highest repute, and that, today as ever, our most eminent citizens stand at the head of the profession. But take care, Crassus, all the same. Make quite sure that, when you are taking so much trouble to dress the law up in a strange and foreign costume, you do not at the same time succeed in despoiling and denuding it of things which by long tradition have been recognized as its true possessions. If you were merely saying that a lawyer can at the same time be an orator, and an orator can at the same time be a lawyer, you would then be assuming the existence of two separate arts, both noble, neither inferior to the other – partners in dignity. But what you are doing instead is to claim that men can be, and often have been, good lawyers without possessing any of the eloquence we are talking about; and yet at the same time you are denying that anyone can be an orator unless he has acquired knowledge of the law. So according to you a lawyer *in his own right* is nothing but a sharp, tricky little practitioner, a mere clerk of procedure, a manipulator of cant formulas, a master of verbal quibbles. But just because a man speaking in court often has to appeal to the law, you have also attached the whole of legal science as a sort of servant and hanger-on at the orator's heels.

'You expressed wonder at the impudence of those pleaders who profess great things when they do not know even small ones, and have the effrontery to tackle the most important court cases though they have no knowledge of the subject and have never studied it. But these phenomena admit of a simple and easy explanation. Consider a man who does not know the form of words of a certain type of marriage contract; there is no reason to feel surprised if he nevertheless proves competent to plead the cause of a woman who has been married according to the formula in question. You cannot compare the two pursuits of oratory and the law in the same terms as you can compare the navigation of a small ship and a large one. In that case, a man who performs the latter task needs the same *sort* of knowledge as the other person. But it does not at all follow that a man who does not know the form of words needed to demand the division of a property must for that reason be incapable of arguing a lawsuit on the same subject.

'Think of those important actions before the Board of One Hundred which, as you pointed out, hinged on judicial questions. All the cases you mentioned could have been argued fluently enough by an eloquent man who knew nothing about the law. And indeed, as it so happened, the legal points involved in every one of the actions you referred to were so obscure that they provoked total disagreement, even among the greatest experts. This was true, for example, of the recent lawsuit in which you represented Manius Curius. It was also true of the dispute about Gaius Hostilius Mancinus, and of the issue concerning the boy who was born to a second wife before the first wife had been sent notice of divorce. The speakers employed on those occasions did not need any familiarity with the law. The victorious advocate was not going to achieve his success by virtue of any special legal learning of his own, but by knowledge he had borrowed from someone else: it was not legal expertise but eloquence that would earn him his victory.

'I often used to hear a story about Publius Crassus Dives Mucianus. When he was standing for the aedileship, Servius Galba, though his senior and a former consul, used to accompany him when he went round canvassing, since Galba had married his son Gaius to Publius Crassus's daughter.[1] On one occasion a rustic came up to Crassus to consult him on a point of law. But when this individual had taken Crassus aside and put the matter before him, he got advice which, although correct, was by no means what he hoped to hear. Whereupon Galba, seeing how annoyed he was, called out to him by name, and asked what he had been consulting Crassus about. Then, after listening to what the man said and observing his distress, Galba remarked; "Evidently Publius Crassus must have been preoccupied by other matters when he was dealing with

1. Publius Licinius Crassus Dives was aedile in about 137 BC. Gaius Sulpicius Galba was an orator admired by Cicero.

your inquiry." And he took hold of Crassus and said, "Look, how on earth did you come to offer an opinion like that?" Crassus, who possessed an extremely expert knowledge of the law, repeated with full assurance that the position was exactly as he had advised, and that there was no room for argument. But Galba, in a humorous fashion, brought up a host of varied analogies and illustrations pointing out the advantages of equity as opposed to strict law. And finally we are told that Crassus, who although a good speaker, was not in the same class as Galba, took refuge in written authorities, pointing out that the advice he had given corresponded with what appeared in the books of his brother Publius Scaevola and the notes of Sextus Aelius.[1] And yet Crassus had to admit that Galba's argument possessed great plausibility – and could almost be described as right!

'Another reason why the orator need not be very strong in knowledge of the law is that a whole mass of cases, in which the legal position is perfectly clear, never get as far as the courts at all. To take a single example, if the head of a family has made a will and a son is subsequently born to him, who would bother to claim an inheritance under the will? Nobody: because it is a well-known fact that the will has been cancelled by the subsequent birth. So this entire branch of jurisprudence produces not a single action in court. Consequently, the orator can safely disregard the whole range of undisputed law – and it constitutes far and away the largest part of the legal field.

'But even when we turn to the sort of judicial topic which does give rise to learned disputes, it will be quite easy for him to discover authorities in support of whatever case he may happen to be defending. They can supply him with his javelins, ready for action; and then it is up to him to hurl the weapons himself – with all the strength of his orator's arm. Now, I do not want to offend your excellent father-in-law

1. On Sextus Aelius Paetus Catus see above, p. 305.

Scaevola. However, you did not find it necessary to mobilize all his writings and maxims, did you, when you were arguing the case of Manius Curius? Surely you followed quite a different procedure, emphasizing the claims of equity against strict law, and insisting on the spirit behind the will, and the intention which had been in the dead man's mind.

'Indeed, in my opinion (and I was often by your side, listening to what you said) you have won the vast majority of your favourable verdicts by sheer wit and charm – and by some very good jokes. I remember you mocking Quintus Mucius Scaevola the Priest for his brilliant discovery that *a man, before dying, first has to be born.* And meanwhile you would whip up a host of relevant points drawn from statutes and senatorial decrees and from everyday life and conversation. Your performances of this kind were not merely shrewd but funny, whereas a strict adherence to the letter instead of the spirit would not have produced anything like the same results. And so the court was full of laughter and good spirits. But what use, I ask, did you make of your legal experience in all this? None, because what served your purpose was something quite different, a remarkable gift for eloquence, supplemented by a marked capacity to provide charm and entertainment.

'Now your adversary on that occasion, Scaevola the Priest, might well have been expected to figure as the upholder of his father's juridical tradition, and as the champion, one might say, of his own hereditary rights.[1] And yet, when Quintus spoke against you on that occasion, not one of the arguments he introduced into his speech bore the slightest sign of having been borrowed from the law. He never recited a single statute,

1. His father Publius Mucius Scaevola (consul 133 BC) had been the first member of the family to win distinction as a jurist, being an authority on priestly law; and Quintus the Priest himself (who, after Quintus the Augur, taught Cicero) set out the whole *ius civile* in eighteen books. See Genealogical Table (I), p. 360.

and entirely kept off any and every matter which the uninitiated might have found obscure. Instead he concentrated on one contention and one only: that all possible weight must be attached to the written word. And yet this is merely the sort of elementary point which boys are trained to debate about in the schools, when they are presented with cases of this kind and told to assess the rival claims of the written word on the one hand and equity on the other.

'And then take the case of that soldier. Are you really going to tell me that, if you had been appearing either for him or for the heir, you would have relied on the *Precedents of Hostilius*[1] rather than on your own powers and gifts as a speaker? Not a bit of it. Had you been arguing in support of the will, you would have arranged matters so that the entire validity of every will in the world would seem to be staked on the result of this one single case. And if, on the other hand, it had been the soldier's cause you were pleading, you would have employed your usual eloquence to conjure up his father from the dead. You would have managed to resuscitate the old man before our very eyes. We should have seemed actually to see him embracing his son, and weeping and commending the youth to the merciful compassion of the judges. The scene would have been enough to extract tears and lamentations from the very stones of the building. And then who would have bothered about all that technical business in the Twelve Tables, starting "As the tongue hath declared"?[2] The legal authority of the Tables, which you claim to prefer to all the libraries in the world put together, would have been neither here nor there; for all the part it would have played in the case it might just as well have been any old formula botched up by some professor.

1. Nothing more is known of this collection of forms of proceeding, which evidently comprised cases affecting wills.

2. A testament was originally an oral declaration incorporated into the legal act.

'And then you censured the young for their laziness, because they do not learn by heart all this law you are so keen upon. To begin with, you declared, the whole subject is perfectly easy. But on that point we must defer to the people who strut about claiming to know all about legal studies – and they make them out to be extremely difficult! Besides, ought you not to consider whether you are being quite logical here? For at one moment you are saying "this is a simple art", and at the next you contradict yourself by declaring that it is not really an art at all, but will become an art one day – when someone unspecified has managed to learn *another* art which can show him how to systematize this one. You then went on to suggest that law makes a very entertaining study. But I am quite sure everyone will be only too glad to leave you to enjoy yourself in that way – without feeling any enthusiasm for this particular amusement themselves. If something has to be learnt by heart, there would be a universal preference for a good play, say the *Teucer* of Pacuvius, rather than Manilius's *Forms for Contracts of Sale.*[1]

'Next you argued that patriotic motives ought to impel us to study the practices invented by our ancestors. But surely it must be quite clear to you that the decisions taken in antiquity have, by now, either fallen into the extreme decrepitude of old age, or indeed may well have been superseded altogether by more recent legislation. And then take your conviction that legal studies make a man good, because the law offers rewards to virtue and punishments to vice. I personally was always under the impression that, if virtue can be rationally taught at all, this has to be done by exposition and persuasion, and not by menaces and force and intimidation. For here, at any rate, is one thing that we surely can learn without having the

1. The *Teucer* was one of the most successful tragedies of Ennius's nephew Pacuvius. Manius Manilius (consul 149 BC) was an eminent jurist who was regarded as one of the founders of the *ius civile*. He appears in Cicero *On the State*.

slightest knowledge of the law: that it is an excellent thing not to behave badly!

'You were kind enough to make an exception in my favour and say I am the only man who is capable of pleading a case adequately without possessing any legal learning. And on that point, Crassus, I should like to offer a comment. Certainly, I never learnt the law. And yet never once, in any case I ever argued before the praetors, have I felt the lack of that knowledge. For even without being a master of some specific subject or art, it is perfectly possible to avoid being stupid and ignorant about the ordinary daily affairs and customs of mankind.

'When one of us manages to snatch an opportunity to walk over his farm and take a glimpse at country life, either for profit or pleasure, he would be quite abnormally unobservant and stupid if he remained in total ignorance of sowing and reaping and the pruning of trees or vines, and the seasons at which these operations take place, and the methods that are appropriate in each case. Supposing, in other words, that we have occasion to go over a property, or give the manager directions about an agricultural matter or instruct the bailiff to do something, must one really first make a thorough study of all the technical writings on the subject by Mago the Carthaginian?[1] Surely we can be perfectly satisfied with whatever ordinary knowledge we have managed to pick up.

'The same applies to the law. We have to endure the wear and tear of every sort of business in the Forum, judicial and otherwise, and we can rest content if we know enough about the statutes to ensure that we do not seem like foreigners and strangers in our own country. Or even if, one day, we should happen to get employed in some lawsuit of a more complicated nature, it would not be all that difficult to get in touch with

1. The name of Mago was attached to a twenty-eight volume Punic work on agriculture brought to Rome and translated by order of the Senate after the destruction of Carthage in 146 BC.

Scaevola here; though in such cases we usually get the necessary information from the opposing parties themselves, who are always ready to contribute all the legal advice and research an advocate might need. And if there is some question of fact, or a problem of boundaries for example – when a visit to the actual spot is not possible – or a point relating to account-books or receipts, then once again we are confronted with complex and often very difficult technicalities which we know nothing about; and we just have to get them up. And when it is a question of mastering statutes or expert legal opinions, the situation is the same. That is to say, we have no reason whatever to fear that our failure to devote very much study to the subject all through the years will mean we cannot contrive to get a grip of whatever may be needed when the particular occasion arises.

'Should we conclude, then, that a speaker will find knowledge of the law entirely useless? Personally I should not be prepared to dismiss any sort of knowledge whatever as altogether lacking in value, especially for a man eager to achieve real oratorical excellence, which is a thing that needs a lot of material to keep it going. But even the qualifications which are absolutely indispensable for an orator are already numerous and extensive enough, and by no means easy to come by, and I would not want him to dissipate his energy over too many branches of learning.

'We should all agree, for example, that a speaker's bearing and deportment will be better for the gestures and grace of a Roscius. And yet nobody would, on that account, urge youthful trainees in oratory to work as hard at perfecting their movements as actors do. Again, the most essential thing of all for an orator is his voice. All the same, no one with ambitions in this direction would be well advised to become a slave to his own voice, as Greek tragic actors seem to be. They spend years and years just sitting and practising declamation; and every day, before giving their performance, they throw themselves down flat on the ground. From there they declaim; and the sounds they utter grow gradually louder and louder. Then, when they have finished their stage appearance, they come back and sit down, and in that position they regain control of their voices, so to speak, by gradually bringing them down from highest treble to deepest bass. If we orators felt like doing this, our clients would already have been convicted long before we had got through the number of chants and arias required.

'Certainly an orator's eloquence depends very largely on his voice. But that does not mean we must give it a disproportionate amount of our time. Gesture, too, is a great help. But we must not exaggerate our attention to that either. In each of these matters we can only attain the degree of proficiency compatible with such small amount of leisure as all our public business allows us. Still less, therefore, ought we to immerse ourselves too thoroughly in the study of the law. In the first place one can get a general grasp of the subject without any instruction at all. And anyway it is not quite in the same category as the other things I was talking about. Vocal powers and gestures are qualifications you cannot just acquire from some external source or other at any time you wish, whereas the points you need from the law, the requirements of any particular case, *can* be picked up from experts or works of reference at any moment you may happen to need them.

'That is why the leading Greek orators, knowing nothing about the law themselves, employ skilled assistants for their cases, men who, as you mentioned a little while ago, are known as attorneys. Our own countrymen, however, have adopted a much better arrangement. In order to give their laws and judicial decisions the finest protection possible they wanted to have at their disposal the most distinguished and authoritative statesmen they could get. However, surely the Greeks, too, would have thought of this idea if they had regarded it as necessary – that is to say, they would, like us, have taught their statesmen and orators a sufficiency of the law instead of giving them attorneys to help them.

'You also remarked that the reputation of being a legal expert saves a man from loneliness when he grows old. Perhaps the possession of a lot of money can achieve just as good a result! However, we are not considering what is advantageous to ourselves, but what is necessary for the orator. In the course of this investigation, we have had occasion to take a good many points of comparison from the acting profession; and let us now do so once again. Roscius, whom we were quoting just now, is fond of remarking that the older he gets the more he wants the flautist who accompanies him to moderate his speed and intensity. Now if Roscius, tied down as he is by definite rhythmical and metrical rules, is nevertheless able to think out some sort of relief for his old age, it should be a very great deal easier for ourselves, too, to quieten our tones down – and even to change them altogether.

*

'For as you are well aware, Crassus, the styles of oratory are many and diverse. Indeed I rather imagine that you were the first person to offer us a practical demonstration of the point, since you yourself, for some time now, have spoken in a much more serene and gentle manner than you employed before. But you are still very impressive, and this milder style commends itself to your audiences just as much as your earlier and much more forceful and passionate approach used to please them. Earlier generations, too, had orators of the same type. For many speakers, including, we are told, the great Scipio Africanus the younger and Laelius, obtained all their effects by raising their voices only a little above the tones of ordinary conversation. They never strained their lungs and shouted like Servius Galba.

'But in any case even if one day you will no longer be able

to manage even this quieter manner, indeed even if you no longer want to speak at all, are you really so afraid that a man and citizen of your calibre will find his home deserted by one and all merely because the litigious members of society no longer have cause to flock to it? On this point my views differ from yours completely. Far from agreeing that the people who flock in for consultations are a prop for one's old age, the solitude you find so alarming seems to me a haven to look forward to. For in my opinion the most splendid asset of old age is spare time!

*

'As you say, the remaining requirements – history, and public law, and antique customs, and precedents of every kind – are useful to an orator. But should I ever feel a need for them, I can always borrow what I want from my excellent friend Congus, who knows all about such things.[1]

'Certainly, if Sulpicius and Cotta act on your advice and read and listen to everything, and take part in every pursuit a cultured person ought to take part in, I shall be the last to raise any objection. But, heaven knows, Crassus, if they are really going to get down seriously to everything you expect them to do, they are going to have their work cut out! Even if the rules you laid down may be virtually essential if our young friends are really going to achieve the heights they are aiming at, were you not perhaps, all the same, being just a little harsh on them, considering their youthful years? For think of the training you required them to perform. It included extempore exercises on stated problems, in addition to carefully prepared set speeches, not to speak of those written compositions which, as you rightly say, provide the finishing touch to the process of instruction. Now all these exercises require a very great deal of strenuous work. And if, in addition, the poor men

1. Junius Congus, a celebrated antiquarian referred to by Cicero elsewhere.

are expected to compare their own productions with what other people have written, and attempt impromptu appreciations of the latter compositions as well, allocating them praise or blame, approval or refutation, their memory and imitative capacity are going to be subjected to very extensive demands.

'Another claim you made really shocked me – and I am convinced it will act as a deterrent rather than a stimulus. I refer to your observation that every one of us ought to be a sort of Roscius. You also remarked that the approval accorded to the good things in a speech customarily falls far short of the lasting disapproval earned by the bad things. Here again I disagree. In my view, speakers are judged less severely than actors. Personally I have formed the impression that, even when our voices are quite hoarse, we can still get an extremely attentive hearing. This is because the interest of the case itself is sufficient to hold the audience. Whereas Aesopus on the other hand, if he shows so much as a trace of huskiness, gets hissed right off the stage![1]

'For whenever you have an art which aims solely at entertainment, at the gratification of the ear, the slightest decrease in this gratification is regarded by listeners as disagreeable. But in oratory the range of things that can provide satisfaction is far wider; and even if any particular speaker may not possess every one of them to absolute perfection, the substantial presence even of a fair number of these qualities will in itself be sufficient to win a high degree of approval.

*

'And now let us return to the point where we began. We may accept Crassus's definition of the orator as someone who can speak in a manner which enables him to persuade people. But the man in question ought to limit himself to the activities

1. Aesopus was a tragic actor who gave the young Cicero lessons in elocution.

which are concerned with the ordinary daily life of the community and the Forum. Noble and glorious though other pursuits may be, he has got to leave the whole lot of them aside.

'Let him take the great Athenian Demosthenes as his model.[1] There was a man whose supremacy as an orator is universally admitted. And his keenness and energy were absolutely indefatigable: as he showed at the outset of his career, by the untiring way in which he persevered to overcome his natural handicaps. One of these disadvantages was his stammer, which was so bad that he was quite unable to pronounce the initial letter of his own art, the "R" in rhetoric. And yet by sheer practice he made himself as fluent a speaker as anyone in the world. Another of his troubles was shortness of breath. However, in time, he learnt to control this so successfully that he could deliver a whole period in one single breath, raising and lowering his voice twice in the process. His own writings indicate as much. Another story tells how he used to put pebbles in his mouth and then declaim a large number of verses as loud as he could without drawing breath at all. And sometimes, during these exercises, he preferred not to stand still in one place, but strode about, or even clambered up a steep slope.

'Provided that this is the kind of training you recommend for making young men work hard, I am with you completely, Crassus. But when we come to all the other qualifications you amassed together from so many different activities and arts, the fact that you yourself have mastered the whole lot of them does not alter my conviction that they are entirely unconnected with the proper function and business of an orator.'

*

1. As Cicero claimed to do (to avoid the opposing excesses of too exuberant or too plain a style). Cicero also translated one of Demosthenes's speeches (*For Ctesiphon*).

After Antonius had finished speaking, both Sulpicius and Cotta were clearly unable to make up their minds which of the two lines of argument seemed closer to the truth. But Crassus had something more to say. 'Oh, Antonius,' he protested, 'you want to make the orator into nothing better than an unskilled labourer. However, I have a strong suspicion that this is really not your view at all. I suspect that what you are doing is to indulge your remarkable taste for contradiction, which has always been a speciality of yours. And this taste for paradox, indeed, is a gift peculiarly characteristic of orators; though philosophers have now taken up the habit too, and particularly those who make a practice of arguing elaborately for and against whatever thesis you choose to put before them.

'Now I, on the other hand, did not think it right, especially with yourselves as my listeners, merely to depict the type of orator who spends his whole life in court and concentrates on the necessities that his cases there required. On the contrary, I had my eye on a distinctly higher idea; and that is why I expressed the opinion that the orator, especially in our own community, ought to possess the most extensive possible equipment. You, however, Antonius, have preferred to circumscribe his entire task within narrow limits. And certainly this will facilitate your task when you let us know your conclusions about his functions and the rules that ought to govern them!

'But not, I suggest, until tomorrow. Today we have talked enough. For Scaevola, who is planning to move on to his own villa here at Tusculum, ought to have a bit of a rest until the day turns cooler; and considering the hour we had better think about our own health as well.'

Everyone considered this a good idea. But Scaevola added a final comment. 'I wish I hadn't promised Lucius Aelius to go and join him today at my place![1] It would have been

1. On Lucius Aelius Stilo Praeconinus see above, p. 303. The

fascinating to hear what Antonius is going to say next.' And as Scaevola rose to his feet, he added with a smile: 'I wasn't so much annoyed when he pulled our law to pieces as amused when he admitted how little he knows of the subject himself.'

---

manuscripts read 'Laelio', but Gaius Laelius (see *On Friendship*) must have been dead long before the date at which the discussion is supposed to have taken place.

# THE DREAM OF SCIPIO

IN 54 BC, a year in which the triumvirs were kept busy – Pompeius trying to keep order at Rome, Crassus planning the eastern expedition against Parthia which was to cause his death, and Caesar undertaking a second reconnaissance in Britain – Cicero began his six volumes *On the State*. The treatise was finished some three years later. It comprises a discussion, supposed to have lasted for three days, between Scipio Africanus the younger (seen as the ideal blend of statesman and philosopher) and Laelius and other members of their circle. The occasion is stated to have been the Latin Holiday (January or early February), during the year of Scipio's death (129 BC). Conscious of the recent failures of Rome's politics in his own day, which had led to the autocratic triumvirate, Cicero lays stresses on constitutionalism, but admits the need of a strong hand to maintain the equilibrium.

*On the State* has come down to us in a fragmentary condition. Until 1820, when Cardinal Mai discovered about a third of the work at the Vatican, nothing was known of it except the *Dream of Scipio*, which is translated here. Originally a portion of Book VI, it has survived without interruption and attracted immense attention, especially in the last days of antiquity and throughout the Middle Ages (p. 36).

The dream which the younger Scipio Africanus narrates is about the heavenly habitation: a brilliant vision which is the climax to the sociological and philosophical analyses in the earlier part of the main work, and sets them in cosmic perspective. Describing his dream, Scipio discloses the nature and structure of the universe, offering a weird but impressive exposition of the sort of astral theology which had been prevalent in preceding centuries, based on the predominance of the Sun.[1] One feature of the system has fascinated many a subsequent European writer – the sounds that emanate from the heavenly bodies on their courses: the music of the spheres.

> Ring out ye crystal spheres.
> Once bless our human ears,
> If ye have power to touch our senses so;
> And let your silver chime
> Move in melodious time;
> And let the bass of Heaven's deep organ blow,
> And with your ninefold harmony
> Make up full consort to the angelic symphony.[2]

Whether this concept of the harmony of the spheres goes back to Pythagoras (p. 348) or not, he is one of the ultimate authorities to whom many of these ideas about the universe can be traced back, as well as the picture of the Transmigration of Souls which also appears in the *Dream*. This doctrine had been passed on to Plato, whose Myth of Er the Pamphylian, dwelling in the other world, helped to inspire Cicero's vision.[3] Cicero's other sources are greatly disputed; for such ideas were generally in the air. For example, there was a tradition, dating back at least to the second century BC, that the Egyptian sage Nechepso had been carried off by a divine being and transported to the heights, where a voice had sounded in his ear and a dark form had appeared to him.[4] And in the generation before Cicero many cosmological speculations that we know from the *Dream* had been collected by the Syrian Stoic Posidonius (p. 27).[5]

1. For a description of this cult see M. Grant, *The Climax of Rome*, Weidenfeld & Nicolson, 1968, pp. 172ff.
2. John Milton, *Ode on the Morning of Christ's Nativity*. Cf. Sir Thomas Browne (1605–82): 'There is music wherever there is harmony, order or proportion; and thus far we may maintain the music of the spheres.'
3. Plato, *Republic*, X, 614ff.
4. Fragment 1 Riess – Vettius Valens, *Anthologies*, p. 241, 16 Kroll.
5. It has also been argued that Aristotle, or alternatively Antiochus of Ascalon, was a principal source for the *Dream*.

These varied traditions are firmly Romanized by Cicero, who declares that the figure who appears before the younger Scipio Africanus in his sleep is his adoptive grandfather, the elder Africanus, conqueror of Hannibal and epitome of Roman glory.[1] The heavenly domain which the great man displays to his descendant is the abode of great and righteous spirits, for whose company the younger Scipio is bidden to prepare himself once his life on earth shall be ended. In the *Dream* we find the doctrine of selective immortality – for those who have deserved well of their country – an idea which was later developed, with further poetic variations, by Virgil in the sixth book of his *Aeneid.* It seems, logically, an indefensible doctrine, 'falling short of the justice demanded by the reason and conscience of mankind' (C. N. Cochrane). Moreover, such beliefs clashed in Cicero's mind with the sceptical tendencies implanted in him by the Academy (p. 29). At other times it seems as if he would find it easier to believe that there is no afterlife except the sort of 'immortality' conferred by fame;[2] although here in the *Dream*, disillusioned about public life and uncharacteristically pointing to its comparative triviality, he is at pains to make the elder Africanus deny the effectiveness or durability of any such earthly renown. Through the lips of the great commander, Cicero, for all his profound consciousness of Roman grandeur,

1. See Genealogical Table (II), p. 361.

2. On fame as the guarantee of immortality see *Philippics*, XIV, 12, 33, etc. In the speech *For Sestius*, 68, 143, this idea is combined with the concept of the survival of the soul: and cf. p. 183 above. In the *Letters*, on the other hand, he interprets death as annihilation; though when Tullia was dead he refused to accept such a view, referring back to his Stoic belief in the divine spark shared by all human souls (*Tusculans*, I, 25, 60). But Cicero, though he often discussed immortality, never quite found an answer to satisfy him. As he himself said, when he was reading Plato's *Phaedo* arguing in favour of it he was convinced, but when he put it down all his agreement slipped away (*Tusculans*, I, 11, 24).

sets all this pomp in its place as a single, diminutive aspect of eternity.[1] For the circumstances in which Cicero wrote encouraged a sombre, disenchanted sense of the transitoriness of human things. Moreover, the dramatic date of the *Dream* immediately preceded and foreshadowed the younger Scipio's mysterious death, perhaps compassed by his enemies (p. 182). At the time when Cicero was writing, the future of the Republic was again shrouded in black clouds, for its free working was eclipsed by dictatorial government: though not yet so totally eclipsed as to dishearten Cicero from uttering his conviction, apparently at variance with his estimate of worldly greatness, that patriotic service is the way to the gods.

1. Compare a similar sentiment in *On the State*, I, 17, 26; cf. *On Laws*, I, 23, 61.

# THE DREAM OF SCIPIO

As you know, I was military tribune in the Fourth Legion in Africa under the command of the consul Manius Manilius. When I arrived there I was particularly eager to meet King Masinissa, who for good reason was a close friend of my family.[1] When I came into his presence the old man embraced me and wept. Then, after a moment, he lifted his eyes to heaven and uttered these words.

'Most glorious Sun and other heavenly beings, I offer you my thanks![2] For before I depart from this life, I am now seeing with my own eyes, within this kingdom of mine and beneath my roof, Publius Cornelius Scipio. The very sound of his name revives my strength. For never a moment has the recollection of his glorious, invincible forbear faded from my memory.'[3]

Then I began asking him questions about his kingdom, and he in turn interrogated me about Rome; and so we spent the whole day in conversation. Afterwards, he entertained me in regal splendour, and we continued our discussion far into the night, as the aged king wanted nothing better than to talk of Africanus. He had not forgotten a single deed the great man had ever done, or a single word he had ever uttered.

1. Manius Manilius, consul in 149 BC, was in command of the Roman force which besieged Carthage at the beginning of the Third Punic War. King Masinissa of Numidia (eastern Algeria) had helped the elder Scipio Africanus to win his decisive victory in the Second Punic War (at Zama in 203). In 150 Masinissa goaded the Carthaginians to attack him, thus provoking the Romans to intervene on his side and start the Third Punic War. He died in 149.

2. The peoples of north Africa paid special attention to the worship of the Sun, which played so great a part in current Mediterranean religion (p. 338).

3. For the Scipio family see Genealogical Table (II), p. 361.

When we finally parted and retired to bed, my journey and the lateness of the hour had made me tired, and I fell into a deeper sleep than usual. As I slept I had a dream, prompted no doubt by what we had been talking about. For it frequently happens that the subjects of our meditations and discussions reappear in our dreams. This happened for example to the poet Ennius; he writes of his dream about Homer, who was naturally the constant subject of his thoughts and conversations when he was awake.[1] And so I dreamt that Africanus was with me; his appearance recalled his portrait busts rather than his actual living self.[2]

*

I recognized him – and trembled with fear. But he spoke to me; and this is what he said.

'Calm yourself, Scipio. Do not be afraid. But remember carefully the things I am about to tell you. Do you see that city there? It was I who made its people submit to Rome. But now they are starting up the old conflicts once again; they refuse to remain at peace!' And from where he stood amid the bright illumination of radiant stars, he pointed down at Carthage, and began speaking once more. 'This,' he declared, 'is the city you have come to attack. At present you are not much more than an ordinary soldier. But within the space of two years you will have been elected consul, and then you will overthrow the place utterly. Thereafter the surname, which you now bear as an inheritance from myself, will be yours by your own right. Later on, after you have destroyed Carthage and celebrated a Triumph, after you have held the

1. A reference to a passage in the *Annals* of Ennius (239–169 BC); elsewhere Cicero quotes his actual words. It was said that Ennius believed himself to be a reincarnation of Homer.

2. In fact, however, the younger Scipio did not know his older relation, since he was born in about the year of the elder Scipio's death (184).

office of censor and undertaken missions to Egypt, Syria, Asia and Greece, you will be elected to the consulship for the second time, while you are absent, and you will win a very great war and raze Numantia to the ground. But at the time when you yourself are proceeding in Triumph to the Capitol, you will find the government in a state of confusion: for which the machinations of my grandson will be responsible.[1]

'After that, Africanus, it will be your duty to devote to your people the full splendid benefit of all your integrity, talent and wisdom. But at that juncture I see two divergent paths of destiny opening up before you. For when your life has completed seven times eight circuitous revolutions of the sun, and when these two numbers, each of which for a different reason is regarded as possessing some quality of perfection,[2] have in their natural course brought you to your supreme moment of destiny, that is the time when the entire Roman State will turn to you and all that you stand for: the Senate, every right-minded citizen, our subject allies, the entire Latin people. The fate of the whole country, at that juncture, will depend on you and you alone. In other words, it will be your duty to assume the role of dictator, and restore order to our commonwealth – provided only that death does not overtake you at the criminal hands of your own kinsmen!'[3]

1. The younger Scipio was consul in 147 BC, destroyed Carthage in 146, held the censorship in 142, headed a delegation in the eastern Mediterranean in c. 140–138, was consul for the second time in 134, and destroyed Numantia in Spain in 133. The grandson to whom the elder Scipio refers is the tribune Tiberius Gracchus, who was killed in the same year (p. 199). Scipio's Triumph was in 132.

2. The idea of 'perfect' numbers went back to Pythagoras (p. 22). There are various contradictory explanations why seven and eight were perfect.

3. After the death of Tiberius Gracchus the younger Scipio had stepped in to check Tiberius's 'democratic' followers, who were trying to implement their dead leader's land law. The Italian allies

At this, Laelius cried out aloud, and a deep groan was heard from all.[1] But the younger Scipio smiled serenely, and went on: 'Hush! Do not, I beg you, awaken me from my sleep. Listen a little longer, and take heed of what my ancestor went on to say next.'

For then he continued speaking. 'But consider this, Africanus,' he said, 'and the thought will make your determination to defend your homeland even greater than it is already. Every man who has preserved or helped his country, or has made its greatness even greater, is reserved a special place in heaven, where he may enjoy an eternal life of happiness. For all things that are done on earth nothing is more acceptable to the Supreme God, who rules the whole universe, than those gatherings and assemblages of men who are bound together by law, the communities which are known as states. Indeed, it is from here in heaven that the rulers and preservers of those states once came; and it is to here that they eventually return.'[2]

By now I was thoroughly alarmed. It was not the idea of death that frightened me so much, but the thought of treachery inside my own family. Nevertheless, I managed to ask Africanus a question. Was he, was my father Paullus, were the other men we think of as having died, really dead? Or were they still alive?[3]

'To be sure they are still living,' he replied, 'seeing that they have escaped from the prison-house of their bodies – that is to

---

resented the law and appealed to Scipio in 129. When Scipio died later in the year, there were rumours of foul play (p. 182), and the names of Tiberius's mother Cornelia, his sister Sempronia and his brother Gaius were among those mentioned.

1. For Gaius Laelius, who was one of the spokesmen in *On the State*, see *On Friendship*.

2. An echo of Plato. For the insistence of the Stoics on the unity of the divine and human mind, see p. 26.

3. Lucius Aemilius Paullus Macedonicus, consul in 182 and again in 168 BC, when he was victor over King Perseus of Macedonia at Pydna.

say from "life", as you call it, which is, in fact, death.[1] Look: do you not see your father Paullus coming towards you?'

Indeed I now saw him approaching; and I burst into a flood of tears. But my father put his arms round me and kissed me, and told me not to weep. So when I had suppressed my tears and felt able to speak, I cried out, 'Since this, most revered and best of fathers, is true life, as I hear Africanus declare, why must I stay any longer upon earth? Why should I not come and join you, with the utmost possible speed?'

'That must not be,' replied Paullus. 'For unless God, whose sacred domain is all that you see around you here,[2] has freed you from your confinement in the body, you cannot be admitted to this place. For men were brought into existence in order that they should inhabit the globe known as the earth, which you see here at the centre of his holy space. They have been endowed with souls made out of the everlasting fires called stars and constellations, consisting of globular, spherical bodies which are animated by the divine mind and move with marvellous speed, each in its own orbit and cycle. Therefore it is destined that you, Publius, and all other righteous men, shall suffer your souls to stay in the custody of the body. You must not abandon human life except at the command of him who gave it to you. For otherwise you would have failed in the duty which you, like the rest of humanity, have to fulfil.[3]

'Instead, then, Scipio, do upon earth as your grandfather has done. Do as I have done, who begot you. Cherish justice

1. The Pythagoreans believed that the soul was a fallen divinity confined within the body as a tomb and condemned to a cycle of reincarnation (p. 22).

2. The word *templum* originally meant a region of the sky marked off for purposes of divination, and then it came to signify a sacred space generally.

3. Plato had compared men who commit suicide to soldiers who desert their posts. But for a different view see p. 115.

and devotion. These qualities in abundance are owed to parents and kinsmen; and most of all they are owed to one's country.

'That is the life which leads to heaven, and to the company of those who, having completed their lives in the world, are now released from their bodies and dwell in that region you see over there, which the Greeks have taught you people on earth to call the Milky Way.' And he pointed to a circle of light, blazing brilliantly among all the other fires.

As I gazed out from where I stood, first in one direction and then another, the whole prospect looked marvellously beautiful. There were stars we never see from the earth, and they were larger than we could possibly have imagined. The smallest was the luminary which is farthest away from heaven and nearest to the earth, and shines with reflected light.[1] These starry spheres were much larger than the earth. Indeed the earth now seemed to me so small that I began to think less of this empire of ours, which only amounts to a pinpoint on its surface.

*

While I looked more and more intently down at the earth Africanus checked me. 'How long,' he asked, 'do you propose to keep your eyes fastened down there upon that world of yours? Look up, instead, and look round at the sacred region into which you have now entered.

'The universe is held together by nine concentric spheres. The outermost sphere is heaven itself, and it includes and embraces all the rest. For it is the Supreme God in person, enclosing and comprehending everything that exists, that is to say all the stars which are fixed in the sky yet rotate upon their eternal courses. Within this outermost sphere are eight others.

1. The Moon. Anaxagoras of Clazomenae had discovered that its light was reflected.

Seven of them contain the planets – a single one in each sphere, all moving in the contrary direction to the great movement of heaven itself. The next sphere to the outermost is occupied by the orb which people on earth name after Saturn. Below Saturn shines the brilliant light of Jupiter, which is benign and healthful to mankind. Then comes the star we call Mars, red and terrible to men upon earth.

'Next, almost midway between heaven and earth, blazes the Sun. He is the prince, lord and ruler of all the other worlds, the mind and guiding principle of the entire universe, so gigantic in size that everything, everywhere, is pervaded and drenched by his light. In attendance upon the Sun are Venus and Mercury, each in its own orbit; and the lowest sphere of all contains the Moon, which takes its light, as it revolves, from the rays of the sun. Above the Moon there is nothing which is not eternal, but beneath that level everything is moral and transient (except only for the souls in human beings, which are a gift to mankind from the gods). For there below the Moon is the earth, the ninth and lowest of the spheres, lying at the centre of the universe. The earth remains fixed and without motion; all things are drawn to it, because the natural force of gravity pulls them down.'[1]

I surveyed the scene in a stupor. But finally I recovered enough to ask: 'What is this sound, so strong and so sweet, which fills my ears?'

1. This was the system gradually elaborated by the Pythagoreans, and described by Plato. The seven internal spheres containing the planets were believed to rotate from west to east through the signs of the zodiac, whereas the outermost sphere of fixed stars rotated from east to west. The reference to Jupiter is based on astrological teaching. In the fourth century BC Heraclides of Pontus had classified both Venus and Mercury as satellites of the Sun. The Sun and Moon are counted as planets. Cicero takes the order of the planets from Archimedes and the Chaldaean astrologers, whereas Plato placed the Sun between the Moon and Mercury.

'That,' he replied, 'is the music of the spheres.[1] They create it by their own motion as they rush upon their way. The intervals between them, although differing in length, are all measured according to a fixed scheme of proportions; and this arrangement produces a melodious blend of high and low notes, from which emerges a varied harmony. For it cannot be that these vast movements should take place in silence, and nature has ordained that the spheres utter music, those at the summit giving forth high sounds, whereas the sounds of those beneath are low and deep. That is to say, the spheres containing the uppermost stars, comprising those regions of the sky where the movements are speediest, give out a high and piercing sound, whereas the Moon, which lies beneath all the others, sends forth the lowest note.

'The ninth of the spheres, the earth, fixed at the centre of the universe, is motionless and silent. But the other eight spheres produce seven different sounds on the scale – not eight, since two of these orbs move at identical speeds, but seven, a number which is the key to almost all things that exist. Clever men, by imitating these musical effects with their stringed instruments and voices, have given themselves the possibility of eventually returning to this place; and the same chance exists for others too, who during their earthly lives have devoted their outstanding talents to heavenly activities.

'The ears of mankind are filled with this music all the time. But they have become completely deaf to its melody; no other human faculty has become so atrophied as this. The same thing happens where the Nile rushes down from high moun-

1. The doctrine of the harmony of the spheres (p. 338) may have originated early in the fifth century BC. Pythagoras had discovered that the intervals of the musical scale could be expressed as numerical ratios; and later Pythagoreans concluded that the arrangement of the heavens was based on the principles of musical harmony. Venus and Mercury were believed to have the same speed.

tains to the place known as Catadupa.[1] For the sound there is so loud that the people who live nearby have entirely lost their sense of hearing. And that, too, is why the mighty music of the spheres, created by the immeasurably fast rotations of the whole universe, cannot be apprehended by the human ears – any more than you can look at the light of the Sun, which is so intense it blots out your power of vision altogether.'

The scene filled me with awe and delight. And yet all the time I still could not help riveting my eyes upon our own world there below. Africanus noticed this, and spoke again. 'I see,' he said, 'that your gaze is still fastened, even now, upon the places where mortals dwell upon the earth. But can you not understand that the earth is totally insignificant? Contemplate these heavenly regions instead! Scorn what is mortal!

'For the lips of mankind can give you no fame or glory worth the seeking. Note how few and minute are the inhabited portions of the earth, and look upon the vast deserts that divide each one of these patches from the next. See, the inhabitants of the world are so cut off from one another that their different centres cannot even communicate with each other. The place where you yourself dwell, for example, is far removed from certain of the other populated areas, both in latitude and longitude; and some people live in regions that are at the very opposite end of the world from yours. Surely you cannot expect *them* to honour your name.

'Furthermore, you will observe that the surface of the earth is girdled and encompassed by a number of different zones; and that the two which are most widely separated from one

1. Catadupa ('thundering falls') is the First Cataract of the Nile at Syene (Assuan). The reference to the mountains is confusing. Pliny the elder and Seneca the younger (first century AD) confirmed the deafness of the inhabitants. The Pythagoreans, however, ascribed human inability to catch the music of the spheres to habit.

another, and lie beneath opposite poles of the heavens, are rigid with icy cold, while the central, broadest zone is burnt up with the heat of the sun. Two others, situated between the hot zones and the cold, are habitable. The zone which lies towards the south has no connexion with yours at all; it represents your antipodes. As to its northern counterpart, where you yourselves live, you will realize, if you look, what a diminutive section of this region can really be regarded as your property. For the territory you occupy is nothing more than a small island, narrow from north to south, somewhat less narrow from east to west, and surrounded by the sea which is known on earth as the Atlantic, or the Great Sea, or the Ocean.[1] In spite of the grand name this stretch of water bears, you can tell from here how tiny it really is.

'And I must disabuse you of any idea that your own fame, or the fame of any one of us, could ever be great enough to extend beyond these known and settled lands. It could never scale the Caucasus mountains (you see them down there);[2] it could never swim the river Ganges. Not one of the inhabitants of all those eastern tracts, or the remote west either, or the far off north and south, will ever so much as hear the sound of your name! And once you leave all these hosts of people out of account, you will have to conclude that the area over which your glory is so eager to extend itself is really of the most trifling dimensions.

'And now about the people who *do* know and speak about us. The point is, how long will this go on? Assume, if you like, that future generations, having inherited our praises from their fathers, will indeed retain the desire to hand them down to their children as well. Even so the deluges and conflagrations which inevitably descend upon the earth at fixed

1. The great stream believed to flow round the earth.
2. The Hindu Kush (Paropamisus, see p. 94).

intervals will make it impossible for any glory we may gain in this way to be eternal – or even to last for any length of time.[1] But in any case why do you regard it as so important to be talked about by people who have not yet been born? After all, you were never spoken of by all the multitudes who lived before you – and they were every bit as numerous, and were better men.

'It is also necessary to remind ourselves that even the people who may in fact hear our names mentioned will not retain the recollection even for as much as the space of one year. I am not referring to the year as it is commonly understood, which is measured according to the revolution of the sun, that is to say according the movements of one single star. But when *all* the stars return to the places where they started from, so that after an immense interval has elapsed the entire heavens finally resume their original configuration, then that great period of rotation can truly be called a year – but how many generations of human life it comprises, I should not venture to say.[2]

'Long ago, when the spirit of Romulus ascended into these sacred expanses, it seemed to those living at the time that a shadow suddenly passed over the sun, and its light was blotted out. When, once again, the sun shall go into eclipse in the very same position and at the very same hour, that will signify that all the constellations and stars have returned to their original positions: and then you will know that the Year has been

1. The Stoics (though not Panaetius) believed in this cycle of periodical destruction by flood and then fire (occurring at winter solstice and summer solstice respectively) or by alternate flood and fire. They attributed the doctrine of conflagration, wrongly, to Heraclitus of Ephesus (c. 500 BC), basing it on his belief that the basic world principle is Fire.

2. This is the Great Year, an idea which goes back as far as Hesiod. It was variously estimated as 30,000, 15,000 and 10,800 years, or as 300,000 generations.

completed. But you must understand that, up to now, not one twentieth part of its course has been run.[1]

*

'As for yourself, do not abandon hope of coming back here one day. For this is the place which offers great and eminent men their authentic reward – and, after all, such fame as you are able to win among mere human beings can evidently be disregarded, seeing that it is scarcely capable of enduring even for a small part of one single year. Look upwards, then! Contemplate this place which is a habitation for all eternity! Then you will not need any longer to be at the mercy of what the multitude says about you: then you will not have to put your trust in whatever human rewards your achievements may earn.

'Instead let Virtue herself, by her own unaided allurements, summon you to a glory that is genuine and real. Feel no concern about what other people may say about you. They will say it in any case. Besides, whatever words they may choose to utter will not pass beyond the narrow limits you now see below you. No utterance of man about his fellow-men has ever been lasting. When a person dies his words die with him. Posterity forgets them; and they pass into annihilation.'

He stopped speaking, and I cried out my assent. 'Even when I was only a boy, Africanus,' I declared, 'I was already exerting myself to the utmost to follow in your footsteps, and in those of my father. I longed to be not unworthy of your fame! And if there is really a path leading right to the entrance of heaven for those who have served their country well, the knowledge of this great goal before me will inspire me to redouble my endeavours.'

1. The traditional date of Romulus's death and departure to heaven, where he became the god Quirinus, was 716 BC, or 567 years before the date at which Scipio was supposed to be speaking.

'Strive on,' he replied. 'And rest assured that it is only your body that is mortal; your true self is nothing of the kind. For the man you outwardly appear to be is not yourself at all. Your real self is not that corporeal, palpable shape, but the spirit inside. *Understand that you are god.*[1] You have a god's capacity of aliveness and sensation and memory and foresight; a god's power to rule and govern and direct the body that is your servant, in the same way as God himself, who reigns over us, directs the entire universe. And this rule exercised by eternal God is mirrored in the dominance of your frail body by your immortal soul.

*

'That which is always in motion is eternal;[2] yet that which communicates motion to something else, but is itself moved by another force, must necessarily cease to live when the transmission of this motion to it has ceased. Consequently the only thing that never ceases to move is something which has the power of starting up motion all *on its own* – it can go on moving because its power to achieve motion depends on itself and itself alone. This, therefore, it must be concluded, is the source and first principle of motion for all things that move.

'Being the first principle, it never had a beginning: since the first principle is what everything else has originated from, it cannot possibly have originated from anything itself. For if it owed its origin to something else, it could not be described as the first principle.

'And since it never had a beginning it will never have an end. For if the first principle were destroyed it could never be reborn from any other source and would no longer be able to

1. An echo of Plato, his disciple Xenocrates of Chalcedon (head of the Academy 339–314 BC), and the Stoics.

2. The passage that follows is a translation from Plato's *Phaedrus*, 254 C–E.

create things on its own account – which is obviously what the first principle has to do.

'The beginning of all movement, then, comes from that which has set itself in motion: which can neither be born nor die. For if that were not so, one would have to envisage the entire heavens and all things that have ever been created crashing down and coming to an end – for that is what would happen if the force generating their motion were taken away from them.

'Since, therefore, it is plain that the self-moving principle is eternal, the same must evidently apply to the human soul. For unlike lifeless objects which can only be set in motion from outside, the soul, by its very essence and nature, is a living thing such as can only derive its life and motion from within itself. And since, uniquely, it possesses this characteristic of self-impulsion, surely it has no beginning, and lives for ever.

*

'Use this eternal force, therefore, for the most splendid deeds it is in you to achieve! And the very best deeds are those which serve your country. A soul devoted to such pursuits will find it easiest of all to soar upwards to this place, which is its proper habitation and home.[1] And its flight will be all the more rapid if already during the period of its confinement within the body it has ranged freely abroad, and, by contemplating what lies outside itself, has contrived to detach itself from the body to the greatest possible degree.

'When, on the other hand, a man has failed to do this, and has abandoned himself instead to bodily indulgence and become its slave, letting the passions which serve pleasure impel him to flout the laws both of gods and of men, his soul,

1. According to Plato political virtue was the highest form of virtue; but philosophical speculation, on which the highest good depended, could only be attained by keeping the soul free from the disturbing influence of the body.

after departing from his body, hovers about close to the earth. Nor does it return to this place until many ages of torment have been undergone.'[1]

Then Africanus vanished; and I awoke from my sleep.

1. Plato estimates this purgatory of the soul at different durations varying between three thousand and ten thousand years.

# APPENDIX I

## *The Philosophical Works of Cicero*

| | |
|---|---|
| ? | Translation of Plato's *Protagoras* (lost) |
| ? 60s BC | Translation of Aratus's *Phaenomena* (poem, fragments) |
| 54–51 | *On the State*, I–VI (incomplete: includes *The Dream of Scipio*) |
| 52 and 46–45 | *On Laws*, I–V (?) (incomplete) |
| 46 | *Paradoxes of the Stoics* |
| 45 | *On the Chief Good and Evil*,[1] I–V |
| | *Academics*, I–IV (incomplete: I from second edition, II from first) |
| | Translation of Plato's *Timaeus* (fragments) |
| | *Consolation* (fragments) |
| | *Hortensius* (fragments) |
| 44 | *Discussions at my House at Tusculum* (*Tusculan Disputations*), I–V |
| | *On the Nature of the Gods*, I–III |
| | *On Divination*, I–II |
| | *On Auguries* (lost) |
| | *On Fate* (part) |
| | *On Glory*, I–II (fragments) |
| | *Cato the elder: On Old Age*[1] |
| | *Laelius: On Friendship* |
| | *On Duties*, I–III[2] |
| | *On Virtues* (fragments) |

1. For the title *De Finibus Bonorum et Malorum* see p. 8, n. 1.
2. *Cato the Elder: On Old Age* and *On Duties*, III are translated in *Cicero: Selected Works*, op. cit.

# APPENDIX II

## *The Rhetorical Works of Cicero*

| | |
|---|---|
| c.82 BC (? or later) | *On Invention* (Rhetorica) |
| 55 | *On the Orator*, I–III |
| c.53 | *The Divisions of Oratory* |
| 52 | *On the Best Kind of Orators* (fragment)[1] |
| 46 | *Brutus: On Famous Orators* |
| | *The Orator: to Marcus Brutus* |
| 44 | *Topica: to Gaius Trebatius* (*Methods of Drawing Conclusions*) |

1. Preface to translations (lost) of Aeschines's speech against Ctesiphon and Demosthenes's reply.

# APPENDIX III

## *Principal Dates*

| | |
|---|---|
| 510 BC | Traditional date for expulsion of kings and foundation of Republic |
| 451–450 | Twelve Tables |
| 280–275 | War with Pyrrhus |
| 264–241 | First Punic War |
| 218–204 | Second Punic War |
| 171–168 | Third Macedonian War |
| 149–146 | Third Punic War |
| 146 | Destruction of Carthage and Corinth |
| 133 | Numantia captured by Scipio Africanus the younger |
| 133 | Tribunate of Tiberius Gracchus |
| 123–122 | Tribunates of Gaius Gracchus |
| 106 | Birth of Cicero |
| 91–87 | Social (Marsian) War |
| 88 | Sulla marches on Rome |
| 87 | Death of Marius |
| 81–79 | Dictatorship of Sulla |
| 70 | Cicero's speeches against Verres |
| 67, 66 | Extraordinary commands of Pompeius |
| 63 | Consulship of Cicero: Conspiracy of Catilina |
| 60 | First Triumvirate (Pompeius, Crassus, Caesar) |
| 58–57 | Exile of Cicero |
| 56 | First Triumvirate renewed at Luca (Lucca) |
| 53 | Death of Crassus at Carrhae |
| 51–50 | Cicero's governorship of Cilicia |
| 49 | Outbreak of Civil War between Pompeius and Caesar |
| 49 | Caesar's first dictatorship |
| 48 | Battle of Pharsalus. Death of Pompeius |
| 46, 45 | Caesar defeats the sons of Pompeius |
| 44 | Caesar made dictator for life and murdered |
| 44 (Sept.) | Cicero's First Philippic against Antonius |
| 43 | Second Triumvirate (Antonius, Lepidus, Octavianus) |
| 43 (7 Dec.) | Death of Cicero |

# APPENDIX IV

## *Some Books about Cicero*

J. M. André, *L'Otium dans la vie morale et intellectuelle romaine*, Paris, 1966

R. R. Bolgar, *The Classical Heritage*, Cambridge University Press, 1954

K. Büchner, *Cicero*, Heidelberg, 1964

*Cicero: Basic Works* (ed. M. Hadas), New York, 1951

*Cicero: Selected Political Speeches* (ed. M. Grant), Penguin Books, 1969

*Cicero: Selected Works* (ed. M. Grant), Penguin Books, 1960 (reprint 1969)

M. L. Clarke, *Rhetoric at Rome*, Cohen & West, 1953

M. L. Clarke, *The Roman Mind*, Cohen & West, 1956

T. A. Dorey (ed.), *Cicero*, Routledge & Kegan Paul, 1944

A. E. Douglas, *Cicero*, 'Greece & Rome' (New Surveys in the Classics, No. 2), 1968

M. Gelzer: *Cicero: Biographischer Versuch*, Wiesbaden, 1969

G. Highet, *The Classical Tradition*, Oxford University Press, 1949 (reprint 1967)

H. A. K. Hunt, *The Humanism of Cicero*, Melbourne, 1954

G. Kennedy, *The Art of Persuasion in Greece*, Routledge & Kegan Paul, 1963

*Marco Tullio Cicerone: Scritti commemorativi pubblicati nel bimillenario della morte*, Florence, 1961

K. Meister, *Die Freundschaft bei den Griechen und Römern*, Darmstadt, 1967

A. Michel, *Rhétorique et Philosophie chez Cicéron*, Paris, 1960

T. Petersson, *Cicero*, New York, 1919 (reprint Biblo & Tannen, 1963)

G. Radke (ed.), *Cicero: ein Mensch seiner Zeit*, Berlin, 1968

J. Rist, *Stoic Philosophy*, Cambridge University Press, 1969

C. L. Stough, *Greek Skepticism*, Berkeley, 1969

W. Süss, *Cicero: Eine Einführung in seine Philosophische Schriften*, Wiesbaden, 1966

# GENEALOGICAL TABLES: 1. THE SCAEVOLAS

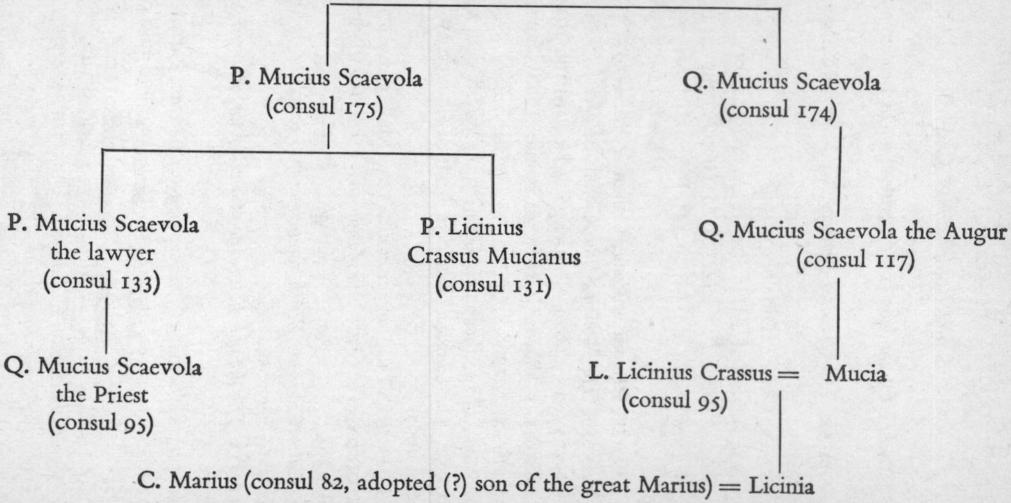

## 11. THE SCIPIOS

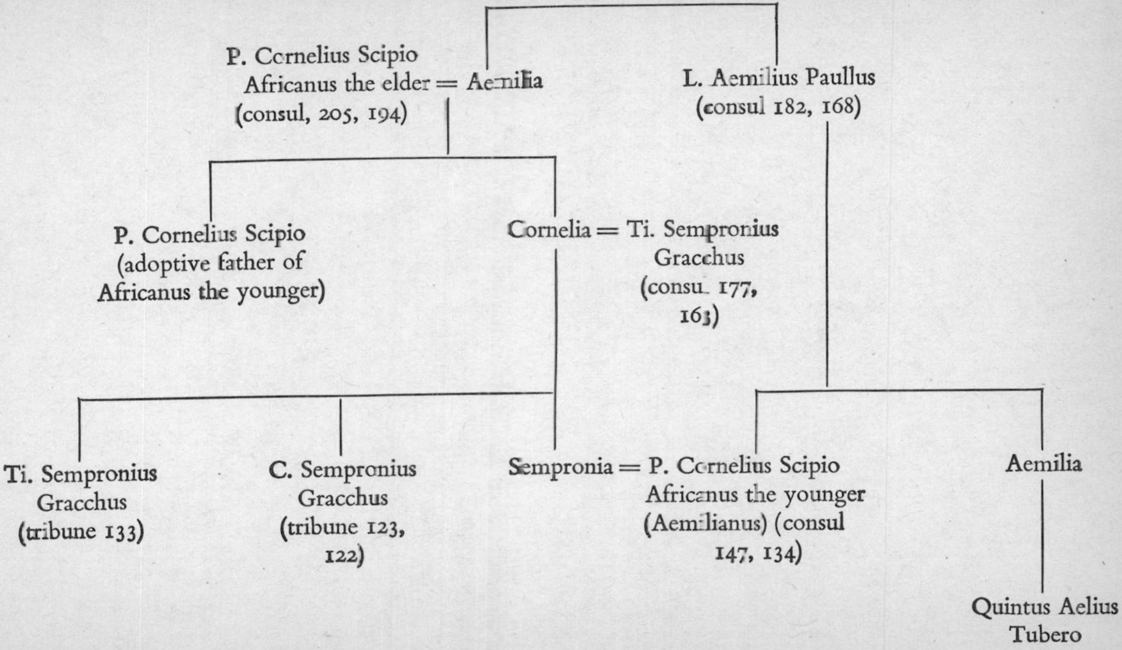
P. Cornelius Scipio Africanus the elder (consul, 205, 194) = Aemilia
L. Aemilius Paullus (consul 182, 168)
P. Cornelius Scipio (adoptive father of Africanus the younger)
Cornelia = Ti. Sempronius Gracchus (consul 177, 163)
Ti. Sempronius Gracchus (tribune 133)
C. Sempronius Gracchus (tribune 123, 122)
Sempronia = P. Cornelius Scipio Africanus the younger (Aemilianus) (consul 147, 134)
Aemilia
Quintus Aelius Tubero

# MAPS

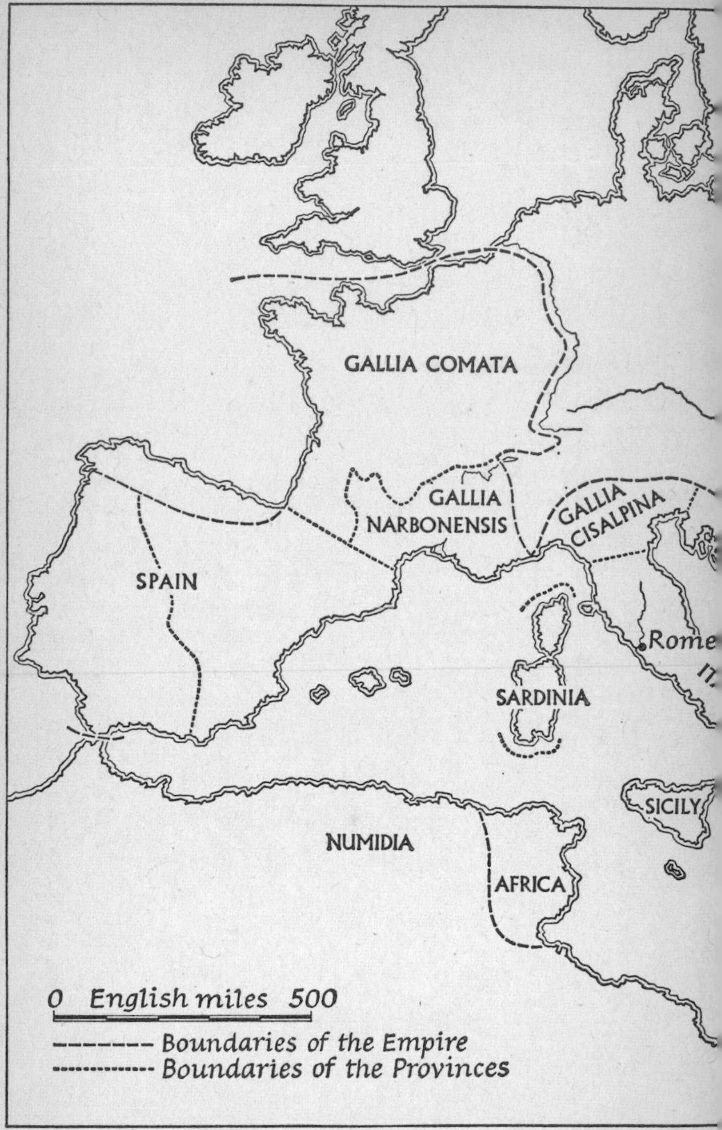
GALLIA COMATA
GALLIA NARBONENSIS
GALLIA CISALPINA
SPAIN
Rome
SARDINIA
SICILY
NUMIDIA
AFRICA
0 English miles 500
Boundaries of the Empire
Boundaries of the Provinces

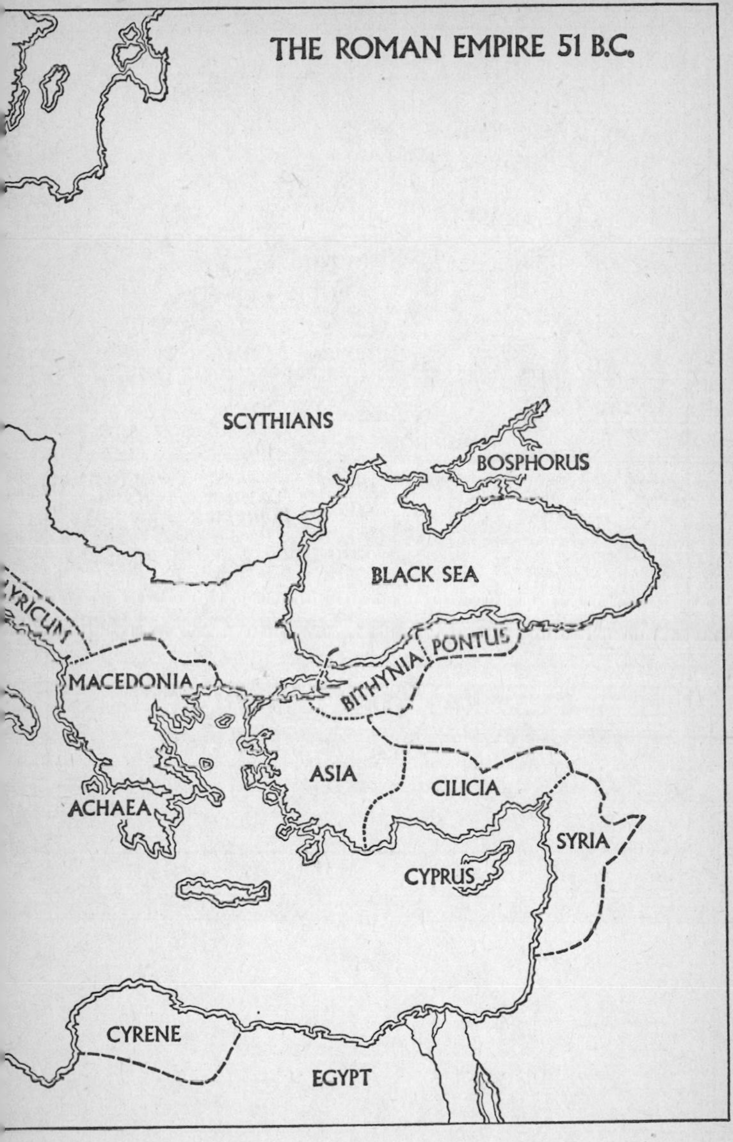
THE ROMAN EMPIRE 51 B.C.
SCYTHIANS
BOSPHORUS
BLACK SEA
YRICUM
MACEDONIA
BITHYNIA
PONTUS
ASIA
CILICIA
ACHAEA
SYRIA
CYPRUS
CYRENE
EGYPT

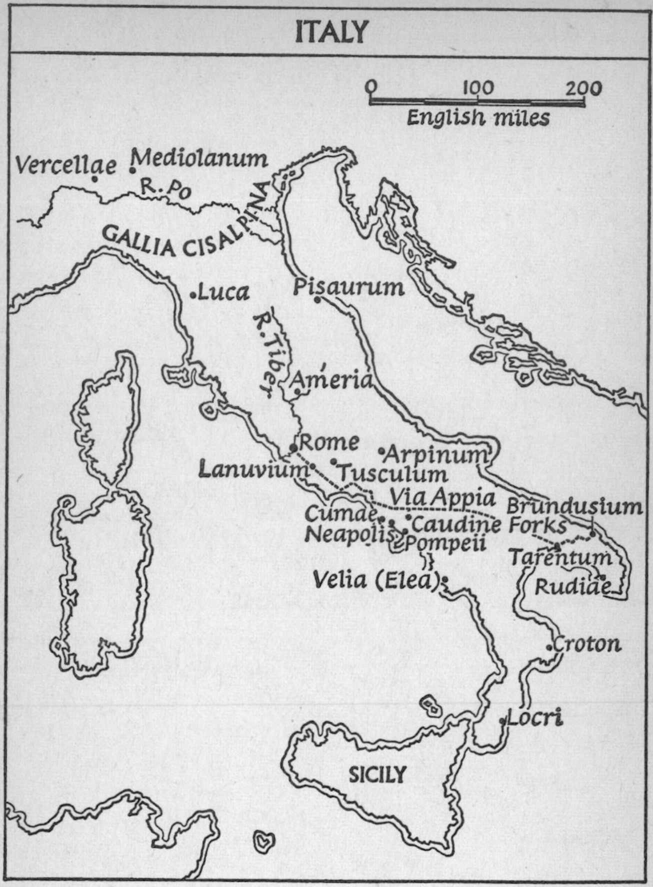
ITALY
0
100
200
English miles
Vercellae
Mediolanum
R. Po
GALLIA CISALPINA
Luca
Pisaurum
R. Tiber
Ameria
Rome
Arpinum
Lanuvium
Tusculum
Via Appia
Brundusium
Cumae
Caudine Forks
Neapolis
Pompeii
Tarentum
Velia (Elea)
Rudiae
Croton
Locri
SICILY

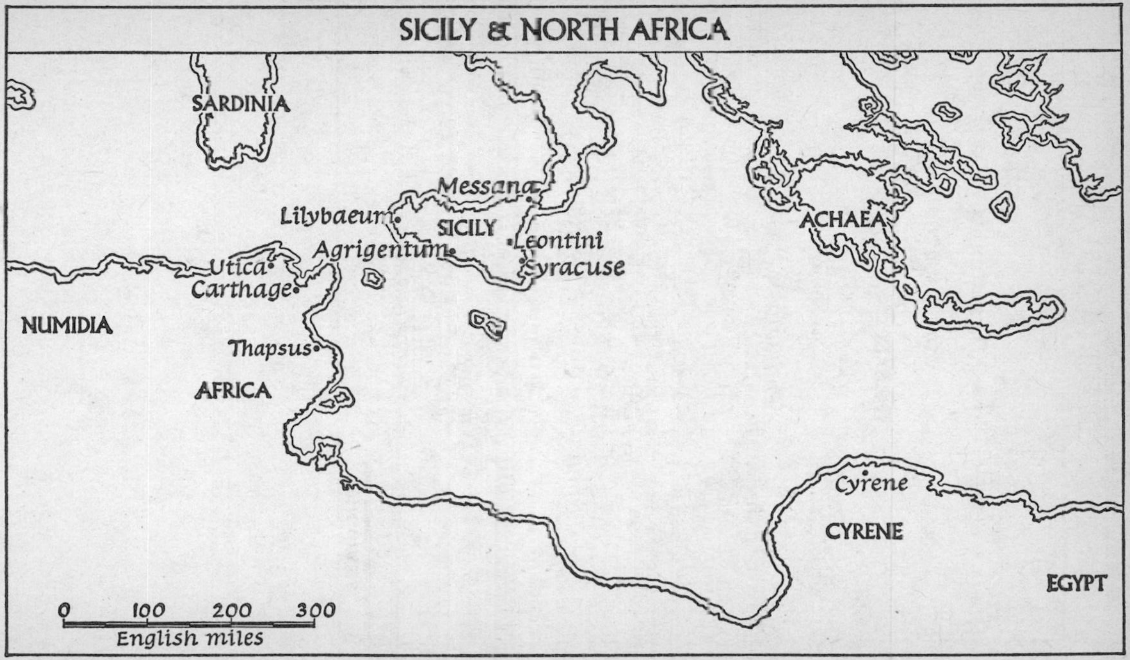
SICILY & NORTH AFRICA
SARDINIA
Messana
Lilybaeum
SICILY
Leontini
Agrigentum
Syracuse
Utica
Carthage
NUMIDIA
Thapsus
AFRICA
ACHAEA
Cyrene
CYRENE
EGYPT
0
100
200
300
English miles

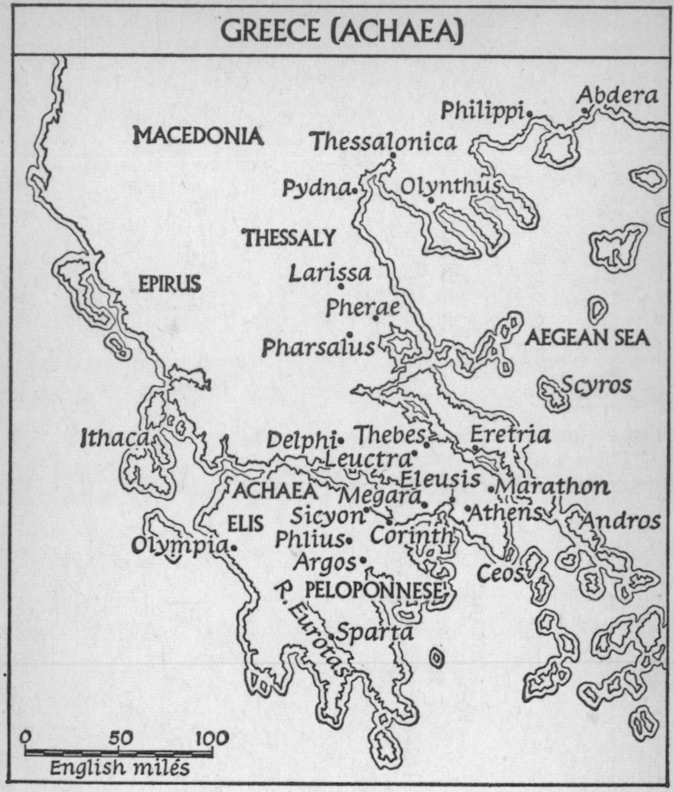

GREECE (ACHAEA)
MACEDONIA
Thessalonica
Philippi
Abdera
Pydna
Olynthus
THESSALY
EPIRUS
Larissa
Pherae
Pharsalus
AEGEAN SEA
Scyros
Ithaca
Delphi
Thebes
Eretria
Leuctra
Eleusis
Marathon
ACHAEA
Megara
Athens
Andros
ELIS
Sicyon
Olympia
Phlius
Corinth
Argos
Ceos
R. Eurotas
PELOPONNESE
Sparta
0
50
100
English miles

WESTERN ASIA MINOR
Sinope
Chalcedon
PONTUS
Lampsacus
Prusa
AEGEAN SEA
Eresus
Mytilene
Lesbos
Pergamum
IONIA
Chios
Clazomenae
Colophon
Samos
Ephesus
ASIA
Priene
Miletus
PAMPHYLIA
Rhodes
Phaselis
0
100
200 English miles

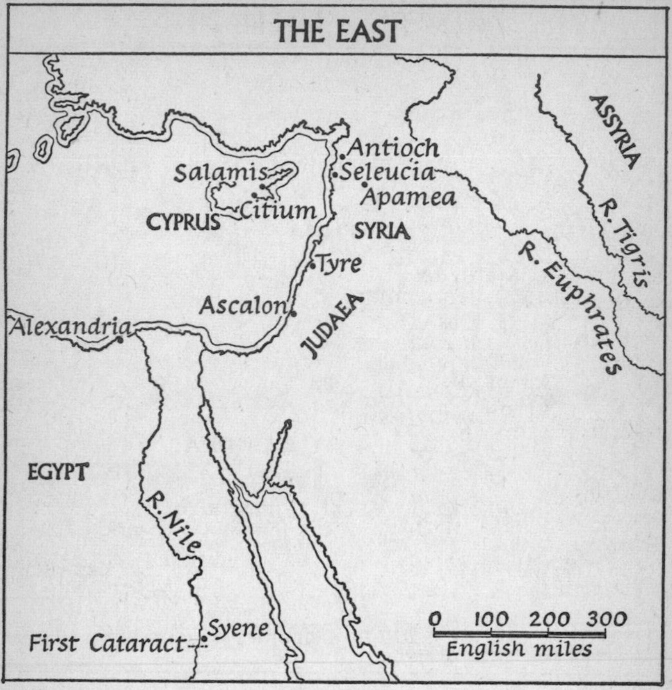
THE EAST
Antioch
Salamis
Seleucia
Apamea
Citium
CYPRUS
SYRIA
ASSYRIA
R. Tigris
R. Euphrates
Tyre
Ascalon
JUDAEA
Alexandria
EGYPT
R. Nile
Syene
First Cataract
0 100 200 300
English miles

THE WEST
BRITANNIA
R. Rhine
GALLIA COMATA
R. Rhone
GALLIA NARBONENSIS
Narbo
Massilia
GALLAECIA
Numantia
CELTIBERI
FURTHER SPAIN
NEARER SPAIN
LUSITANIA
0 100 200 300 English miles

# INDEX

The following abbreviations are employed: A.: Aulus, Ap.: Appius, C.: Gaius; Cn.: Cnaeus, L.: Lucius, M.: Marcus, Mam.: Mamercus, Man.: Manius, P.: Publius, Q.: Quintus, Sex.: Sextus, Sp.: Spurius, T.: Titus, Ti.: Tiberius

# INDEX

## MORE ABOUT PENGUINS

*Penguinews*, which appears every month, contains details of all the new books issued by Penguins as they are published. From time to time it is supplemented by *Penguins in Print*, which is a complete list of all books published by Penguins which are in print. (There are well over three thousand of these.)

A specimen copy of *Penguinews* will be sent to you free on request, and you can become a subscriber for the price of the postage. For a year's issues (including the complete lists) please send 30p if you live in the United Kingdom, or 60p if you live elsewhere. Just write to Dept EP, Penguin Books Ltd, Harmondsworth, Middlesex, enclosing a cheque or postal order, and your name will be added to the mailing list.

Note: *Penguinews* and *Penguins in Print* are not available in the U.S.A. or Canada